Judgment in administration

Judgment in administration

Commemorative Edition

Ray E. Brown
(1913-1974)

DIVISION OF TEACH 'EM INC.

Chicago 1982

Library of Congress Catalog Card Number:
82-82148

International Standard Book Number:
0-931028-31-0

American College of Hospital Administrators
840 North Lake Shore Drive
Chicago, Illinois 60611

Pluribus Press, Division of Teach 'em, Inc.
160 East Illinois Street
Chicago, Illinois 60611

Printed in the United States of America

This book is dedicated to that legion of practicing administrators in industry, education, health, and government who have both knowingly and unknowingly helped me confirm the observations and notions about administrative conduct that I have recorded in this book.

Contents

Commemorative edition foreword

It is with pleasure and pride that the ACHA joins with Pluribus Press to republish Ray Brown's important work, *Judgment in administration*. Since its original publication in 1966, passages from the book have been quoted extensively by speakers and authors in a wide variety of disciplines and industries. More importantly, Ray Brown's words have served to encourage and prepare countless men and women to serve more effectively in their hospital and health administrative positions. Truly, the book has had significant positive impact upon a whole generation of administrators. With this republication, it is our hope that another generation will be so affected.

Ray Brown was a leader. He was ahead of his time. Review of his published bibliography reveals a man of many talents who appreciated the complexities of administration. His works are both pragmatic and theoretical as well as both discipline-specific and highly integrative across many disciplines.

His leadership skills extended far beyond the literature. Both the AHA and the ACHA were guided by his firm hand from the position of the chief elected officer. A permanent legacy of his foresight is the ACHA Congress on Administration, the largest management-oriented program of its kind. A tribute to Ray Brown's leadership in the creation of the Congress follows this foreword.

As a graduate student in the 1950s, I was influenced by Ray Brown's words and thoughts. *Judgment in administration* was published early in my career as I served as an assistant hospital administrator. Ray's influence continued. I heard him speak and shook his hand, but never really knew the man. For those privileged to have known him, this republication will stimulate the memory and create an opportunity to relive an important part of the past. For the newer generations, this book will provide valuable insights which will make us better administrators.

Stuart A. Wesbury, Jr., Ph.D., FACHA
President
American College of Hospital Administrators

Ray E. Brown and the Congress on Administration: an appreciation

This is one of those rare occasions that allows all of us to reflect on the past history of this fine professional organization and to appreciate what exceptional leadership can accomplish. This is the 25th anniversary of an event unprecedented in our history. The Congress on Administration is the centerpiece of an educational banquet left in perpetuity by Ray Brown for all of us.

"A. J." Swanson of Toronto, Frank S. Groner of Memphis, and Tony Eckert of Perth Amboy, were the chairmen officers of the American College of Hospital Administrators in 1957-58; they wanted a signal, auspicious event to emphasize and recognize the then silver anniversary of the College. Ray Brown was a Regent of the College at the time, and he was selected to head a committee to plan and implement a special event. The Congress on Administration was the answer.

Ray Brown was probably the best known hospital administrator of his era and his time. He followed Dr. Arthur Bachmeyer as director of the Graduate Program in Hospital Administration at the University of Chicago in 1951. At the same time, he was superintendent of the University of Chicago Hospitals and Clinics. His administrative staff included Irv Wilmot and Dick Wittrup, both of whom he involved in planning the Congress program. Ray subsequently left Chicago to direct the Department of Health Administration program at Duke University, went from there to what is now the Affiliated Hospitals System in Boston, and then returned to Chicago to head the McGaw Medical Center of Northwestern University.

Ray was an uncommon man: an astute administrator, influential educator and a prolific writer who knew the health care field and understood his audience. His audience consisted of: trustees, bewildered by a stewardship of the most saleable product in the world, many of whom still thought that trusteeship in a hospital was similar to trusteeship at the YMCA, Salvation Army, the opera, symphony, or the local church; auxilians, committed to voluntarism; government, overwhelmed by the continued increase in the cost of health care; and a prepayment system engulfed by a cash-flow unprecedented in the insurance business. It was a time when the Hill-Burton program, the Blue Cross movement, and the field, as we know it today, were in adolescence. It was a time never seen before or since when the leaders of our field exuded confidence and genuinely believed the future was theirs. The challenges of health care technology and science gathering momentum on the horizon were perceived by only a few.

Ray Brown, however, was one of those visionary few. He was in the mold of the George Bugbees, the Andy Pattullos and the Don Cordeses, Roy Houses, and Bob Cunninghams. He loved the business, the people in it, and took a prideful view of the developing role of the hospital manager: the health care executive and statesman. He represented what you and I dream about, fantasize, and work a lifetime to emulate. He was the man of his profession! He was the Ali, the Reggie Jackson, the Kissinger, the Admiral Rickover, Bishop Sheen — at the height of their fame and career performance. Indeed, Ray was an ideal choice to head the planning group for the College's first Congress, scheduled to begin February 13, 1958 — a quarter century from the date the professional society was founded.

When apprised of the College's interest in a special anniversary educational program, Dr. Edwin Crosby, director and secretary of the American Hospital Association, pledged his support to this new educational endeavor and expedited a $5,000 contribution by the AHA toward the total undertaking.

To assist with the presentation of the first Congress, Ray Brown, as chairman of the planning committee, enlisted the help of a distinguished group of leaders in the College and in the health field, many of whom have continued their roles as statesmen in the profession. For example, he appointed Jim Hamilton, then director of the University of Minnesota Graduate Program in Hospital and Health Care Administration, as chairman of the Book of the Year Award Committee, whose membership included Mort Zimmerman and Vernon Forsman. Alden Mills of Santa Monica, California, was named chairman of the Article of the Year Award Committee; Milo Anderson and Don Cordes were among its members. Ray's own planning committee included such leaders in the field as Dr. Gary Hartman, Dick Johnson, Boone Powell and Dick Stull.

The first Congress provided the appropriate occasion for remembering the past and commemorating the memory of those who had contributed to the College's formation and development. Tributes were paid to Editor Matthew Foley, Dr. Malcolm MacEachern, and the first president of the ACHA, Charles Wordell, all members of the original founding group and all deceased at the time.

Today, only Charter Fellows Dr. Robin Buerki, John Mannix and J. Dewey Lutes survive from that initial band of founding fathers.

The year of the first Congress — 1958 — was the heyday of the educators, and four from the era who were prominent, Charlie Berry, Colonel Fred Gibbs, Bob Hudgens and Dr. Herluf Olson, all attended. Those of us who were present at the time can remember the heady experience of rubbing shoulders with the general officers and the admirals of the hospital industry, basking in their presence and formulating dreams of future personal accomplishment. Many of us left the Congress inspired with a determination that there was nothing that we could not do.

The general program sessions of that first Congress mirrored the times: "Operations Research, A Management Resource" and "Strategy for Administration Reaction," for example. Dr. Herbert Simon, winner of the first book award, spoke on salient features of his work, *Administrative Behavior*. Ev Johnson, a Gary,

Indiana, administrator at the time, and his committee chose twenty-five seminars on subjects that included, "Line vs. Staff Responsibility," "The Ideal Group Size," "How to Listen Effectively," "Scientific Management for Small Organizations," "The Art and Science of Long Range Planning," "Lay Interference, an American Principle," and "The Administrator's Role in Setting and Maintaining Standards."

What other highlights of that first Congress come immediately to mind? There are many. Here are a few — from my personal recollections:

... Tuition to the Congress was modest: $25 for meetings held on a Monday and Tuesday at the then appropriately named Congress hotel.

... Midway Airport was very busy that year and many of us flew to the meeting on DC6s and 7s — on Constellations and Convairs. Many others came by train.

... The College's offices at that time were located at 620 North Michigan Avenue. There was no zip code.

... Paul Douglas, the U.S. Senator from Illinois, was the banquet speaker. His topic: the dangers inherent in the continued manufacture of atomic and hydrogen bombs. He digressed long enough to pay special tribute to the contributions of a colleague, Senator Lister Hill of Alabama.

... "Chuck" Goulet, current Executive Vice President of the Chicago Blue Cross Plan, then an assistant professor in hospital administration at the University of Pittsburgh, scheduled a luncheon meeting with the key administrators who served as preceptors for his graduate program.

And, finally ... the first Congress cost $25,000 to produce; when it was finished, it showed a surplus of $1,200.

The first Congress clearly identified for us attendees the opportunities for professional development, uplifted our career horizons, expanded our vision of the world about us, and exhilarated our confidence.

Consider! Here was the ACHA, a professional society of *health* administrators, recognizing an author acclaimed for his *business* organization expertise — surely more properly a role for the American Management Association. We were listening to a U.S.

Senator speak about world-wide problems and possible solutions
— a topic certainly more appropriate for a fund-raising campaign
of a political party in an election year. We were talking for the first
time not to ourselves and about our problems. We were talking
about organization principles and their application to all business.
We realized we were a part of a larger community with the same
personnel, fiscal, and management problems that all businesses
experience. The Congress faculty, representing a wide-ranging
background far transcending the health field, reaffirmed it for all
of us.

The architect of this extraordinary experience, the first Congress, of course, was Ray Brown, the tough, warm, chain-smok-
ing, card-playing Southern roughneck, who was the right man, at
the right time, in the right place to play a role that has indelibly
marked him for a honored niche in our professional history.

It has been a privilege on this occasion of the 25th anniversary
Congress on Administration to share this historical perspective
with you. It also provides an opportunity to remind all of us that
we are reaping the harvest from fields of health care delivery —
that were planted a quarter century ago by Ray Brown and nurtured through the years by many, many others.

There is a new and growing prestige and stature in being a hospital and health services administrator. We are all most fortunate
in having as a role model Ray Brown, whose productive career
personified the ideal to which we might all aspire.

I hope the spirit of that first Congress, and its promise for your
future is present with all of you this afternoon.

Ray Brown died in Chicago on May 4, 1974, at the age of 60.

> *Bernard J. Lachner, FACHA*
> *President*
> *Evanston Hospital*
> *Evanston, IL*

Presented: March 4, 1982
25th Congress on Administration
American College of Hospital Administrators

American College of Hospital Administrators
Chairmen Officers/President
1981-1982

Chairman
Charles T. Wood, FACHA
Director
Massachusetts Eye & Ear Infirmary
Boston, MA

Chairman-Elect
Earl G. Dresser, FACHA
President
Methodist Hospital
St. Louis Park, MN

Immediate Past Chairman
Donald R. Newkirk, FACHA
President
Ohio Hospital Association
Columbus, OH

President
Stuart A. Wesbury, Jr., Ph.D., FACHA
American College of Hospital Administrators
Chicago, IL

American College of Hospital Administrators
Board of Governors
1981-1982

American College of Hospital Administrators
Board of Governors
1981-1982 (cont.)

District 5
Howard M. Winholtz, FACHA
Executive Director
Rochester Methodist Hospital
Rochester, MN

District 6
Arthur L. McElmurry, FACHA
President
Wadley Hospital
Texarkana, TX

District 7
Austin Ross, FACHA
Vice President
Virginia Mason Hospital
Seattle, WA

Preface

Arriving at a title for this book represented quite a difficulty to both the author and the publisher. The title that was finally adopted accurately describes what the book is about, but it may be misleading as regards what the author is attempting to accomplish. The title might give the impression that the book is a scientific treatment of a rather abstract subject. This would be a grossly inaccurate impression. It is intended that the book be a very practical treatment of a very practical subject. It is concerned with the practicing judgment of the administrator.

The book is a bit unusual in that it concerns itself more with causes of failure in administration than with causes of success. This is the only way that a useful book on judgment in administration can be written. One can preach salvation only by preaching about sin. Good judgment is achieved by avoiding and overcoming the causes of bad judgment. This does not mean the author has attempted to develop a manual of do's and don't's on judgment for the administrator. The approach is one of attempting to mark out the hazards and pitfalls to good judgment.

The book was written to be read by anyone who is interested in developing and improving his understanding of administration and his ability to practice it. It is the conviction of the author that there is an art of administration and that it is learnable. Said another way, this book is predicated on the notion that the administrator is a craftsman and that his craftsmanship is an acquired thing. Stated still another way, the author holds the firm belief that administration is a thinking man's game, and this book is an attempt to help the administrator practice in a more thoughtful manner.

The notions expressed in this book were derived from observing my own conduct as an administrator and that of a host of other individuals active in various types of administration. It has been my good fortune to have been both a participant and a spectator in administration for some twenty-five years. During this period I served first as the director of a large university hospital and then as a vice-president of that university. At the same time I served an active role as a professor in the graduate school of business. This dual role provided me the unique opportunity of experiencing what I was teaching. It also conditioned me to observe closely the administrative conduct of colleagues, acquaintances, and former students. This book reflects those observations and the meanings I derived from them. I suspect, however, that a rather considerable portion represents reflections on my own conduct as an administrator.

The Preface is traditionally used as a means of acknowledging the author's obligations and appreciation to those who provided assistance in the production of the manuscript. The number of individuals who have significantly contributed to the production of the ideas making up this book are legion, and it would be impossible to list them all. This impossibility is partially the result of the limitations on space that can be used for such a purpose, but it also results from the fact that I cannot name them all; an individual's domain of thought is made up of an amalgam of experiences, observations, discussions, and readings. The time, place, and source of much of the amalgam represented in this book are not identifiable.

Very direct thanks are due the several journals and business publications which have permitted me to use material in this book from some of my previous writings. I am also grateful to McGraw-Hill for the patience and assistance they have bestowed on my efforts. Acknowledgment must be given to Professor Mark Ashin of the University of Chicago for his assistance in reviewing the manuscript and keeping the number of split infinitives within acceptable limits. The same is true for Miss Elsie Farr of the University of Chicago and Mrs. Linda Pethia of Duke University, who typed the manuscript. Most of all, much credit is due my wife, Mary Witherspoon Brown, who has permitted me to work late hours and who has endured the ordeal of listening the book through, sentence by sentence.

Ray E. Brown

Introduction: the role and nature of judgment in administration

I Good judgment is said to be the child of wisdom. This must mean that bad judgment has other parents. It is these other parents with which this volume on the administrator's judgment is concerned. Such concern with the administrator's poor judgment should not be taken as a lack of confidence in the quality of the administrator's usual judgment. On the contrary, the administrator's usual judgment is usually good. The difficulty lies in the fact that the administrator's judgment is not evaluated on the scales of what is usual. His judgment is much more easily observed, and severely evaluated, because it is much more exposed and has much more important consequences for other people. The consequences of individuals' judgment in their private, everyday lives usually go unnoticed, even by their friends, because they do not affect too many people in an important way.

The fact that the administrator's judgment is usually good may be difficult to prove to the various individuals and interests affected by his judgment at different times. They are not the same

1

people and interests each time; they may be personnel, subordinates, colleagues, superiors, owners, customers, and any number of other individuals coming into contact with the enterprise. Some of these diverse contacts may be one-time relationships. All this means that the administrator has a number of different report cards on his judgment, and he is not given credit for the good grades on one card when his grade is being recorded on the other one. He is not usually permitted the benefit of an average grade, and each test of the administrator's judgment is treated almost as a final exam. Somebody gives emphasis to each act, and even a single error in judgment may wreck his career. Although a cat is said to have nine lives, the erring administrator is at times fortunate to have even a second chance.

Good judgment is the most prized attribute of an administrator. It is the attribute most often mentioned when references are requested, or given, for individuals under consideration for an administrative position. The same is true when people discuss the performance of an administrator. The role of judgment is so pervasive that critics tend to evaluate the total administrative performance in terms of it. Under such circumstances judgment is used as a kind of blanket term that sums up the effectiveness with which a man uses all his attributes and skills. It is considered a sort of integrate of all the other characteristics that the individual possesses. This importance assigned to judgment in administration is no doubt well placed. The administrator is a practitioner, and all practice depends upon the use of judgment. It is something that every practitioner uses in his every act. It isn't all he uses, but it always guides him in whatever else he does use. Since people know that judgment is one element that is always present in any act of the practitioner, all his actions are likely to be credited to good or bad judgment. This isn't ever fully correct, but it is sufficiently descriptive to provide a stranger with an idea of a particular administrator's general competence.

Despite the crucial importance of judgment in administration, it has received scant attention in management literature, and the word is scarcely mentioned there except as a correlate of decision making. This is all right as far as it goes, but it does not go nearly far enough. Judgment affects far more than the decision. It qualifies the results of the decision as well as the decision itself. Judgment is as much a controlling factor in the implementation of the decision as it is in the production of it. Deciding is not the same as doing. The decision helps determine the direction, but it does not assure passage to the destination. Good judgment cannot guarantee the ends either, but it can provide indispensable assistance along the route.

Psychologists have not contributed very much to the administrator's understanding of judgment. They apparently have been more interested in the man than in his product and more concerned with his characteristics than with his actions. This has been the general approach of most of the behavioral scientists. The administrator as a person has been largely ignored, while the attributes and traits of some impersonalized image of an administrator have undergone very precise measurement. Said another way, the interest seems to have been more in what the administrator was, or seemed to be, than in what he was doing. This statement is not necessarily a criticism of the behavioral scientist. His research has been aimed at identifying and classifying the specific traits and characteristics of the individual, and he has sought to particularize the attributes of the individual. This is good for the advancement of science, but it has not helped much to improve the administrator's judgment. Judgment is a composite process that brings into play the totality of an individual's traits and characteristics and represents a configuration of these traits rather than the simple sum of them. Also, judgment is a product of a particular situation; it represents a particular response made in a unique circumstance. One can never be certain which traits an individual will use in a given situation or that the individual's response will be the most appropriate and relevant of which he is capable. The responses that a given situation arouses in an individual may at times represent his worst traits rather than his best. One of the themes of this book is the belief that a person does not always come up with his best judgment.

Judgment is the result of a highly complex psychological process that has never been clearly defined. Fortunately, it does not seem that an understanding of the process is necessary for the exercise of good judgment. Some individuals almost always demonstrate a high level of good judgment; every normal individual demonstrates a great deal of it. If the latter were not true, we could not conduct even our private, everyday affairs. The problem lies in the lapses in good judgment that everyone suffers,

more or less infrequently, and in the fact that the general level of
a given individual's judgment may vary over periods of time. It is
these lapses that require examination if the administrator is to
improve the level of his judgment. This thesis is based on the notion that good judgment is natural to the process and that poor
judgment represents an interference with the process. If the interferences can be identified, the individual may be able to improve
his judgment by avoiding them or at least by minimizing their
influence.

This book is about the administrator's use of his judgment and
is not intended to take the place of many pages of technical discussion about the process of judgment. It is not intended to be
technical at all. It will not even attempt to provide any specifications for good judgment. The effort will be to examine the causes
of poor judgment as observed in the performance of many administrators in various fields of administration. The approach will be
to examine the work of the administrator and to attempt to
identify those aspects of his work that make him peculiarly vulnerable to errors of judgment. While no attempt will be made to
define precisely the judgment process, some of its general characteristics will be examined in order to help provide a context in
which to discuss the hazards to effective administrative judgment.

Essentially, judgment represents a matching of facts with
values. It can be likened to a filtering process in which the individual screens the facts he receives through a set of values that he
has adopted. This means that the quality of an individual's
judgment is dependent upon the quality of the facts and values
used in the judgment process. But it also depends upon the quality of the process. The best of facts and values can be adulterated
if the filter becomes clogged with interferences. The quality of
the administrator's judgment is dependent upon three fairly
independent variables, and any of these can independently
impair it.

The evaluation of the administrator's judgment may not even
be based on the best product of the process, however. It is based
on what the administrator exhibits. As far as others are concerned, the administrator's judgment is expressed in the actions
taken by the administration, and thus it can be evaluated only in
terms of what was actually done or not done. Further, the quality
of the administrator's judgment is decided by others. If the judg-

ment of the administrator is to be approved, it must reasonably conform with the way his observers think they would have acted in the same situation. The fact that they might not have acted in that way at all is not pertinent. The way they would actually have acted may have little relationship to the way they would have wanted to act, or the way they believe they would have acted. This means that for all practical purposes the administrator's judgment on each occasion is evaluated by those who are using their own best judgment.

The fact that the administrator's judgment is subjected to the test of comparison with the best judgment of those evaluating his performance places the administrator at a heavy disadvantage on several counts. They are judging him on his act rather than his thought. As stated above, the observers can evaluate the administrator's judgment only by his actions, that is, what he does or does not do, in a given situation. But what a man thinks and what a man does are not always the same thing. There is a difference between appraisal and response. The appraisal embodies the individual, while the action conveys him. The action may be something by, rather than of, the person. There are many reasons, to be discussed throughout this book, why we do not always use our best judgment. All of us can recall many instances of doing things even though at the time we knew better. When the administrator acts, he must reckon with realities beyond himself, but those sitting in the safety of their box seats can pass a judgment on his acts unfettered by the emotions and events that led him to act as he did. Also, because the administrator's judgment is evaluated after the act, it is likely that additional facts will have become available. The observers will often have the wonderful advantage of perfect twenty-twenty hindsight and, somewhat as in bridge, one peek at the full hand will tell much more than two finesses. There is still another temporal difficulty. This has to do with the time span involved in many decisions of the administrator. The administrator's judgment is often subjected to evaluation by a short-run yardstick for long-run decisions whose consequences require years for fruition.

Contrary to the impression that the above might give, the degree of success of a particular action is not the sole, nor perhaps the major, determinant of the evaluation placed on the administrator's judgment. The fact that those observing do apply the test of their own best judgment when evaluating his actions means they neither blame, nor credit, him for unwarranted or unintended consequences. For instance, the head of a shipping company may order one of the company's ships to make a trip up the Great Lakes that will extend beyond the usually accepted date for safe, ice-free passage. The fact that an unusual break in the weather permitted the ship to complete the trip will not prevent the order from being classified as one resulting from bad judgment. It will only be said that the company head got away with it. Likewise a freak storm that destroys a ship in a period of expected good weather will not result in the incident being charged to bad judgment. It will probably be said that the administrator in question was the victim of circumstances.

Because judgment is a mental process, it is often closely associated with intelligence. Actually, except at the lower extreme, there does not seem to be a close relationship between the level of intelligence and the general level of judgment demonstrated by different individuals. Above the lower extreme, there seems to be significant variation in the quality and consistency of judgment among individuals with apparently equal intelligence, and the variations seem to be accentuated among individuals with high intelligence. Obviously, higher intelligence increases an individual's ability to assimilate and understand complex facts. Other things being equal, this ability should serve to increase the competency of an individual's judgment. Higher intelligence should also enable him to drink more deeply of what he sees and experiences. However, these same factors may serve to seriously impair the range of his judgment. The person with high intelligence often specializes his interest and knowledge and thus narrows both the background of information and values available to the judgment process. A narrow range for judgment may be adequate in specialized professions and occupations, but it is likely to prove inadequate for the purpose of accommodating the traffic of diverse problems that confronts the administrator of even relatively small activities.

The notion that there is no necessary correlation between the level of the administrator's intelligence and his judgment is logical when one considers that intelligence is the product of the intellect. The intellect is that quality of the mind which enables the mind to acquire and retain knowledge. It is the quality that is used to process facts into knowledge by adding a perception of their meaning. Intelligence is what remains after the intellect has acted on the facts and thus represents stored-up knowledge. A test of the amount and kinds of stored-up knowledge is used to determine an individual's intelligence. Intelligence tests are knowledge tests. While knowledge is much more than facts because the intellect has performed the vital function of giving meaning to the facts, intelligence still represents only acquisition and retention of prepared or processed facts. If knowledge is to be translated into action, it must still go through the judgment process of being related to values. It is this matter of values that prevents any necessary correlation between the level of intelligence and the level of judgment. Good administrative judgment must fit the circumstances for which it was produced, and it is values which provide the criteria by which to measure the fit. Intelligence, as the product of intellect, is concerned with knowledge per se and in itself is devoid of the feelings which constitute one major component of an individual's values. This characteristic is recognized in the term "cold intellect," which is often used to describe the production plant for intelligence and emphasizes the fact that the intellect is not supposed to be warmed by considerations of feeling.

Knowledge is itself, of course, a kind of value in that new facts must be sized against already known facts in order to determine their meaning. The intellect can assign meaning to incoming facts only by relating them to the stored-up meanings possessed by its own intelligence service. In a way, a person never gets a brand-new understanding—he just adds to old understandings. A thing must fall within a person's "ken," or existing knowings, if it is to have a meaning for him. For instance, to get the meaning of a joke, we have to know both the normal situation and what is different, or "funny," about the situation around which the joke revolves. If we don't know the normal, or unfunny, situation with which the circumstances in the joke are being compared, we do not get the point and the joke falls flat. Knowledge represents an impersonal value for the judgment process, however. Like a road sign, it can tell how far it is to a particular town, but it can't tell us whether that is where we want to go. That is a function of our personal value system. To use a simple illustration, if we see a ten-year-old Rolls-Royce priced at a certain figure, we must weigh the matter of correctness of price against our knowledge of the prices being generally charged for ten-year-old Rolls-Royces in similar condition. This is an impersonal matter and has nothing to do with us as individuals. But if we consider buying the car, we will then have to weigh the matter against our personal values, which dictate why we want an old Rolls-Royce and why we might want it more than the many other things we might otherwise use our limited resources to purchase.

Admittedly, an argument could be made that one's personal values represent knowledge. Such an argument would be right, however, only with regard to the values that had been subjected to the clarifying process of the intellect and bleached of any feelings that would otherwise discolor them. The other part of one's values, and perhaps the far larger part, would have to be classified as unbleached beliefs, or opinions. This doesn't mean that a great many of our values aren't rational and wouldn't hold up under the bleaching process or that some color in our values necessarily spoils our judgment. In the present discussion it just means that most of our values can't qualify as knowledge because they have not been intellectually certified.

Any discussion of the role of knowledge in judgment must sooner or later involve the question of the influence of formal education on the level of judgment. Formal education seems to be in about the same company as intelligence with regard to the extent and manner of its influence on judgment. If individuals have a reasonably adequate command of the language, there does not seem to be any direct correlation between the levels of education and the levels of judgment demonstrated by different individuals, except on matters where technical knowledge is required. The reasons for this lack of direct correlation are probably the same as those involved in the relationship between intelligence and judgment. Formal education is concerned primarily with the transmission of knowledge. It is an efficient method of increasing the individual's inventory of knowledge because it uses the accumulated experiences of others and does not have to depend upon the individual's own experiences. This means that the inventory can be built up much more rapidly and that it can be much more selective. Also, it means that the ability and capacity to acquire knowledge can be increased because the complexity and difficulty of the material can be organized to best sharpen and stretch the intellect. Education increases the individual's store of knowledge and thus increases his capability for good judgment, but its actual influence upon his judgment is very probabilistic and can vary significantly between individuals.

Formal education can produce a learned man, but it can't in itself produce a wise man. A learned man knows many things, but a wise man knows one big thing that the learned man might not know: the ways of the world about him. "Wise" comes from an Anglo-Saxon word meaning way, manner, or mode, and a wise man is a man who knows the ways and manners of people. The word connotes an experienced man who has been through the mill and who has likely paid for the trip; "sadder but wiser" is a phrase that is as natural-sounding as "ham and eggs." The word also connotes mellowing or aging. We say "wise beyond his years" when a young person acts wisely. In general, wisdom could be said to represent knowledge ripened by experience. In the same light one might also say that knowledge serves as testimony for judgment and that wisdom serves as the jury to determine the utility of the testimony. Because knowledge transmitted through teaching represents vicarious experiences for the learner, it can qualify only as hearsay testimony borrowed from others. It may be quite accurate, but it isn't fully acceptable. Like a borrowed hat, it just doesn't sit well because it doesn't exactly fit the fellow who borrows it. This is the notion conveyed in the use of the term "academic" to imply that an idea hasn't been empirically decorated. Experience is a conforming process that serves to shape the things an individual learns to fit the real life to which the learning will be applied.

The fact that it is difficult to learn to make love from a book is in no way an indictment of plagiarized knowledge. To achieve the broad knowledge necessary in administration, the administrator must be a constant cadger. If he has only his own experiences to feed him, he quickly can become self-impoverished. Also, his knowledge can lose the balance so badly needed in administration. Experience is, in large part, a fortuitous thing and is marked by randomness. It is a conforming process, but it can deal only with what comes to hand. Perhaps most importantly, an individual must rely on a background of knowledge provided by others as a foundation on which to store his own new experiences. This is especially true for the administrator since he must demon-

strate common sense in decisions about many things that have
been uncommon, or at least superficial, within his personal
experience.

Common sense can only be common if it coincides with the
judgment of all people sufficiently knowledgeable to pass competent judgment on a particular question. This is quite different
from saying that common sense is the sense demonstrated by the
celebrated "common man" or the "man on the street." It is the
sense that a man would demonstrate if he had the facts and the
training required to understand a given situation. We can credit
this kind of common sense only to the "man on a particular
street." Thus we would expect the judgment of a banker on a
problem of foreign exchange to be shared by most other bankers
who are involved in foreign exchange. Likewise, we would expect
the judgment of a nuclear scientist on a problem of applying nuclear power for industrial use to be shared by other nuclear scientists possessing competency in that specialized field. On a problem
concerned with nuclear power, we would not expect the judgment
of the specialist in foreign exchange to be shared by the specialist
in nuclear power. This logic is not always followed, however. We
don't always distinguish between the pronouncements of the specialist on his specialty and those he makes on matters outside his
specialized field. There is a tendency to ignore the fact that judgment is exercised in every situation and that each specific situation has its own unique set of facts to be interpreted. In matters
where we have no competency ourselves, we tend to give credit
to the judgment of another individual just because he has high
competency in an unrelated field. In those circumstances in which
we can't determine the truth for ourselves, we seem to equate
creditability with "bigness." That is, we accept as truth the beliefs
we hear repeated most often; or those shared by the largest number of those around us; or those stated by the biggest names we
know. That there is a disposition to associate great wisdom with
great names was stated in an admonition to those of great name
by Franz Josef Gall, himself a great name in anatomy, more than
150 years ago when he said, "Men who enjoy a great name should
more than others guard themselves against spreading hazardous
ideas, for however erroneous they may be, they will be repeated."
Evidently his own name wasn't great enough to transform this
idea into an accepted truth, for too often the specialist seems

5521

willing and eager to have others believe in the versatility of his competence. This is demonstrated by the physical scientist who speaks as if his mastery of nature has made him a master in economics, and by the minister who talks as if his mastery of theology has made him an expert in labor relations. An individual who is highly trained in economics or labor relations will attach very little validity to the judgments of either of these individuals on problems in his own field. He will say they are out of their environment. He might very well listen to them on matters outside both his and their fields, however. The fact that he is highly critical of ideas in his own field doesn't seem to make him skeptical about other fields. One can produce more than a little evidence that expertness may produce credulity concerning matters outside the expert's field.

As an aside, the comment can be made that businessmen are being urged to assume a similar role of omnipotence in judgment. They are being told that they should actively engage in politics and seek to control the development of general public policy. Such a venture on a wide scale by our business leaders could not help but have unfortunate consequences. A concerted effort of this sort on the part of businessmen would probably lead to the formation of a labor party and a political division by class rather than ideas. Also, it would mean a dilution of the time and energies of the businessman away from his important and vital role of carrying on the business of the nation. Public affairs are too complex to be considered only from a business point of view, and the businessman would have to be prepared to study and understand the full range of public issues. Unless he did this, he would be exposed as a novice in the many complex fields of social policy in which he lacks the special competence required to exercise good judgment. Despite what businessmen might think, and how the fiction writers might depict them, the businessman's judgment is highly regarded by most people. This is because he has, in general, restricted his public use of it to matters in which he possesses special competence, and when he has attempted to influence public policy, he has generally restricted his efforts to affairs of business which he knows something about. Those who have opposed him have at least respected his competency to make judgments on those matters. But if he is going to enter actively into politics, he will be required to take a stand on all public policy questions. This will not only expose his lack of competence on many complex and difficult issues but it will compromise his freedom as a critic on those issues on which he is an authority. In order to maintain a public following, he would have to acquiesce to popular solutions of social problems, and this would muffle his voice in opposing those he might otherwise consider unsuitable. Of course the businessman has the right, and the obligation, to form his opinion on all matters of public policy and to express these to his neighbors and at the polls. This is a different story from an organized, public effort to enforce his political judgment on others, or from an expansion of the duties of his public relations staff to include thinking up solemn pronouncements to be issued in his name on virtually any subject. This latter course can cost him the public respect for his judgment that he must retain if he is to be permitted the freedom to continue to make judgments about the conduct of the nation's business.

To get back on the track after this philosophical side excursion, a brief examination of creativity is merited because creativity is also a member of the mental league. Used in its restricted, dictionary meaning of invention, of bringing something new into existence, creativity seems to lack any direct correlation with the quality of an individual's judgment. Because of the great emphasis being placed on creativity and how to stimulate and develop it as an ability of the administrator, the matter of definition is of more than passing importance. It may be that this growing interest represents another of the romantic fetishes to which administration seems peculiarly susceptible. But more important, it may mean that quite serious errors will be built into the programs for recruitment, promotion, and development of administrators. The basis for this assumption lies in the distinction between invention and application. The creative process produces something new, something that never existed before. If not for the danger of appearing facetious about an important process, one could best describe it as making something out of nothing. The creative product is the novel idea—not the act that issues from it. The judgment process, on the other hand, does not create ideas. It measures them. Thus one can have very good judgment and never have a novel idea. This would indicate that effective administration does not depend upon the inventive ability of the administrator. Administration is the implementation of ideas rather than the conception of them. The effective administrator makes ideas work, but he need not make them. He must be imaginative, but that is a conceptual skill and is concerned with the unseen rather than the unborn. Also, he is innovative, but this means a readiness to use the untried rather than the ability to conceive it. The effective administrator seeks new ideas and new arrangements of old ones, but he is more likely to be a miner of them than a maker of them.

Any strong correlation that exists between creativity and administrative judgment is likely to be an inverse one. There are logical reasons why this should be true. Persons who are highly creative are that way because they are conditioned to see things differently from the way things are usually seen. They have to strive to see things in a new way unless they are to see only what everyone else sees. Creative persons are by habit of mind uninhibited by the culture around them and the conventions that the culture utilizes for its own cohesiveness. All of this means that the truly creative are prone to be out of step with accepted ideas, even on matters unrelated to their work, and their judgment reflects such "out-of-stepness."

Although highly creative individuals may not score high on judgment, they are precious assets of the enterprise with which they are associated if their abilities are meaningfully and productively utilized. However, creativity and good administrative judgment are two different things, and they seem to be more incompatible than compatible. The good administrator must, of course, be imaginative and possess a high order of conceptual skills. These are putting-together skills, however, rather than discovery skills, and are in themselves important elements of the judgment process. The field of industry offers numerous examples demonstrating the dichotomy between creativity and administrative effectiveness. Seldom has an inventor been able to administer successfully an enterprise founded on his invention. Often the enterprise is highly successful for the short period of time during which the new product's competitive superiority obscures the effects of the way the enterprise is possibly being administered. Later, either growth of the enterprise or of competitive products creates problems that usually result in loss of administrative control and sometimes of ownership.

The matter of being in step, mentioned earlier, probably

represents the largest single characteristic by which the administrator's judgment is evaluated. It was stated earlier that judgment is a mental process which matches facts and values. This matching must, however, make sense to those around the administrator if it is to be accepted as good judgment. This means that the administrator must, in practice, apply the values of those around him if he is to meet this test of consensus. (This statement can raise all sorts of moral and ethical issues, but they are not pertinent to this particular discussion. The concern here is that the administrator understand how his judgment is evaluated rather than how far morally he should go to have his judgment approved or followed.) Because the administrator's judgment must make sense in terms of the values of those the administrator wishes to influence, it must have grounds common with their own. This is what is meant by "common sense" and is the reason that the term is used interchangeably with good judgment. In a very real way the administrator has to think himself into other people's shoes.

The above indicates that there is a provincial quality to good judgment. A simple illustration of this quality is seen in a problem concerning what dress should be prescribed for bank clerks in a Honolulu bank. The bank administrator in Honolulu might recently have been transferred from Boston, where he was conditioned to respect formality in dress, and thus be personally opposed to the habit of wearing sport shirts to work, which is done in Honolulu. Good judgment requires, however, that he use the values current in Honolulu. This illustration suffers from the fact that most situations requiring administrative judgment are more complex and most values are considerably more subtle. We are not conscious of most of the values we use or of the values used by those around us. Also the administrator does not have time to think of all the values to be matched in the judgment process. Still his judgment must take into account the controlling values of the particular environment in which it is being exercised. This means that his judgment must at times be shaped by environmental values which are not his own.

The foregoing indicates that the administrator's judgment is greatly dependent upon an acculturation with the particular environment in which he is practicing. This again brings up the role played by experience in the judgment process. "Acculturation" encompasses the complete impact of the environment on the individual, but here it is the best term to express the subtle role experience plays in the judgment process. Values are a way of looking at things, and we generally look at things through the spectacles fitted upon us by those around us. To a large extent, the values of a person are an unlisted inventory of the encounters he has had with his society. Through unwitting observation, whole clusters of outlooks and insights are gained bits at a time as the individual becomes experienced in the ways of his environment. His values become rooted in the numberless explanations and justifications continuously provided him concerning all that is happening about him and are further shaped as he gives explanations and justifications to all those around him. Most of this acculturation goes on without his knowledge, but this is because of the nature of the process and the limitless scope of it and not because it is voluntary on his part. Normal individuals seek to conform and to adjust to their environment. Even the beatnik, who pretends to rebel, holds tightly to most of the ways and outlooks of those whose attention he is attempting to attract. If for no other reason, life around the individual is simpler if it is institutionalized and he is in step with it. This is undoubtedly one of the reasons a person seeks affiliation. He seeks to assist acculturation by checking his beliefs and determining the rightness of his position. He is especially anxious in novel or ambiguous situations to see how others act and what opinions they hold. This also may be one of the major reasons we are reluctant to change. We are fearful of being caught out of step. We do not necessarily absorb all of the controlling values of those around us but we develop a feel for them, a sort of "weather eye" that permits us to take the values of others into account effortlessly.

In addition to the actual advantages the administrator gains from familiarity with a particular environment, he receives a bonus in the credit which people seem to automatically give for such familiarity. Added weight is given to the opinions of those raised in a person's own neck of the woods. There may be some truth to the definition of an expert's being a person from a distant city insofar as his technical knowledge is concerned. However, it is usually a different story when deciding the course of action to be taken with regard to the expert's recommendations. The recommendations of the expert usually have little weight until they pass the test of provincial judgment. We also tend to favor the judgment of those with the same religious or racial backgrounds as our own. The familiarity factor is in part the reason extra attention is paid to the judgment of older people. We feel perhaps that older people should know more about things because they have been around things longer.

Said in another way, a requirement for good judgment is that it be indigenous to the environment in which it is exercised. This means it must be compatible with the ways of those affected by it. What goes in a business firm may not go in a university, or what goes in city hall may not go in a bank. Good judgment can occur only when the frame of reference in which it is being made is taken into account. The precepts of environmental relativism must be observed since administrative actions are social contracts, and a fair contract pretty well has to involve each party's knowledge of the other's attitudes and goals. We cannot be sure our actions make sense to others unless we know what might make nonsense to them, and we cannot know what will be accepted as rational unless we have a notion of what will appear to others as irrational.

Compatibility of judgment does not refer to agreement about the decision but, instead, to the conventions observed and the criteria used in arriving at the decision and in implementing it. Good judgment is a function of the social process but does not necessarily conform with it. The definition of good judgment is concerned more with the process than with the product. In general, one would expect a high percentage of agreement under conditions of compatibility, but agreement is not the imperative. The imperative is that those affected by the administrator's judgment have confidence that he takes into account the values with which he contends.

As the first chapter of this book has developed, the reader may very likely be getting the impression that too much emphasis has been placed on the administrator's ability to say and do the correct thing at the proper time. It may seem that the administrator's judgment has been treated as the errand boy for everyone else's values and that more concern has been shown for keeping the drain pipe in good repair than with what comes through it. The remaining chapters should help to dissipate any such impression and to establish the fact that judgment does indeed represent a dominance of thought and consideration over opinion and personal whimsy. The remaining chapters will not, however, contradict the notion that, administratively speaking, our judgment is in great part what other people think it is. This does not mean the administrator is not responsible for doing what he thinks needs to be done. It is simply a matter of defining the race in which the administrator runs.

To say that judgment must meet the test of consensus does not mean that it must be popular to be evaluated as good. What a man believes and what a man likes are not always the same thing. Members of the organization expect those in authority to demonstrate good judgment and will not have respect for them if they fail to do so. This is true even if the bad judgment brings advantages to the individuals concerned. They may exploit the advantage, but they will not admire the administrator. While in the short run some individuals may, because of overriding considerations, choose to go along with bad judgment and even support it, most people will, in the long run, rebel against repeated instances of poor judgment. This fact has been learned the hard way by administrators who have chosen the popular way out and found that out was ultimately where they did indeed find themselves.

The above may encounter opposition on several counts. One of these has to do with the long-term popularity of politicians who act against their own better judgment by supporting legislation in the special interests of their constituents. The error here is in the analogy and not in the discussion. It is the same error made by those who write on the subject of leadership and confuse the politician with the administrator. The legislator deals directly with the rank and file and is not required to secure performance from them. He does not sit at the apex of a hierarchy but is a proxy holder for his constituents and is evaluated by the way he represents their special interests. He is expected to be partisan and to show favor to those he represents. It should be noted, however, that no such favoritism is permitted on the part of those who administer whatever special-interest legislation might be passed. Another widely held concept that might be raised in opposition to the previous discussion is that individuals will consciously rationalize their personal interests into good judgment. Undoubtedly, a person's judgment is significantly influenced by his personal needs

and biases, but to the extent that they do in fact fool his judgment, they are unknown to him. He unconsciously may search
harder for those facts that will bolster his case and may knowingly try to dodge those that will weaken it, but this only
demonstrates that he desperately needs to prove his case to himself and that he cannot consciously kid himself. He must be right
in his own mind if he is actually to think that he is right. He
may seek always to justify his actions to others, but it is highly
doubtful that he succeeds very often in consciously spoofing
himself or even tries to do so very often.

The statement was made early in this chapter that the administrator did not always demonstrate his best judgment. Much is
made of the fact throughout this book. Much will also be said
about the administrator's failure to permit his best judgment to
form. Both the formation and application of administrative judgment involve skills that can be improved. There is every reason to
believe that skill in the use of judgment is like the skill of a physi-
cian, a musician, a bridge player, or any other professional, and
must be practiced repeatedly if the skill is to become good and
remain good. Conscious, meaningful practice can improve the
administrator's skill in the use of his judgment in a number of
ways. It can increase his dexterity of judgment by increasing his
ability to spot the significant and his speed in bringing his knowledge and values to bear on the facts. It can give him an administrative savvy that provides him with prior or ready-made understandings, available and usable at any given moment. Problems
have a family resemblance, and even though they are never
exactly alike, they are never totally different. A wide acquaintance with problems can help him become a sort of administrative
man-around-town whose judgment has the jump on situations as
they start to occur.

Experience gained through practice provides seasoning for the
administrator's judgment and permits it to function properly in
the face of upsetting or provocative circumstances. This seasoning
can produce the sort of administrative *sang-froid* that will help
prevent him from getting "buck fever" in untried and novel situations. Experience can help develop the mental poise that gives
the administrator self-possession and clearheadedness in the face
of confusing and disturbing conditions. This can come in part
from the confidence he develops in his judgment from seeing it

tested and repeatedly proved under fire. Experience is also a tempering process that matures the administrator's judgment and provides it with the sort of dispositional and temperamental control that produces evenness and prevents excess. It not only helps maintain a proper balance between mind and emotion but it can help develop the sort of maturity that introduces the qualities of sobriety and seriousness into judgment.

Just what effect experience actually has on the administrator's judgment, however, is a very dependent variable. It depends upon what he has a chance to experience. Experience that is meaningful to growth must be innovative and not just repetitive. A person can't get much more out of his experiences than is there. Growth from experience depends also upon one's openness to his experiences. Most people are strongly inclined to seek the traditional and proven and to read into their experience what they have learned to expect there. It is difficult for the administrator to gain more than he is willing to take, and some individuals seem to gain much from experience while others seem to gain very little. Most important, the gain depends upon the meaning the administrator gives to his experiences. He will pick up notions from his experience, but there is always the question of what he will pick up. To learn a lesson well is not the same as learning a good lesson. Actually, experience may warp one's judgment because both the duration and degree of the effect of experience are greatly dependent upon the intensity of the particular experience. Experience is a random thing, and the most intense experience may be the least meaningful for purposes of sizing up a subsequent situation. Because of its deeper impression, however, it is likely to be overemphasized. This overemphasis is aided by the fact that no experience is fully permanent, and we are gradually shaping and reshaping our thinking all the time. Since the impressions of our less intense experiences fade rapidly, the more intense ones remain to interact with the new experiences and thus their influence is magnified still further out of proportion. The unbalance in experience is further abetted by the fact that we automatically supply more than was actually experienced in a situation in order to fill out an otherwise incomplete picture. Because a person can supply only from what he has, he is likely to build up his new experiences with the most enduring parts from the old.

Perhaps we will never understand the wonderful process by which man sizes up a confusing mass of perceptions and preconceptions and grasps meaning from them. If we ever do fully understand it, it is quite probable that it will not help us utilize the process any better. Apparently, one does not have to understand too much about the process to use it successfully. As with electricity, the user may need to understand only a few of the characteristics of the process in order to get the most out of it. The fact that all normal people seem to exercise a fair amount of good judgment indicates that the process usually works unless it is inhibited. The fact that those usually known to demonstrate excellent judgment sometimes exhibit poor judgment further shows that good judgment can be inhibited. All of us know, too, that there are many times when we do not use our best judgment but lose our head and override our better judgment. We often, with truth, tell ourselves that we knew better.

All of these characteristics of judgment lead to the notion that poor judgment results largely from an interference with the judgment process and that the exercise of good judgment depends in large part upon controlling such interferences. This notion is admittedly an oversimplification of a very complex problem, but it does have the very important advantage of offering an opportunity for the administrator to consciously improve the level of his judgment. This means of improvement consists of identifying and removing, or at least quarantining, the inhibitions to the exercise of good judgment.

If one observes his own administrative conduct and that of other administrators, he can recognize tendencies common to all administrators which interfere with their judgment. They are common to all administrators because they are human tendencies. Some are not bad in themselves and represent an asset to the administrator if their influence on his judgment is controlled. Some are quite necessary for the effective practice of administration. Some can be said to be conflicting, and the administrator's judgment is at times "torn" between them. This too is not bad, since such tendencies help keep each other under control. It is only when certain tendencies grow too strong, or become too habitual, that the level of judgment deteriorates. They are accentuated in administrative conduct because the administrator is confronted with so many situations in which they may exert themselves.

Some of them recur so often that they can be tagged and a conscious effort made to censor and control them. This book is an attempt to examine those tendencies the author has found most prevalent in his own work as an administrator and in the work of other administrators in diverse fields which he has observed. If the author is correct, the reader will recognize them from his own experiences although he may not have specifically identified and catalogued many of them. The value of this book will be in helping the reader to become more aware of these interferences with his judgment and to exert a conscious effort to control them. Watching them and controlling them is the administrator's best answer, for it is his only answer. He will never completely eliminate them.

Stress can distress
good judgment

2 Coolness and calmness are known as bosom companions of good judgment. This is because judgment is a process that depends upon a clear mind which filters facts through values. Strong emotions can gum up the mind and cause judgment to become adulterated by fouling up the filtering process. But, like other adulterants, emotions usually settle down and keep out of the way unless they are stirred up by heat and agitation. This means the mind needs to be cool and calm in order to keep the emotions under control. Friction from mental stress and strain tends to produce heat and tension, however, and this chapter will attempt to examine some of the influences of stress upon the administrator's judgment.

Certain physical factors are among the most obvious hazards to the emotional stability of the administrator. Some of these factors are the result of disease and may represent a chronic and permanent handicap to good judgment. It is not within the scope of this volume to discuss such diseases, since their influences are largely beyond the control of the individual himself. The influence of disease on emotional stability must be recognized by the administrator, however, and he should seek medical assistance to prevent and control such diseases. Modern medicine can cure many of them and can help the administrator combat the effects on his judgment of many of those that cannot be cured. Good health is in every way a valuable asset of the administrator, and he should treat it as such. Bad judgment is blamed on the administrator personally, irrespective of its cause.

Physical factors that produce short-term emotional obstacles against good judgment and are controllable by the individual are usually more important to the administrator than those that might be classified as pathological. This is true, if for no other reason than that the administrator who suffers from chronic and uncorrected impairment of his judgment will most likely be weeded out of administration. In any event, the consequences of his bad judgment usually will not be too pronounced, since his judgment will not be fully trusted. Because repeated errors in judgment will cause his judgment to be suspected, the organization will most likely develop ways and means of reviewing and even bypassing it. It is the occasional and temporary lapses in good judgment on the part of an individual whose judgment is usually respected that do most damage to the enterprise. Other members of the organization will not scrutinize his actions closely, and the occasional error will not be recognized. Or, if any members do feel an error in judgment has occurred, they will be reluctant to challenge it because the administrator's record of good judgment will make them uncertain of their own evaluation. Such sporadic instances of bad judgment can catch the organization off guard and perhaps going under full steam in the wrong direction.

There are several nonpathological physical factors which can occasionally but significantly affect an individual's judgment. One of the most common is fatigue. When an individual is tired, he simply doesn't think clearly. His mental processes are clouded, and his span of attention is greatly restricted. Worse, the chances are that he will suffer fatigue most often at the times he can least afford its effects on his judgment. These are the times when he is faced with important problems or is under the greatest pressure. Long hard hours in study of the problem, plus sleepless hours in worry over it, leave him at his dullest when he needs to be at his sharpest. This condition can affect him in either of two ways. He may take the one extreme of submission to decisions or conditions that are against his better judgment because he lacks the energy to resist unwise moves that may have strong backing or does not feel up to the hard task of implementing a change. On the other and more likely extreme, he may give way to the irritability and loss of temper that on most occasions accompany tiredness and serve to blind or override his better judgment. The effect of fatigue on judgment, as well as on all the other activities of the administrator, is so clearly detrimental that keeping reasonably fit is a must for him. This is more easily said than done, since the nature of his work means that the administrator can almost never get all his work done. This is literally true, since there are no set limits to the added gains that might accrue from added planning and added review by the administrator. At the same time he must realize that administration is a dangerous hangout for a tired man and that bad judgment can often be worse than no judgment. The economics of marginal utility apply to the administrator's use of his own energy as well as to his use of the other resources of the enterprise.

A low stress level is a very vulnerable flank for the administrator, and fatigue is only one of many contributing factors. It is both a psychological and physiological condition and may represent both inherited and acquired tendencies. Low tolerance to stress is often manifested as anger in the individual's conduct. It is the control of such manifestations that is important administratively, and, from the evidence, this control can be developed or acquired to a high degree. Training has a powerful effect on anger, both in stimulating motivation toward it and in repressing it, and lack of control thus represents either the development of poor habits or the failure to develop the proper ones. All of us have seen enough of our own conduct and the conduct of those around us to learn that the use of a hot temper is in part, at least, habit-forming. Each time we let go, it becomes easier to let go the next time. The fact that we are "letting go" is proved by the fact that even the worst-tempered individuals seem, to some extent, to choose the occasions and the individuals against whom they take off the stops. As the habit grows, however, they become less discriminating about the time and place in which they dare display their temper, and unless the practice is checked, it becomes habitual and the explosion level is set increasingly lower.

Individuals who let their tempers outgrow them sometimes fall back for an excuse on the doctrine inherited from the philosophers, and now used by some behavioral scientists, that their temperament is inherited. An individual's temperament is admittedly an important element in the way a person responds. Its importance, however, is more related to the mode in which he responds than to the character of his response. Temperament tells only half the story of what an individual will do. A person may have a "quick" temperament, but that doesn't indicate what he will be quick about. He may be quick in his thinking, but slow to reply, and he may be quick in his reply, and still be kindly and solicitous in what he says. Also, there is a difference between being quick-tempered and being high-tempered. There may be divided opinion among behavioral scientists regarding how much of an individual's mode of response is hereditary, but what he reacts with depends upon his character, and this is acquired and changeable.

An explosive temper is damaging to the administrator's effectiveness in a number of ways. People cannot help reducing their respect for him when they see him chronically lose his poise and self-control. Control of situations and of individuals is the major purpose of administration, and it naturally follows that the administrator cannot expect to retain control over others unless he can first control himself. It also follows that the fear of his temper on the part of his colleagues will serve to isolate the administrator from the flow of information and ideas so vital to his effective performance. Things will not be brought to his attention by his colleagues and subordinates for fear of creating a scene. His direct requests for information will be answered more as he wants them answered than as they should be answered. In a manner of speaking, his communications will become fouled up by the sugarcoating from the messages he receives. Those with contrary ideas will be reluctant to present them, and he will forfeit his match with their minds by insisting they tangle with his temper. Continued demonstrations of unreasonable anger will ultimately eliminate even the one advantage that the administrator might gain from a display of temper. The organization will become accustomed to such manifestations and adjust to them. Irritation

on his part will then lose any significance as a means of demonstrating substantial displeasure with organizational or individual
performance. People will still dread his temper, but they will not
be able to interpret it. The administrator must exhibit displeasure
with inefficient and inadequate performance in order that everyone may know the level of performance expected. If the situation
warrants, it may be necessary for him to exhibit anger in order to
demonstrate extreme displeasure. But the administrator must remember that anger as a weapon for obtaining mastery is a self-
feeding device, and if it works once, it is likely to be tried again
and again. Things are relative, and a big thing quickly becomes a
normal thing if it is the only thing people ever experience. Administration by tantrum can be effective only so long as the
tantrum represents a change of emotional pace.

Anger produces some very disturbing effects on the administrator's judgment. In the first place, it often will cause him to ignore
or override his best judgment. He will do and say things that he
knows at the time he should not do and say. All of us can recol-
lect instances in which anger caused us to act against our better
judgment. This is because of the rash position anger leads one to
take and the necessity of acting up to that position. It is a matter
of acting out a role of courageousness adopted under the heady
stimulation of anger. Also, anger keeps us from allowing our
judgment to form. In such instances we act without taking time
to think. We lash out at the provocation, or at the nearest substitute if we either cannot recognize the real provocation or are
afraid of it. At such times we are more interested in getting even
than in acting evenly. This is shown by the strong remorse we
feel when our anger cools after we have given our judgment an
opportunity to operate. Unfortunately, we can neither erase
words that are spoken in anger nor undo actions that are taken
when anger blocks our judgment. Some of us may be big enough
to eat crow and admit we acted emotionally, but a steady diet of
crow doesn't nurture effective administrators.

Anger inhibits whatever judgment the administrator does form,
by fixing his mind. The person or thing he is angry about monop-
olizes his attention and prevents a rounded judgment. He develops
a fixation on the affront and reviews it again and again. His mind
goes round in circles and is dominated by the incident rather than
the circumstances which surrounded the incident. He can't have

an open mind because his mind remains filled with the fixed ideas that hot anger has welded there. He can't have a balanced perspective on the particular problem because he keeps viewing things from the same angle. He keeps seeing the thing that made him mad rather than the things that need to be done about the problem. For these reasons a brooding mind is no spot for breeding new ideas or new possibilities.

The effects of a brooding mind on the judgment of the administrator go much beyond the fixation of his thinking on the affront or hurt that has been done him. The tendency to seek retribution —to get even—is a natural and compelling correlate of anger. We get mad about things, but we get mad at people. We blame things on people and usually focus our anger on the individuals we connect most closely with the things we resent. The extent to which we blame the individual does not seem to be related to how greatly he was involved but rather to how great is our resentment. Sometimes we even hunt for someone on whom to take out our anger. There seems to be some sort of law of human physics that says we must avenge an injustice with an indignity of equal size on another human being. This is probably what we mean when we talk of "getting even." It is perhaps also involved in our desire to "take it out" on someone. The "getting even" process is unusually injurious to the work of the administrator. Because he is involved in so many things, there are many opportunities for things to go wrong; if he lets his paranoia get out of hand, he can easily see a vandal behind every problem and spend all his time getting even with people rather than getting on top of his problems. It doesn't take too much of such activity to produce an actual vandal behind each problem, since those around the administrator have the same human tendencies and will feel the same urge to get even with him. His desire for revenge will unite those around him, but the united front he needs so badly will be against him instead of for him.

The united front against the revenge-minded administrator will not be limited to a private club consisting of those he "has taught a lesson." The administrator is under the constant scrutiny of all members of the organization, and his actions are weighed by each individual in terms of the meaning and import of those actions to the individual's own welfare. This means that even the most thoughtful and considered actions of the administrator are often misconstrued and cause unnecessary apprehension on the part of different members of the organization. Such scrutiny makes the members doubly sensitive to any arbitrary and capricious action he takes. They may not be affected directly by the particular action, but the result is almost the same so far as their attitude toward him is concerned. They realize they may be the next target. Capricious action, like lightning, is uncontrolled and irresponsible and may strike anywhere. The administrator who, out of anger, insists on teaching a lesson to the offender often has a larger class than he thinks, and he may be teaching more about himself than about the topic he thinks he is covering.

Administration by spite leaves its marks on the administrator in several ways. Soon he is carrying a chip on his shoulder and looking for a fight; and if the people around him are worth their salt, he most likely will find the fight for which he is spoiling. The ultimate result is a weakened organization as the fighters move out of the organization and are replaced by those with less courage and strength. The administrator will probably be unaware of the damage he is doing to his organization because he naturally will have pictured those leaving as troublemakers. He sees himself as a man of goodwill, and by this definition, those who left the organization are not. He will also be unlikely to discriminate between opposition to his personal attacks and opposition to his ideas and will be prone to write off those who leave as incompetent as well as uncooperative.

The chances are good that those who habitually taste the administrator's anger will oppose his good ideas as well as his bad ones. There is a chain reaction to anger and we usually meet rage with rage. It may be that this behavioral reciprocity is a universal feature of all human relations because we usually get back our change in whatever behavioral coin we give. This is shown by the compelling stress we place on the intentions of others in deciding what our reactions will be. We can graciously accept even serious injury from another if we believe it was unintended, but the slightest indignity will usually upset us if we think it was intentional. To be convinced of this, one only needs to recall how easily we bristle at the sound of a car horn behind us at a changing stop light and how quickly our scowl becomes an embarrassed smile when the driver pantomimes the fact that the toot was an accident by pointing to his horn button.

Ill will seems to be characterized by longevity. There may be several reasons why this appears to be true. Apparently, irritation has a fermenting quality. It seems to mount rather than subside, and its growth is hard to stop short of an anger explosion. Because of some sort of preservative factor, resentment keeps for a long time, and we can harbor ill feelings for a lifetime. Even when we apparently get over our hard feelings toward someone, we do not give them up. They may lie dormant for years and then be reactivated, strong as ever, in a single moment or by a single incident. Ill feelings that are not discharged continue to accumulate, and the larger the pile, the more quickly it seems to ignite. This is why we are sometimes shocked by witnessing a violent display of temper over what appears to be a minor matter. This also indicates that the larger the accumulation, the weaker the spark needs to be in order to explode it. Further, ill feelings seem to have a "substitution" quality. When we are upset for one reason, we can use that reason to trigger an explosion of pent-up feelings which were developed over entirely different issues and against entirely different individuals. The verbal tendencies of anger enhance its long life expectancy. When we are angry, we take off with our tongue and quickly expose our stored-up bad feelings to the other person. We dress the individual down by dressing the current incident up with all our past peeves against him. This is, of course, an invitation to the other fellow to dredge up all his past grudges toward us and dump them onto our emotional corns. Because ill will, unlike old soldiers, seems neither to die nor fade away, an ounce of prevention is worth several times the effort it requires. The administrator works with the same people for long periods of his career and cannot afford the psychological overhead that goes with maintaining a perpetual inventory of ill will. Working with people is difficult at best, and he needs to spend his time figuring out how to get along rather than in plotting on how to get even. Somehow, he must learn to carry the high tensions of his job without becoming high-strung.

Administrators who manifest rash and extravagant loss of temper may impair their exercise of good judgment in an opposite manner from those who hold grudges. Some individuals may demonstrate a spirit of contrition rather than retribution. All of us can recall times when we have been ashamed of having lost our tempers and of the attack we may have made upon the person we blamed in our anger. This shame, and a sense of fair play, caused us to seek to make amends and to demonstrate that we were sorry. Such a reaction on the part of the individual who loses his temper is both normal and noble and represents a sort of emotional hangover. It can, however, become a definite handicap to the exercise of good judgment on the part of the administrator. Administration by contrition can inhibit his use of his best judgment as much as administration by retribution. This is because it mortgages the independence of his judgment. If the administrator, to make amends for an anger spree, says yes when he should say no he is compromising his responsibility. If he feels obligated to another member of the organization, he will hesitate to exercise critical judgment so far as that individual is concerned. It is a case of doing penance for his personal acts at the expense of the enterprise.

Frustration is another feeling that belongs in the same company as anger. It serves to erode the individual's stress level and is often translated into anger. Like anger, it is commonly associated with aggression, but it sometimes produces manifestations the opposite of aggression. In this hearing, however, we are examining only its close association with anger, and that is enough to convict it so far as administration is concerned. Because of the nature of his work, the administrator has a wide-open exposure to frustration. He deals in ideas that he must depend on others to carry out. He is faced with problems that he does not create, but for which he is held responsible. Often he can see the way to go but cannot get the organization to go with him. To a very large extent, the administrator's success is what others decide it shall be.

In one sense, administration is defined as a matter of problem solving. Problem solving is an adaptive process that consists of finding ways to move around or over obstacles that are always getting in the way of the organization. Frustration is a result of the inability to adapt. It occurs when we feel that we are trapped by the obstacles confronting us and are unable to see a way around them. When we cannot see a clear way to attack the problem, we have an impulse to strike blindly at it. Because it will not yield to our judgment, we are prone to retaliate with our hottest emotions. By the queer sense that seems to accompany frustration, we think that if we blow our top, it will somehow blow the obstacle out of our way. But usually when we blow our top, we only succeed in blowing our chances ever to properly solve the problem.

If one is permitted to make such a comparison, blind anger which has been aroused by frustration is the most unprofitable sort of anger. Unlike the anger that one directs against his tormentors, it does not always help whip back into line those whom it hits, since those it hits often are not out of line. Because it results from bafflement rather than disagreement, it really has no target and thus carries the stigma of misplaced anger. Most important, it cannot even claim the justification of serving as a lightning rod for the administrator's overcharged tensions. Anger is a counterfeit emotion so far as frustration is concerned. It is a bogus expression for what is actually personal bewilderment and helplessness, and a lightning rod is no good for siphoning off a mental fog. Frustration results from a mix-up in the administrator's feelings toward himself, rather than from a mishap in relations with others. A flare-up between two individuals can, on occasion, use up the static generated by the way the individuals rub each other.

When the hamstrung administrator starts looking for his tormentor, he will be smart to look in the nearest mirror, since frustration is a state of mind and therefore strictly a product of the individual's own thinking. It is a very relative thing, and its degree depends largely upon the level of accomplishment the individual sets for himself. The effective administrator is by nature highly achievement-oriented, but he usually controls his frustrations by chaining them to the realities around him. He knows that some problems have no solution and that both he and the enterprise must accommodate to them. However, he does attempt to recognize his problems. Not only does he consider it a matter of propriety to know what he is living with, but he realizes that undefined problems can also be a cause of frustration. He knows that the way to avoid frustration lies not in ignoring the problem, but rather in defining and facing it and, if necessary, consciously accepting it.

The successful administrator realizes early in his career that there is no place for heroes in administration and that success comes from the grubby job of delivering the goods day by day. This means that he has to restrain his desire to take on more work

than he can handle or work that others can handle. An overburdened administration is frustration laden. Hard work is satisfying work, but unfinished work is the opposite, and it is the work
that doesn't get done that can cause the administrator's ulcer. A
lack of time can gnaw at his conscience as well as his stomach,
since it may mean the work is being done only halfway. This
means that when he finds his appointments overflowing his calendar, he should audit his activities. It may be that he needs more
assistants or needs to delegate more, or it may be only a matter of
the way he is scheduling his time; but if he is smart, he will see to
it that he is using his time instead of its using him.

Strangeness can create uncertainty and frustration in the administrator's mind. This is demonstrated by the tendency we
demonstrate to criticize the methods, policies, customs, and individuals we find when we move to another organization. We are
bewildered by our lack of familiarity with the new landscape and
respond by attempting to knock it rather than to knock for information and direction. This is perhaps the reason why a new
broom sweeps clean. The more things a new administrator can
change, the less dependent he becomes on the new environment.
He won't need to learn his way around if he can change things
around his way. The administrator does bring new perspective
and new ideas to a new job, and he ought to use them; but he
needs to remember that futile feelings can be confused with
fertile ideas when he is in a strange environment.

A low stress level can have still other effects on judgment. One
of these is fear, which sometimes blinds judgment more than anger
does. It is seldom manifested in such extravagant forms as is
anger, but it plagues every administrator to some degree. In its
milder and controlled forms it can be considered an asset to the
administrator because it can serve as censor for his judgment and
his actions. It is a reminder to the administrator that he is not a
freewheeling agent, but that his actions have consequences he
must face. The normal person learns to live with his fears and to
both observe and control them. Experience teaches him what
fears to respect and what risks to take. Because of his large exposure to pressures and risks, it is necessary for the administrator
to learn to exercise a high level of self-control, so that he will not
panic in the face of opposition or uncertainty. If he allows his
fear to become fright, his reason and his scruples can be over-

whelmed. Fear can confuse his judgment and also prevent him from exercising what he knows to be his best judgment.

The urge to act from expediency is a form of fear. It may result from factors such as a lack of administrative time or energy, but it most commonly represents the administrator's concession to pressures he is unwilling to face. It can represent an attempt by the administrator to buy his way out of problems by yielding to immediate pressures and ignoring the long-run effects of his purchase. It often results in the administrator's being stuck with a policy he can't live with. If the administrator repeatedly yields to expediency, he will permanently weaken his influence in the organization, since yielding to the pressures of the moment is the same as issuing an open invitation for an attack on his authority by the most aggressive and vocal members of the organization. The result is a sort of "cafeteria administration" in which everyone strong enough to do so selects his own policies. This will be seen by all members of the organization as evidence of indecision and uncertainty on the part of the administrator, and, organizationally speaking, about the only thing that could be worse than a bad decision is the demonstration of indecision. It will demonstrate a lack of convictions about long-run goals and an unwillingness to stand up and be counted on issues important to the welfare of the organization. It will show he can't stand his ground because it will show he has none. It will finally result in administration by default and the administrator's becoming an agent instead of the boss. A policy of peace at any price has seldom produced peace, but it can be counted on always to raise the price. In this connection it should be pointed out that administration is not a popularity contest and that many administrative decisions, of necessity, represent choices between opposing views within the organization. While all members of an organization may have the same long-term interests, their ideas concerning how best to achieve those interests are not always so clear and unified. Under such circumstances it isn't possible to have all sides like all administrative decisions, but it is possible and important that they respect them. Such respect comes only if the decisions follow some logical pattern obvious to all parties affected by them.

Failure to see the implications to the organization of decisions based on expediency may produce several unfavorable results. As in all cases where the treatment is aimed at the symptoms rather than the cause, it may mask the basic cause of the problem and thus prevent a solution at the time it might be most easily accomplished. Administration is not a game of solitaire, and it cannot ignore the rights that individuals develop through precedent and in established practices within the organization. The results of expedient decisions may not come to a head until long after strong organizational habits have been developed and strong claims staked out on the basis of those decisions. Corrective measures will usually take an even longer time to put into effect if upheaval and strife are not to result. If circumstances are not corrected at first notice and are encouraged to grow into situations, the trauma to the organization is bound to be greater when correction is finally attempted. The reformation of organizational habits and practices is a tedious and slow process at best, and the road back is long and hard. The administrator can expect a full dividend of antagonism, even under the best of circumstances, as he attempts to redeem the past.

A second unfavorable result from decision making on a first-come–first-served basis is the damage to continuity of policy. The essence of organizational effort is coordination. If there is to be unity of effort, an effective organization can go in only one direction at a time. Perhaps no requisite is as important to coordination as predictability of administrative reaction, because it is the only way the administration can influence the hundreds of decisions which have to be made at all levels in even the smallest of organizations. It is tough enough to develop an organization that wants to do what the administrator wants done, but it is impossible to accomplish the administrator's wishes unless his wishes can be predicted. Without consistency in decision making at the top level, there is no basis by which those at other levels in the organization can predict administrative wishes. If a man undoes one day what he did the day before, no one can ever understand what he does or what he wants done. Others won't be able to stand by him because they won't know where he stands. If the administrator continually bows to pressures and becomes a quick-change artist in decision making, he must expect to lose his following. "Broken field" decision making imposes an intolerable burden on those who have the task of keeping in line with the leader. Ad-libbed policies for the sake of pleasing the critics can only cause the rest of the cast to lose their places in the administrative script.

In addition to the *ad hoc* type of administration that results from acting from expediency, there are likely to be other undesirable side effects on the administrator's judgment. He cannot hide from himself the fact that he stampeded psychologically when the going got rough. It may be that he can convince everyone else that he had good reasons, but in his own heart he knows they were not the real reasons. This can damage his self-respect and cause him to stampede even more quickly on future occasions when his judgment is challenged, since an abject administrator is usually in no position to object. This disgust with himself can produce an opposite reaction that is both unfair and unwise. He will have a tendency to assuage his pride by "taking it out" on a weaker member of the organization, or, in an effort to reestablish his administrative manhood, he may arbitrarily say no to the next request that happens along, just to prove his courage and recapture his self-respect. Usually anger leads one to want to fight and fear leads one to want to escape, but a strong enough feeling of inadequacy can reverse the urge of the fearful administrator and cause him to engage in senseless fight. This can occur when his fear is turned into frustration because of his inability to find a way to escape a serious problem. It is not a matter of suddenly gaining courage but rather of finally getting cornered. If his sense of inadequacy becomes sufficiently ingrained, he may feel permanently cornered and change to growling instead of groveling. Because fear and anger have a common parent in stress, it may be that the two are really twins and the difference in expression is simply due to the difference in the direction in which each is looking. Fear is always looking at the future and anger is always looking at the past. Both are running away from stress, and probably they are running in different directions only because they got headed that way. The notion that the distinction between the urge for fight and the urge for flight may be one without a difference is supported by the fact that we never seem to have a strong urge to do either when we are winning. It is only when the tide is turning against us that we stop using our head and start swinging or running. In other words, it is only when we think we are inadequate for the circumstances confronting us that we lose our heads and begin to use our fists or our feet. It isn't material whether we choose to blow or to blow off; the fact is that it is our own inadequacies that confront us.

If there is any merit to the above notion, then a great part of the answer for the administrator's excess anger and fear lies in his properly perceiving his adequacies. This is a matter of personal definition, and he controls that definition. For instance, the Sunday golfer doesn't get upset when he fails to break par, nor would he be fearful of being beaten if he were playing with the club pro. However, he might get angry if he didn't break 100 or he might suffer from fright in a playoff for the Class C cup. This doesn't mean that he would not be trying to break par, or not trying his best against the club pro. It just means that he would not be trying to prove he was good enough to do these things. It is in the proving, rather than in the trying, that our self-esteem determines the danger to which it is exposed, and it is this same place that marks the difference between trying to show we are not afraid and having to prove that we are not failures or cowards.

There is, of course, a time for fear and a time for anger. If the administrator has placed his self-esteem in the right place, then he should react strongly when someone tries to run over it. Where to place his self-esteem is a difficult problem. As with all human behavior there are no specific rules; all the administrator can do is try to observe reality. His important guideline is the frequency with which he finds himself getting angry or becoming overly fearful. If his self-esteem gets hit too often, it is logical for him to assume that it is overexposed and should be moved to a safer spot. There is a time to attack, but there is also a time to retreat, and the administrator can do little but come to terms with things beyond his abilities or his control. It is worse than useless for him to try to stand his ground where he has none.

When he moves his self-esteem back to a less exposed position, the administrator needs to be sure he isn't moving it too soon or too far. It may be that he hasn't been giving it a sufficient chance to look after itself. Responses made out of anger and fear are much more rapid than those made out of consideration and agreement, and they can be triggered before the full story is out if the administrator develops the habit of beating the gun. Further, once anger and fear have been triggered, they cut off any further reception, no matter what the full story might be. Too, the administrator must recognize the extent to which his own attitudes toward others may be causing him to see hostility when it doesn't exist and to exaggerate what does exist. Our attitudes are self-reinforcing, and the more one expects another to be hostile, the more hostile he himself becomes. The administrator is likely to encounter hostility to some degree at any time and must learn to accept some amount of it as normal. People's feelings toward each other are inescapably a mixture of liking and disliking. The administrator must deal with the hostile interests as well as the harmonious ones; it isn't whether hostilities exist, but how he deals with them, that counts. He can't always control how other people act, but he can control how he lets it affect him.

The administrator must recognize the extent to which his own actions provoke and frighten others and serve to create some of the hostilities toward himself. Unless he can be sufficiently receptive to the opinion of others without becoming defensive or hostile, he is bound to build up a full sick bay of hurt feelings. The terrible thing about liking and disliking is that both turn on such small differences. Lifelong friendships can be formed while waiting for a bus, and lifelong feuds can be started by disagreement about who gets the vacant seat. This fragile difference between liking and disliking doesn't mean that the administrator must tiptoe his way through the organization or hold his breath as he holds the organization in line. It does mean that he can profit if he learns to raise his eyebrows instead of the roof and remembers that the other fellow also needs a little self-esteem to go along with his bread and butter.

Whether the administrator runs up the white flag from fear, or runs up his temperature from anger, he is running the risk of turning stress into distress when he permits his emotions to get out of hand. Many emotional hazards can be avoided by the administrator since he can to a significant extent control the occurrences or control the behavior occasioned by them. This can be done in one way by avoiding fatigue and by observing other good health practices. Also, he can learn to recognize his own boiling point and the symptoms that precede it. This will enable him to get a grip on his emotions or to delay further action until he can do so. In any event, he should never take up an issue while he is strongly upset over it. Most of us are prone to do the opposite and rush into those situations that are hottest on our minds. These may be in no way the important problems, and if we hold off our attack until we have regained our self-control, we may find that a problem never even existed in the way we thought it did. Such cooling-off tactics will not appeal, however, to the administrator who lacks the courage to face an issue unless he has achieved an appropriate rage level. This will probably be the same individual whose judgment is most affected by fear. He will never have learned to trust his judgment to win his battles for him because he will have been too fearful to ever put it to the test. Nor can his judgment ever be well done because his hot temper will always scorch it.

The fear of losing
can take the joy
out of winning

3 It is a fact of life that the administrator occupies a perch at the apex of the organizational pyramid. Even those who advocate "bottoms up" concurrence in administration have found no other spot for him. Both the organizational optics and acoustics make this so. If he is to hear and see the entire organization, and if the entire organization is to hear and see him, he has to pitch his tent on the highest spot of the organizational landscape. By virtue of his position, the administrator has an exalted address on the summit, but the notion that he stands on such a high place can also give him a bad case of high-altitude jitters and freeze him to his lofty perch.

It is easy for the administrator to become preoccupied with the danger, rather than the dare, of his position and grab for the nearest railing. The higher he climbs up the organizational ladder, the more precipitous becomes the route he is following and the greater the distance he can fall. Also, the higher his position, the more exposed his judgment and action become. Likewise, the higher his position, the larger the number of individuals affected by his decisions and the more critical the way in which those individuals are affected. For these reasons much consequence is attached to what he does and much scrutiny is given it. These are real and obvious occupational perils, and the administrator who starts looking downward can become more concerned with the distance he can fall than with the distance he has come.

Because of his vulnerable position, the administrator feels a strong pressure to win consistently. Experience has taught him that the winner's circle is the only place in administration where blue ribbons are awarded and that the score on administrators is kept in terms of those ribbons. If he got to his present position by merit, he got there by being a consistent winner. He won because he was aggressive and worked hard to win. He saw the fate of the Little Lord Fauntleroys as he passed them on the way up, and this impressed him with the fact that administrative life was not like a tennis game and competition did not end with the opponents leaping the net to embrace each other fondly. Because he sees that life is real and plays for keeps, the administrator can, without knowing it, start to worry more about losing than about winning. This may sound like hair splitting, but there is a profound difference between the two. The desire to win is a very human and very worthy characteristic of normal individuals. Those who lose it lose the spark that makes life worthwhile. One needs to win on enough occasions to maintain that spark and to make life tolerable. Frequent defeat can destroy the spirit of even the strongest of individuals. Those of us with children realize this fact and are careful to let them win some of the time when we play games with them. Adults probably need to win even more than children do, and it is unfortunate for some individuals that real-life situations cannot be arranged so that they can be sure to win their share of the time.

Fortunately, one does not have to win all the time in order to keep his self-esteem, and it sometimes can be as harmful to the individual's development to be a constant winner as to be a chronic loser. However, the fear of loss is quite different from the desire to win. Whether one plays to win or plays to keep from losing determines the sort of game he plays and the sort of rules he will keep. Those who really want to win will try to keep within the rules because they know that this is the only way one really does win. Those who fight primarily to keep from losing are not restricted by the rules because their goal is actually one of beating the game. They are sort of like the person who fudges on himself in a game of solitaire.

The administrators who keep score by their losses rather than their victories develop tendencies and practices that adversely affect their judgment and effectiveness. These can take any one of several directions. One good way to keep from striking out is never to go to bat. Probably every administrator has on many occasions wished that he could avoid some of his most trying problems and some of the seemingly very trying people. Those with a dread of losing are likely to yield to the urge to run for cover, while those with a zest to win are likely to take their chances. The latter know that only those who take a chance can ever have a chance. They also know that one seldom tries to avoid one difficulty without bumping into another and that many of the administrator's toughest problems are actually not so hard to solve as they are to face.

When a problem that ought to be solved is shelved, the administrator may still be charged with a time at bat. There really is no escape from choice, since not making a choice is itself a choice. Life goes on, both inside and outside the enterprise, and the administrator is always involved in option making whether he realizes it at the time or not. Administration is not a spectator's game, and the administrator cannot hope to be a bystander. There is no place for neutralists in administration. If the administrator is to accomplish his purpose of influencing people's behavior, he must be for something and this must be clearly recognizable. Problems that are at all important need to be settled in keeping with the administrator's notion of the overall direction of the enterprise, and this can be done for sure only if others in the organization know what he wants the solution to be. Neither will he win any friends by being neutral, since the winners will feel no obligation to him and the losers will suspect that he opposed them. At least, they will know that he did not help them. Holding still too long on important issues can prevent the administrator from holding on to his control of the organization.

Another way for him to keep from losing is to pick his opponents and his problems. This way out is taken in administration much more often than the administrator realizes, or at least than he is willing to admit to himself. He can take this way out by turning his head as well as his cheek when confronted by problems or individuals too tough or too strong for his handicap and confining his fire to those problems that look like sitting ducks. There are other ways out which at times tempt the administrator. Some administrators refuse promotions, or job offers from other organizations, because they are unwilling to face the chance of failing in a new position. They are willing to pay in terms of career opportunity for the right to stay in a league where they are sure they can win. Others may take the promotion but attempt to avoid hard tests of their skills by resisting change and holding the job down to their own fighting weight. Others choose to do it by a sort of vicarious losing. When the administrator simply passes the buck by delegating the hardest and meanest problems to his subordinates, he is utilizing the honorable principle of delegation for a not-so-honorable purpose. This permits someone else to test the difficulty for him and soften up the problem before he enters the fray, or it allows someone else to be blamed for the failure before the administrator officially enters the picture and can be charged with the loss. There is an appealing difference between seeming to be the expert who cleans up a mess and being the duffer who created it.

Administrators who are more interested in protecting their batting average than in raising it are likely to be allergic to new ideas. Because the chance to innovate also represents a chance to lose, they are reluctant to increase their exposure to losing. They tend to become overly cautious and seek their administrative exercise from pushovers rather than push-ups. They see change as a threat to their organizational bliss and pull down the shades when they think change might come calling. They never catch on to the fact that there is no refuge from new ideas, but only a race to see who can have them first and use them best. They fail to realize that administrators are blamed just as much for what they fail to do as for what they fail in doing.

Neither new ideas nor difficult problems can faze those administrators who play ostrich when trouble develops and deny, even to themselves, that the problem exists. These administrators use the philosophy of "what you don't see can't hurt you" and ignore unwanted findings and unpleasant conclusions. They grow to prefer part-truth because it is easier to live with. If the pressure of unfaced problems becomes so great as to force them to remove their heads from the sand, they will use "group decide" as an administrative fox hole in which to hide. Fearful of the administrative dark, they venture out only in the company of a committee. If the appointment of a committee doesn't provide a sufficient sense of security, they call for a study or pass the buck to a consultant. When they have exhausted all other means of escaping responsibility, they try to lose the problem in a crowd of new objectives. But basic problems don't get lost easily when unattended and most times thrive best when ignored and obscured. When allowed to go unattended, they usually become so critical that they start erupting and the administrator is permanently cast, if he survives, in the role of firefighter.

If he can't hide himself from the problem, the apprehensive administrator will at times try to hide the problem from others through the use of the "crisis" technique. Problems will be blown up far out of proportion to their significance to the organization or to their difficulty of solution in order to attract attention away from more basic problems whose solution has either eluded the administrator or outweighed his courage. This kind of administrator will push the panic button on minor problems in order to get his subordinates so occupied that they can't raise their heads to see the unattended major problems. If the red-herring problems don't prove sufficiently distracting, the desperate administrator actually may go so far as to create major situations solely to obscure his personal inadequacies. But whether created or overly magnified, the effect of such "decoy" administration is to divert the attention and energies of the organization away from the more significant problems it faces. To chronically cry out the "sky is falling" also wears out the administrator's influence. Like the townspeople in the fable of the shepherd boy who cried "wolf" too often, the organization will become used to the administrative false alarms and cease to respond with vigor and enthusiasm to the real, as well as the invented, problems it encounters.

The administrator who gets overly concerned with his own expendability has a natural tendency to work at becoming indispensable. But his overconcern will usually cause him to work the wrong way. A major result of this overconcern is a "do it yourself" type of administration. This takes the form of the administrator's failing to delegate responsibility and his attempting to be a one-man administrative gang. To his mind, this not only demonstrates how hard he is working but it keeps anyone else from being able to replace him. By playing everything close to his chest, he maintains a situation in which he is necessarily the master because the affairs are incomprehensible to everyone else. This sort of administration leads to increased insecurity rather than less. Because he can't get all his work done satisfactorily, the administrator has good reason to feel more and more inadequate. Also, because he has not shared the information and the problems with others, he cannot share the risks. A "round table of one" provides very little company for the fearful administrator.

Direct involvement in problem solving serves a larger purpose for the insecure administrator than just that of keeping things to himself. It is also a way of demonstrating his importance to the affairs of the enterprise. The individual who isn't sure of his grip on the organization has to keep proving, to himself and to the organization, that he is important by personally tackling every problem that heaves into sight. Even the best of administrators must constantly fight the urge to become involved in the minor problems of the day to the exclusion of attention to the major problems of tomorrow. Immediate problems offer the security and satisfaction of tangling with the tangible, while long-term problems are generally vague and undefined and offer frustratingly few exposed parts of their anatomy into which to sink one's teeth. The need for an anchor with which to secure one's place in the organization may account in part for the trivia which occupy much of the time of certain administrators in even some of our largest enterprises. Some of them insist on performing such minor clerical tasks as opening their mail. They explain that these routines are followed in order to keep them "in touch." One could make a strong argument that this yearning for detail is a misdirected effort to keep hold of something concrete. But whether one is attempting to keep in touch or to keep hold, involvement with trivia isn't going to accomplish it. Someone learned long ago to grab a bull by the horns, instead of hanging onto his tail, if he wanted to be in charge of the bull.

Timorous administrators do not always play their cards close to their chests. Some do the opposite and substitute a personal cabinet for the round table of one as the central piece of their administrative furnishings. They hesitate to make a move until they have checked it with the inner circle. Seeking advice from the best informed and most responsible sources is a major virtue, but the inner circle doesn't always, or perhaps even usually, fall into that category. It is like an accretion to the official hierarchy, and it quarantines the influence of those who have formal responsibility. It is a product of natural selection and mirrors the administrator rather than the organization. The personality of the chief largely determines the personality of the people he will admit to his sanctuary, and getting advice from his inner circle is almost the same as getting it from himself. Those in the inner circle are admitted to it and remain there because of their loyalty rather than because of their ability. The trouble with such an arrangement is that, like most circles, it leads the administrator nowhere. Loyalty of those around him is a must, but the advice that he receives can become musty if the administrator separates loyalty from ability in choosing those to whom he listens.

Those who use loyalty as the dominant criterion in evaluating those around them risk losing the very allies upon whom they have become dependent. The possession of authority has a natural tendency to create a wariness that can easily turn into distrust and suspicion. Loyalty is an attitude, and its existence is determined largely by the absence of defections. This means we have to watch for disloyalty in order to determine how loyal a person is to us. Once we start looking for disloyalty, we are likely to keep looking harder, since we have a tendency to keep trying to find whatever we are looking for. Before the administrator realizes it, he can become overly suspicious and overly sensitive and begin mistrusting his own palace guard. Attitudes are catching, and those people in catching range won't take long to become infected with equal suspicion and doubt of the administrator's motives toward them. Also, the administrator who seeks his security in the loyalty of others had better be pure of heart if he expects any peace of mind. Our attitudes toward others actually reflect our own behavior, and we really trust others only if we know others can trust us. Our interpretation of another person's attitude toward us depends largely upon our own previous behavior toward him. If I am loyal to the other person, I am more likely to think he is being loyal to me. Said another way, the distrustful administrator probably cannot trust himself.

The overly dependent administrator will at times attempt to bolster his hold on those he depends upon by increasing their sense of dependency upon him. He practices a "cloak and dagger" sort of administration and uses "the goblins will get you" technique to create the feeling that enemies are lurking in all corners of the organizational framework and are being held off only by his shield. He talks about the ominous intentions of "they," but seldom specifies who "they" are because he doesn't know and because he wants his henchmen to be fearful of everyone but himself. Incidents are interpreted to his supporters in a way that indicates ulterior motives against them on the part of everyone involved except himself. He can point out to them more angles in the ordinary daily affairs of the organization than can be found in an unabridged geometry book. If the scare routine wears thin because of failure of the boogeyman to materialize, this sort of administrator may give his story substance by creating factions within the organization. This will not be hard to do since he will already have set the stage by sowing the seeds of fear and distrust. Neither will it lack appeal to the inadequate administrator, since an intraorganizational hassle will take the spotlight away from his inadequacies and also justify his failure to attack some of the tougher problems confronting the organization. However, the smart administrator will take a second look before he yields to that appeal. To divide and conquer is an acknowledged strategy that may have its merits under certain circumstances, but one of those merits is not that of providing a camouflage for the inadequacies of the administrator. Another and stronger argument against the administrator's creating an organizational cleavage is the selfish one that the administrator may fall into the cleavage himself and get caught between the factions he has created.

The use of the "let's you and him fight" strategy has a special appeal to those skittish administrators who feel the hot breath of able and fast-coming subordinates on the back of their necks. These administrators search for points of stress where they can get something started among those regarded as threatening. They sometimes seem to foment differences among subordinates deliberately to cause them to keep each other at bay. More interest is shown by the administrator in checking, rather than fostering, their capacity for outstanding performance. He sets up an administrative structure designed less to aid the members to help each other than to provide a sure way of putting his fears to rest. The effort they spend in fighting each other represents a double loss to the enterprise. It is not only wasted effort but it is an added handicap to getting the work done. Also, the opposition that the administrator fosters among his subordinates can backfire on him when it inevitably gets out of hand. There is an old saying about the fact that the wind that blows out a candle can also fan a fire. Most opposition seems to be habitual rather than intellectual and to feed on itself rather than on the things it opposes. Once set into motion, it is always seeking something to oppose, and, being general rather than specific, it is not too discriminating in what it chooses. The administrator who sows the seeds of organizational dissension is likely to reap much of the harvest himself.

The administrator who searches out of fear for a way to bind the members of the organization securely to him may attempt to buy them if he can't frighten them. He may make promotions and retain individuals in their positions on the basis of their loyalty and uncritical support of the administrator. Such purchases almost never represent a bargain to the administrator. If the individuals are not qualified, they can never make the administrator look good, and he will consequently never really feel good or secure. Inadequate administrators can hide some serious shortcomings if they are backstopped by able subordinates, but the best of administrators cannot overcome the handicap of inept and inadequate assistants. The inadequate seller of his loyalty will not feel good over the transaction. If he does not measure up to the demands of his position, he will be frustrated and unhappy. He will recognize that his security depends upon how well he kowtows rather than upon how well he does. His efforts will be concerned more with improving his position than with improving his performance. Such improvement of his position may involve a switch in loyalty just at the time when the administrator needs it most. Loyalty that is bought is a bogus imitation of loyalty that is won. It is somewhat like the difference between the mercenary and the patriot. This analogy is not comprehensive, however, because it does not suggest the effects of favoritism on other members of the organization who observe it. The administrator cannot expect those individuals to enthusiastically support his efforts or those of his henchmen. They will recognize that the private clique carries a privileged clout and will be careful to stay out of reach. This will mean that it will be hard for the administrator ever to enlist the full interests and capabilities of those outside the select circle. The teacher's pets are poor emissaries for extending the influence of the administrator.

The inability to face our losses causes some of us to become skilled in excuses. We try to convince others, and even ourselves, that there was outside interference, bad breaks, circumstances beyond our control, or any one of an unlimited number of extenuating circumstances. Under this sort of alibi administration we will question reality itself, if it leaves us no other excuse, by skirting the facts or trying to dodge them if they get in our way. We spend the time that would permit us to lick the current problems explaining why we failed on the past ones. When this form of administration becomes habitual, we find it impossible to overcome our deficiencies because we never recognize them. Even if we want to recognize them, we find it difficult since we have never faced them.

The internal pressure which compels us to avoid losing is often demonstrated by all of us in the attempt to win a "moral victory" even after our actions and decisions have been clearly discredited. In these circumstances we try to prove we were right by forcing the organization to continue an unworkable or obviously inefficient idea. This can be described as administrative face saving, but too much emphasis is given in administration to the necessity of saving face and not enough thought is paid to the problem of saving respect. The administrator may silence, but he cannot fool, those responsible for carrying out an impractical decision. If face saving is really important, it would seem to be better strategy for the administrator to admit his errors and dispose of them as soon as possible than to give them the prominence that results from the disgruntlement and ill will of those compelled to operate with them. As every kid knows, the best thing to do with a lemon is to make lemonade out of it. It is surprising how many improvements can come out of things that go wrong, and it is quite possible that all of us learn much more from our failures than from our successes. Mishaps that are admitted generally cause one to review the round and to correct his swing. If one knows why undesirable things did happen, he has taken a long step toward knowing why desired things did not happen. Our natural tendencies are in the other direction, however, and often we seem more eager to get out of situations than to get something out of them.

The effort to perpetuate an error can eat heavily into the time and energy of the administrator. Because it is not an efficient and effective answer, it will of course require more than ordinary effort to implement. It will likely suffer also from the halfhearted efforts of those responsible for trying to make it work. If the feelings below are strong enough against the idea, it is not unlikely that there will sometimes be deliberate obstruction. Even the best of ideas can be sabotaged by slight effort, and a poor idea needs only to be left on its own to fall on its face. The refusal to give an inch under such circumstances can easily cost an administrative mile.

The determination to make a poor idea look good can draw heavily on the administrator's judgment and disposition. This is demonstrated by the feeling of relief, and even pride, one experiences on those occasions when he is big enough to admit he was wrong. This is perhaps the answer to those who worry about face saving and protection of the administrative myth that the king can do no wrong. Not only do we feel the noblest on those occasions when we are able to muster the courage to admit we goofed, but a good bit of the respect we have for the men we do respect can often be traced back to the times they were wrong and simply said so. It is quite likely that in such instances the administrator makes other gains. The admission of error is one of the best means of taking the fight out of the opposition, since there really is very little left to say to an individual who admits he erred unless one wants to be guilty of jumping all over a penitent. If we are going to admit to error, however, we should do our confessing when we first recognize the error and not put the organization to the painful task of proving us wrong. We can expect no green stamps for admitting the proven.

If we are going to lose, we should attempt to lose gracefully, but our tendency is to saddle up a scapegoat to carry our blame. We admit the error, but we try to admit it as someone else's. Given enough expendable people to hide his errors behind, the administrator can, at least temporarily, exhibit an impressive scratch sheet. The chances are, however, that the scapegoat will ultimately carry off most of the respect the organization has for the administrator. The code by which the organization judges the

administration calls for the members of the hierarchy to take the
rap in proportion to the authority vested at each level. The administrator is regarded as the chief counsel for the defense of
those under him, even for errors for which he is not responsible.
This does not mean he should not hold individuals responsible for
their failures, but it does mean that he must be prepared to shoulder the blame for the errors of others as well as the blame for his
own.

Because we do not develop the art of losing gracefully, in too
many instances we not only lose our point but we succeed in losing the goodwill of those involved. Even when we know we are
going to give in, we do not always salvage as much as possible
from the situation. We seem to want to salve our own feelings by
clouding the other person's victory. In a way, we try to rub his
nose in our loss. (This fact was illustrated by the conduct of a
store manager I witnessed recently. A customer was insisting that
the store pick up a defective gas stove that had been purchased
some weeks before. The manager agreed that the guarantee period was still in effect and that the customer had full legal right to
return the stove. He insisted on emphasizing to the customer,
however, that the store had gone to the expense of delivering and
installing the stove and was now faced with the added cost of
picking it up. It did not seem to occur to the manager that he was
losing the customer's goodwill as well as the sale.)

The administrator's obsession to win at all costs can be one of
the largest deterrents to full participation by colleagues and subordinates. There can be no battle of ideas within the organization
if the reward is disfavor and ill will from the boss. About the only
method available for pretesting of administrative ideas involves
the willingness and ability to permit ideas and decisions to be discussed and pulled apart before committing the organization to
follow them. The administrator deals in ideas, and these, unlike
goods and things, cannot be tested in the model stage before
being placed on the market. Discussion can be a sort of administrative "wind tunnel" for experimentation with ideas before they
are forced upon real people in real situations. Ideas that are implemented only after full discussion with those who can best
check them may take longer—but they also last longer.

Prior review of ideas and decisions by affected members of the
organization can often serve a larger purpose than a pretesting.

Two minds may produce new approaches and insights that neither would have generated separately. Often, two different experiences and two different outlooks fit together to produce a novel answer to problems of long duration. To get such an administrative extra, however, the administrator must exhibit patience and tolerance toward the organization's independent thinkers and their ideas. Admittedly, this can be very trying to the most patient of administrators. Independent thinkers are not the most tactful and persuasive of individuals and are likely to rub the shine off their ideas by rubbing the administrator and their colleagues the wrong way. Independent thinkers are also likely to be independent in most other ways and are deservedly in the administrative doghouse part of the time. The organizational mavericks can be a bothersome cross to the administrator, but if he can carry it, he may find at times that it is worth its weight in gold.

The justification for participation in decision making by those responsible for implementation is not made from the standpoint of human relations. Permitting the appropriate colleagues and subordinates to participate is not so much a favor to the participants as it is a favor to the administrator. It not only permits pretesting of decisions by exposing them to the scrutiny of those who will have to use them, but it most often assures support instead of sabotage. Human nature being what it is, there is no better way to insure support than to involve others. For those who are opposed to an idea this permits a preventilation of feelings that, if muzzled, might later explode against the idea when adopted. Having been spent in discussion, such feelings won't stand so strongly in the way. Even those who come away unconvinced after having participated in the discussion of an idea are convinced to follow it by the responsibilities that go with identification and alliance. Said another way, even if the other person is strongly antagonistic, he will be less inclined to risk shaking and sinking your boat if he is in the same boat with you. This represents what might be called "conspired" administration, and such administration is probably the most cohesive of all. It helps provide the common interest required for common effort, and individuals cannot participate productively in a common task without such effort.

A passion to dominate often affects the judgment and action of the administrator. This feeling is related to the obsession to win but it is not the same thing. Actually, this desire at times may be better satisfied by defeat if the defeat focuses attention on the administrator and gives him a sort of martyr's role. Such dramatic opportunities are not too frequent in most organizations, however, and usually the passion to dominate has to be satisfied in success situations. The administrator can easily become egocentric if he confuses his position with his self. The position does make him the center of gravity in the organization, and the lines of communication, which follow the lines of authority, radiate out from his position. The important questions of the organization are referred to him, and his answers are deferred to by the important members of the organization. Fortunately, he usually gets used to being the center of attention and adjusts to the aura of the rug in his office before the dazzle blinds his insight.

Kudos make a spicy dish, however, and unwittingly the administrator can start poaching off limits for more than his share. Unless checked, his appetite for attention can get out of control and he will pick the platter clean, leaving nothing for the others who must also feed their pride at the organizational table. It can mean that he will start taking personal credit for the ideas and accomplishments of his subordinates. Instead of acclaiming the contributions of his staff, he will execute an administrative version of a Castro "intervention" and claim their contributions as his own. To legitimize his steal, he sometimes will apply the "antiquities" statute and claim that the idea has been under consideration for a long time. In the long run he is not fooling anyone, except perhaps himself, but he is stifling initiative and building up resentment. His pickings will grow leaner because such expropriation of credit will cause a flight of ideas from the organization as the idea producers seek a more rewarding climate or become infertile because their own diet is so barren of recognition. Some of the most effective administrators feel so strongly about this fact that they, on occasion, give credit down the line for ideas that actually originated in their own mind. These administrators are acting wisely as well as generously. They realize that they are in reality giving nothing away, and that the honor and glory of a job well-done can be compared to a radio beam which allows everyone to tune in without dimming anyone's reception.

This urge to always be "front and center" can result in the administrator's becoming the master of the monologue. Because he is the boss, his histrionics have the benefit of a captive audience until a good excuse permits his listeners to stop being an audience. Some administrators seem compelled to do all the talking, and this extends even to casual and social conversation. Even when he isn't talking, he is so occupied in looking for an opening to take over the conversation that he doesn't listen. He breaks into a discussion when the other person pauses, even though it is obvious to others that the speaker is in the middle of a point. His inattention to the conversation is also demonstrated by the irrelevance of the thing of which he says the speaker has reminded him. The power of suggestion can apparently produce some high voltage for an individual searching for an opportunity to overpower every conversation, but the organizational acoustics for such an administrator perform no more than an echo function.

The need we seem to feel to justify to everyone else all that we do, even those things that are obviously good, can importantly affect the administrator's attitude toward losing. This need accentuates our fear of failure because of the odd way it causes us to look at failure. Our failure in someone else's eyes seems to be much more important to us than failure in our own. We are able to tolerate major losses if no one else knows about them, and for this reason most of us will go to great lengths to hide our losses. Because we place our self-esteem at the mercy of those around us, many of our personal goals are set by others, and we can become more closely attentive to those expectations than to our own preferences. This means that we judge ourselves by what we feel others think of us—by the image of ourselves that we create in our own mind from others' opinions. Actually, we seldom have any direct evidence about what others do think of us. We develop our own notion of what others should think of us by constantly comparing ourselves with other people. (This thought is supported by our proclivity to be "joiners" and belong to numerous organizations in which we have no strong interests. Our gregariousness may be due as much to a desire to evaluate our fellowmen as a desire for their friendship and company.) Said another way, we judge ourselves by what we know about others, and this is a very incomplete and perhaps inaccurate measurement. We can only compare the parts because we have no access to the whole. Most often, we use the other person's strongest parts because they are the ones that we are likely to remember when we

grow worried about our weakest parts and want to measure just
how they do stack up.

The administrator's search for approval is not an idle one.
Every man wants to be approved by his fellows, but the administrator has to be approved, to some extent, by everyone in the
organization. He achieves his purposes only through the responses of others, and the quality of the response he can get determines the quality of the things that he can get done. The quality of the response he gets depends to a large extent upon the
esteem in which he is held. This means he must determine the
appropriate image for gaining esteem and then seek to fill that
image. Because he actually comes into contact with so few members of the organization, his influence comes largely through the
image others have of him. For this reason he must develop an
image that will secure the best response from those he is attempting to influence. This is in no way hypocrisy, but rather a matter
of grafting an appropriate administrative personality over his ordinary one. For instance, a university president may or may not
be intrinsically a patient person, but in his role he must act patiently. It doesn't matter whether he is truly a Job, but he must
act like one because patience is expected of him in his role. The
same individual, whether by nature patient or impatient, could
not survive as head of a highly competitive enterprise and exhibit
the same level of patience. This means that the administrator
must create the image of himself that is required by others in
order for them to do best what is required of them.

The fact that he measures himself by borrowed expectations
can lead the administrator to develop such a distorted image of
himself that he can't fulfill it or such an idealized image of what
he should be that he finds himself seriously wanting. A distorted
notion of what others expect of him can cause him to dread any
encounter that might expose his inability to measure up to what
he thinks others think of him. Every administrator, being human,
has times of discouragement and uncertainty about himself, and
the neurotic residue can leave him with a chronic case of the administrative shakes if he begins judging himself too harshly. He
needs to remember that not only must he hold the organization
together but his own self-esteem as well.

The effort to measure up can lead to the administrator's out-
smarting himself by failing to ask questions of others because of

the fear of exhibiting ignorance. All of us mistakenly demonstrate a strong reluctance to reveal that we don't know things, even things we aren't supposed to know. We evade questions, or even use guesses as replies, rather than admit the perfectly defensible truth that we don't know something that we have had no opportunity to learn. By a strange sort of logic, we admire other individuals when they frankly admit they don't know something, but we are afraid we will lose their respect if we don't show that we know everything. It is not the possession of facts that is important in administration, but rather the acquisition of them when they are needed. Actually, there are times when the administrator needs the benefit of an ignorance that causes him to ask questions. Along with the facts he can also catch the nuances that may be more important than the facts. He can also gain the high favor and regard of the person of whom he asks the information. Few things seem to flatter people as much as being asked for information, and even fewer things seem to provide as much pleasure as the chance to tell someone something. The administrator needs the fortitude to face the facts, but he also needs the greater fortitude to ask for them.

The greater function of the administrator is not to answer questions but to ask them. It is only by questions that problems can be defined or, more importantly, most times even be discovered. The answers the administrator gives can be little better than the answers he receives, and those answers can be little better than the questions the administrator is asking. To a large extent, the sorts of questions the administrator asks determine the sort of administrator he is. Perplexity and puzzlement are trademarks of effective administrators, and no administrator should be embarrassed to display them. Wondering for information is not a sign of ignorance, but wandering for lack of information is a pretty fair proof of it. Asking questions is such a major function of administration that if it ever becomes an organized profession its proper coat of arms should be the question mark.

Overanxiety about losing can adversely affect the administrator in two quite different ways. At one extreme it can cause him to give in too quickly. Those who are harried by apprehensions are likely to see problems as difficulties rather than as opportunities. They are prone to stop at the lowest level of possibility rather than push toward realization of the full potentiality of a situation.

Everyone has a tendency under trying circumstances to take the first idea that comes along. If our anxieties are sufficiently aroused, we are likely to satisfy our critical faculty too easily and too quickly. Because the major concern at such times is not with solving the problem but with escaping the dilemma, we confuse doing something with getting something done. It is easy to imagine the potential advantages of doing almost anything when you are experiencing the actual disadvantages of a situation. The role of the administrator is a decision-making one, but it is also one of not making decisions for the worse. At times, it may even be one of not making any move. There are occasions when it is best to ride out the storm and let nature take its course.

Apprehension over the consequences of losing can sometimes have an undesirable effect in the opposite direction by causing the administrator to try too hard. This can result in his redoubling his efforts at a time when he should be restudying his goals. The resources of every enterprise are limited and must be utilized to obtain maximal results. This means that there is a limit to how much it is worth to solve a particular problem. For the administrator to go beyond that limit solely for the sake of winning is an unwise and improper use of the enterprise's resources. It is also a losing proposition for the administrator even if he wins. Working his head off to solve low-priority problems is no way for him to prove that he has a head. Working "smarter" is often better than working harder. Some problems have no solution, and there comes a time when it is wise for the administrator to admit the fact and adapt the enterprise for coexistence with the problem. It is, of course, essential that the administrator recognize the problem so that he can know what he is living with and what he is detouring around. Administratively speaking, however, a problem is something you can do something about, and if there is no solution then, administratively, there is no problem. But soluble or insoluble, the administrator must at times ask himself not only whether he can win, but what difference it will make. Somewhere between the two poles of selling out too soon and shelling out too much the administrator must find the best bargain for the enterprise.

The administrator who tries too hard to prove his excellence is tempted to concentrate more on the proof than on the excellence. This can put a "guilt-edge" on his ethics and lead to tactics marked more by their sham than by their sheen. Some at times set up straw man problems that they can easily knock over in order to get a pat on the back for doing so. At other times they will disturb smoothly functioning operations for the purpose of demonstrating mastery in putting them together again. If such stacking of the deck does not sufficiently exalt their rank, they will attempt to make up the difference by the degradation of the rank of others. Those who can't stand on their own record seem to think they can improve their standing by jumping all over the other fellow's. Some, however, do not have to disparage the success of others because they have taken the simpler course of depreciating success itself. They become so fearful of failure that they attempt to emotionally prepare themselves for it by denying that winning makes any difference. This constructed indifference may inure them against some of the worry over losing, but it can also take the taste out of winning. A heavy serving of sour grapes is not the best appetizer to whet the administrator's desire for success.

Some measure of sour grapes is perhaps necessary in the attitude of the well-balanced administrator. It can help temper the inevitable losses that even the best of administrators occasionally suffers. It can also help him restrain his expectations. A sense of failure is a relative thing and depends upon the expectations the individual sets for himself. How well he meets his expectations depends upon the aspirations he develops and his abilities for achieving them. For this reason the administrator ought occasionally to audit his aspirations and determine if they are within the bounds of the organization's and his own possibilities. Paradoxically, continuous success can engender anxiety more strongly than failure. The more successful the administrator is, the more he has to live up to. The increased pressure forces him to be concerned not only with continued success but also with accomplishing increasingly larger successes. For most individuals there is a constantly shifting relationship between achievement levels and aspiration levels. The accomplishment of one goal leads to an upgrading and rearrangement of priorities of all other personal goals. We say that "success breeds success," and one reason it does is that it keeps the individual on an "aspirations" treadmill that keeps him striving just to stay even with his own ambitions. The fact that a person never catches up with his ambitions represents one of the most valuable qualities of human nature. It makes life an interesting and productive experience and means that an individual always has an urge for further growth and development. It is an especially valuable trait in the administrator if he is to provide the purposeful, aggressive sort of leadership necessary in effective administration. But his ambitions for the enterprise and himself can get out of hand and grow into unreasonable anxieties. While he must set his goals high and give a hard try to everything he does, he must learn to judge himself on balance and not feel that his full esteem is at stake every time he comes to bat. Some of the problems that confront the achievement-minded administrator are bound to be too much to reasonably expect anyone to handle adequately, and there will come times when just being able to pick himself off the floor will be a proper cause for self-congratulation.

Anxiety has been described as fear in search of a cause. It can cause the administrator to borrow trouble and pay unnecessary interest on it. It is true that the effective administrator is marked by a sense of restlessness that prevents him from ever being completely satisfied with the way things are going. But this is an eager rather than a foreboding dissatisfaction. It is the difference between worrying about what might happen and looking forward to what can happen. In much of what he does, the administrator has no precise way of telling how well he is doing. Since what he does is prologue and must run its course before it can be fully evaluated, he is perpetually uncertain as to what is going on. Unless he is to become more concerned about what may have been left undone than with what can be done, he needs to develop a sense of fatalism that will permit him to quit worrying about things he has put in the laps of the gods. Those administrators who spend more time fearing the past than facing the future can at best serve only as "drovers" and not as leaders. They are much better at plotting a rearguard action than in planning an attack. Because they have eyes only in the back of their head, they are ill-equipped to ever be forward looking.

Some degree of anxiety on the part of the administrator is inevitable. It is a built-in feature of his position, and it is doubtful if any effective administrator is ever fully free of it. A dash of anxiety is necessary in order for him to properly respect the obligations of his position and the implications of his actions. It will also help him keep his feet on the ground and prevent his occasional mishaps from being so unexpected as to be devastating. If he becomes too confident, he is more likely to come apart at the seams when he does encounter obstacles that he cannot handle. Some worry will help keep his position from going to his head and remind him that he is not omnipotent, since one of the greatest deterrents to the administrator's attempting to play God is the recognition that his own job is at times more than he can handle. But anxiety also establishes a beachhead for fear and can cause the administrator to concentrate more on minimizing the probability of failure than on maximizing the likelihood of success. If he keeps his ear too close to the ground listening for trouble, it is bound to limit his vision. It will help the administrator control the gnawing fear of losing if he remembers that many times the thing that he is running from is easier to handle than the thing toward which he is headed, and that what is won, even when he apparently loses, often turns out to be more important than who won.

Feelings are a common cause of failings

4 Judgment is an affair of the mind—a mating of the facts of a situation with the values of the individual. Good judgment requires a good marriage of the facts and values. Good marriages, however, have a deep-seated allergy to third parties. The most insidious of these are the administrator's emotions, which seem to have a special affinity for coming between his facts and his values and thus upsetting his good judgment. This does not mean that his emotions are all bad or that they always act badly. They provide the spice for his experiences and give a taste to whatever life serves up for him. Without the flavor provided by his emotions, his reactions would be cold and sterile. Too, a dash of emotions adds desirable seasoning to the individual's judgment. However, good judgment is not a spicy affair, and too much spice can upset it.

In the preceding chapter, some of the emotions from the family tree of ill will were discussed. Ugly feelings are not the only danger to a good relationship between facts and values, however. They are probably less dangerous than their fancier cousins from the goodwill side of the family. The pretty ones are likely to have greater appeal, and to have a higher social standing, than their uncouth cousins. This means they will be welcomed in more places and their wayward tendencies less suspected. This chapter will attempt to identify some of the tendencies which some of our more respected feelings have toward interfering with the administrator's good judgment.

The goodwill family of feelings has been given top billing in recent years because of their important role in human relations. Since World War II the topic of human relations has been a best seller in administrative circles, and the number of books and journals devoted to the subject has boosted the backlog of the printing industry. The audience has been both large and attentive. The increasing complexities of organizational life and a concern with the motivational effects these complexities were having on the members of the organization caused the practicing administrator to develop a compelling interest in the subject. The fact that the material with which he dealt was human nature and that his practice was based on the behavioral sciences was being increasingly brought home to him, and he read and listened eagerly to the flood of material released by the rapidly growing army of both "head candlers" and head counters who had packed their briefcases and bivouacked out in his plants. With all this effort on behalf of human relations, the practice of administration should have been much improved. But most observers would agree that the practice of administration has not demonstrated such improvement. Administrators have attempted to use the new understandings presented to them, but somehow they are not getting the expected results. They are in somewhat the same spot as the weekend gardener who faithfully follows the directions on the seed package, but who is never able to grow tomatoes like those pictured on the package. Employee performance is not noticeably better, and employee job satisfaction seems to have worsened.

The fact that the contributions to administration of a greatly expanded knowledge of human relations have been little more than word deep is in great part due to the manner in which the administrator has tried to use the new knowledge. Many of the findings of the behavioral scientists have been grossly misunderstood. The scientist studies human relations as a phenomenon and as an end in itself. The fact that he has learned what produces harmonious relations doesn't mean that all tension can or should be eliminated. The fact that he has found out how to communicate well doesn't mean that organizational performance will be improved just by the administrator's communicating well. The quality of the dispatch remains as important for administration as the fidelity of the reception.

The emphasis given to human relations in administration has encouraged both misuse and overuse of the administrator's finer feelings. These have been highly advertised as remedies to be kept in his administrative medicine cabinet, but the advertisements have not always warned of the dangers of overdosage. The administrator has been an easy mark for some of the pitchmen for administrative patent medicines bottled under the name of human relations and sold across the counter without benefit of professional prescription and advice. Because good feelings and goodwill have such proven success as lubricants in human relations, administrators have sometimes been easy to sell on the mistaken notion that they are also a surefire tonic for organizational performance. The administrator's infatuation with the supposedly all-purpose quality of human kindness has led at times to irrelevances as well as excesses in its usage. Through being reduced to the status of stratagems in the battle for the allegiance of personnel, such honored feelings as friendliness, kindliness, sympathy, and brotherly love have in some quarters become more of a farce than a force in the practice of administration.

Because the administrator has such intense occupational need to get along with people, he has unusually strong tendencies toward letting his best feelings become his biggest failings. They can be his biggest failings because they are the most binding and the most entangling of feelings. They can tie the administrator's hands by tying him to individuals rather than to the whole organization and its purposes. They may make him a captive of the very situations he is supposed to command and cause him to become a prisoner of his best impulses.

One of the most common and formidable blocks to the administrator's good judgment is the failure to maintain an impersonal status in the organization. The administrator sometimes forgets that good psychological fences make good organizational neighbors and that he must work to protect a large enough area of personal detachment within the organization to permit him to think and act impersonally. Admittedly, he must be responsive and friendly so that others will not hesitate to approach him and will feel that he has their interests at heart, but both he and those with whom he works must see the difference between the administrator's liking them and liking everything they do. This means that he must learn to set himself apart while still remaining a part of the group around him. Close personal relationships represent one of the most effective set of "mindcuffs" the administrator can wear. The more personal the relationship, the more serious is its restraint on the exercise of good judgment. If we have a close attachment to an individual, it blinds our judgment because we take much more for granted. We do not practice a healthy sort of skepticism, so necessary in good judgment and in good administrative practice, because we are prone to equate the likelihood of people's success with our liking of them. We place confidence in what an individual does and says because we have confidence in his friendship. In a way, we assume that our closest friends are the smartest persons around and commit the error of seeing their goodwill toward us as good judgment.

Often close friendships adversely affect the reliability of the counsel that is given the administrator. It is not that close friends mean to be dishonest with each other. It is simply that none of us relish the idea of hurting a friend, so our advice becomes candied instead of candid. We want him to feel good so we tell him the things that we think will make him feel that way. This causes us to fail to tell him the things that will cause him to feel bad. We protect our friends from the truth out of a mistaken notion that it is better that they feel good than that they be good. At times our motives may be concerned with more than providing protective custody for the feelings of our friends, since no one likes to risk the tangible values that friendship with the administrator carries. Some administrators recognize this fact and go outside the organization for advice. This point is illustrated by the legend of the king who always sought the advice of an unknown oracle who stayed hidden in a cave. The king found the oracle's advice to be good because it was unvarnished. It was unvarnished because the identity of the oracle was unknown, and thus he did not have to fear loss of the king's favor. The king treasured the arrangement and was smart enough never to seek to learn the identity of his oracle. Every administrator at times longs for such an oracle but does not always create a climate in which the oracle can survive.

The members of the organization closely observe the actions and attitudes of the administrator and are quick to catalogue his friends. In fact, they have a tendency to be too quick in doing so and at times assume that certain individuals have an "in" with the administrator simply because the ball bounced that way in certain situations. Those who lose by the way the ball bounces have a strong tendency to look for motives in, rather than for merits of, the case, and even the best adjusted of individuals have to resist the temptation to rationalize their setbacks and to feel the deck was stacked. The easiest explanation to ourselves, and to others, is to blame setbacks on favoritism. When close friendship does exist, the case is pretty tight against the administrator, no matter what the facts might be. Few things the administrator can do are as bitterly resented as favoritism, imagined or real, and the resentment is not restricted to those directly affected but is shared by those kibitzing from the sidelines. To some extent the organization will tolerate inconsiderateness and even injustice on the part of the administrator if all members of the organization are treated the same. The organization adjusts itself, to a degree, to such treatment as long as nothing personal is seen in it. Any variation in treatment of different individuals in the organization, however, is taken as favoritism, and it is doubtful that any organization can ever accommodate itself to such double standards in administrative conduct. If the administrator wants to be sure that he isn't accused of carrying favors, it will be necessary for him to check his close friendships at the door.

One of the few sure things about human nature is the fact that people take things personally. The closer the bonds between individuals, the more likely they are to think that there is something personal in the actions or remarks of the other person. Our resentment seems to bear a direct relationship to the extent to which we think something was meant to be personal. Most married men learn early that they cannot criticize or give advice to their wives because of the strong personal ties between them. For this reason a man will almost always tell his wife that her new hat is a bargain and that it is very becoming. She may insist upon having the husband's opinion but will tolerate it only if it seconds the motion. At the same time, however, she will accept objectively the comments of the strange salesgirl who waited on her at

the hat store. The administrator can afford to gild the relationships he has at home and with his friends outside the organization. He cannot, however, be effective, if he persistently does this
at work. Personal relationships that inhibit detached evaluation
and proper criticism represent a disservice to all concerned. Criticism is fundamental to improvement, and every member of the
organization has a right to expect that he will be told when his
performance needs improvement. Few things seem to shake the
morale of an individual or an organization as much as the sudden
lowering of the boom without prior warning. The rules of fair
play are applied in an organization more strictly to the administrator than to anyone else, and these rules require that a person
be told where he stands and why.

Criticism is hard to take, but people do want to know where
they stand. Nobody likes to play a game and not know the score.
Naturally, people like to have the score in their favor and prefer
praise to criticism, but the worth and validity of praise for a job
well done can be maintained only by criticism for a job poorly
done. This doesn't mean that people want a reading on their performance every hour on the hour or a lecture on every minor mis-
cue. The administrator is smart to hold back his criticism for the
times when people are out of line rather than exhausting its effectiveness on the times when they are only temporarily out of step.
It may be that it is a fine distinction that separates nudging from
nagging, but the administrator needs to observe it unless he is to
impair the usefulness of his criticism. Admittedly, because appropriate criticism is as hard to give as it is to take, there is a
danger that the administrator may bank up his irritations with an
individual's performance and then spend them all on a small, in-
consequential misdemeanor. Because the administrator feels
responsible for the total performance of the organization, he is
prone to take personally any misperformance on the part of any
member of the organization and become personally upset instead
of administratively concerned. Because he finds it difficult to give
out criticism without giving in to his own feelings, there usually is
a direct ratio between the level of his disapproval and the difficulty he experiences in voicing it. This difficulty is both physical
and mental and is quickly communicated to the person being criticized. If the administrator is to get improvement rather than
antagonism, he must be able to demonstrate disapproval without

demonstrating hostility, and to do this he must be able to reserve a sufficient margin of personal detachment to permit him to be emotionally casual in expressing disapproval.

The demonstration of disapproval of inadequate performance is a way of defining the limits and dimensions of expected behavior and is about the only way the organization can determine the level of performance expected by the administrator. Whether the administrator means to or not, he becomes a sponsor for the things he permits or tolerates. The range of toleration a person experiences works out the boundaries of behavior and the permissible deviations for him. Most individuals find it difficult to separate their idea of good work from the boss's acceptance of it. On the average, people live up to the demands of their environment and little further. People will usually do what they think is expected of them, but few will, over any long period, do more than they think is expected. They are willing to pay the going rate, but they don't like to be a "sucker" and pay more than the asking price. This price must be indicated by the administrator's refusal to accept poor performance, or they will never know what it is. They cannot be expected to live up to their responsibilities unless they know what is expected of them.

Perhaps one of the big reasons that people want to do what is expected of them is that they want to know what to expect for themselves. There is usually little doubt that as long as a person does what is expected, he can know what to expect from others. His big worry is to know what is expected of him by others. For this reason, a heavy emphasis on the permissive approach to administration can easily destroy the initiative it is supposed to foster. A lack of firmness leaves the individual in a quandary concerning what really is expected of him. One only has to take a new position, or get a new boss, or experience the frustration of inadequate direction from a superior to realize how much his sense of security depends upon a firm hand instead of a free hand. Uncertainty about what is expected leaves the individual with a limited, rather than a wide, choice of behavior. For this reason, disapproval should never be veiled or vague but should be sufficiently specific and definite to help establish the boundaries within which the individual can move on his own. The best hunters never go hunting without a proper license.

A great amount of permissiveness in an organization is a logical impossibility. The only basis for administration is the assumption that human behavior is caused, and its purpose is to cause the sort of behavior that will best accomplish the objectives and ends of the particular enterprise. This means that part of its purpose is to interfere with behavior that does not conform to the adopted pattern. Organizational behavior is obtained or secured behavior and not spontaneous or random behavior. If every member of the organization always did on his own what was most appropriate for the enterprise, there would be no need for administration. James Madison said, in another connection, in one of the *Federalist* papers, "It may be a reflection on human nature that such devices should be necessary to control, but what is government itself but the greatest of all reflections on human nature. If men were angels, no government would be necessary." However, Madison's statement is not really applicable to administration. Administration is not a reflection on human nature and is not concerned with the level of angelic qualities possessed by the members of the organization. If men were angels, there would still be a need for administration. Even angels can have honest differences of opinion over ways of doing things. Administration is necessary wherever there is a chance of a difference of "mind" between members of an organized activity, and this chance exists wherever two or more individuals are involved in an activity.

Even more important is the fact that organizational behavior is contrived as well as controlled behavior. It is behavior that was rationalized before it occurred. The role of each member of the organization was conceived in terms of the total job to be done and in terms of the individual roles of all members. Organization is concerned with prescribed relationships and represents an effort, through structural determinants, to make the individual's behavior synonymous with his assigned role. It is a behavioral device that is rationally contrived to carry out preconceived conduct. This means it is a synthetic device set up to obtain synthesized behavior. In this sense organization is a prefabricated structure of assumed conduct, and to the extent that it projects conduct, it permits assumptions as to what each of its members will be doing. To the extent that it inhibits unplanned innovations, its members can proceed deliberately from a recognized point of departure.

The above statement on the purpose of organization may be,

to some degree, contradictory to the prayers sometimes said for the "organization man." Because of the defense made in some circles for the organizational nonconformist, it is well to take a close look at a concept that asks administration to abdicate the right to insure conformance. Those who exalt nonconformance are, of course, interested in fostering the more positive virtues of creativity and individuality. But the route of nonconformance doesn't lead to those virtues. Aside from the detrimental effects on the individual himself and the adverse impression he gives to others, the organizational nonconformist violates the only rules by which individuality can be achieved. Without conforming behavior there can be no organization, and without organization everyone is faceless and equal. The basis of organization is differentiation, and the method of organization is to differentiate between individuals. Organization provides a means for measuring and recognizing individual differences and succeeds only to the extent that it expresses and emphasizes these individual differences. The fact that organization restricts the area of an individual's choice does not prevent him from demonstrating excellence. Asking the guard on the football team to block left, instead of right, doesn't prevent him from being an outstanding guard. The fact that he is asked to play guard does, of course, prevent him from demonstrating excellence as a fullback. But he would have no chance to be recognized for anything if he did not have a place on the team.

Those who argue that the organizational requirement for conformance stifles creativity and prevents the maximum personal contribution by the members of the organization place blame on the wrong factor. Any stifling of ideas at any point within the organization is the fault of the manner in which the organization is being administered rather than an inherent defect in the concept of organization. Effective administration encourages the evolution of ideas and maintains an organizational structure that expedites their transmission. It attempts to utilize organization as a device with which the enterprise gains the advantage of the ideas generated at all levels within the organization. This does not mean that it adopts all ideas that evolve up and down the hierarchy. One function of the hierarchy is to screen and distill ideas as they move upward. Effective administration welcomes any battle of ideas that is confined to the staging area but permits no such battle in the action area. Said another way, the organization needs the obedient rebel who thinks on his own, but it cannot tolerate the rebel who acts on his own and who has no sense of the responsibilities to which he is committed as a member of the organization.

Too often, it is not organization that stifles the able but rather those who would tie its hands by making it a sin to separate the sheep from the goats. Strangely enough, those who speak the loudest in behalf of individuality are usually those who most often preach the sort of equality that emphasizes seniority, equal pay, and security. Such people ask that administration perform the astonishing trick of making the individual feel he is nine feet tall by losing him in a crowd. If we really do believe in a fair chance for the individual, we should permit the ablest to win by letting the organization perform its proper function of leveling upward rather than downward.

The doctrine of equality in formal organization represents a misapplication of the concept of democracy. Because men are created equal, there seems to be a presumption that we have to force them to stay that way. The egalitarian base for democracy has been spread far beyond things civil and is now being ruthlessly applied to all our affairs and activities. It appears the thinking man is supposed to prove his thoughtfulness by disdaining, rather than honoring, merit and accomplishment. This extension of political equality to private endeavor can defeat the goal of individual justice that democracy is intended to achieve. Except under the law, men are equal in no respect, and it is an injustice to treat them as if they were. Fair treatment is possible only if unequal treatment is provided for unequal ability and effort. As said earlier, such differentiation is a function of administration, and it is such a key function that administration can be rightly defined as the treatment of differentials in a differentiated way.

The notion has developed in some circles that there is ominous sociological significance to the fact of the subordinate's recognizing he has a boss. This idea has given rise to an advocacy of the administrator's working undercover rather than his working the organizational deviants over. The iron hand in administration has been appropriately indicted on many counts, and the scramble to become disassociated from authoritarianism has caused some administrators to take up administrative legerdemain and substitute the hidden hand for the iron hand. Much has been written of administration as if it were a sort of confidence game in which the employee is fooled into meeting his responsibilities. It seems to have become more appropriate to appeal to the subconscious, to act covertly rather than overtly, when seeking desired behavior from personnel. This administration by seduction is somehow expected to maintain the dignity and self-esteem of the worker. Actually, it would seem that nothing could possibly degrade the individual more than this sort of attitude toward him. The rights of individual decision and personal responsibility are basic to human dignity. These imply a conscious choice among options, each of which should be expected to produce different consequences so far as the individual making the choice is concerned. Administration affects human behavior by modifying the causes of that behavior through a system of inducements and, no matter what else one might like to call those inducements, they are a matter of rewards and penalties. The individual attempts to maximize the satisfaction of certain of his personal needs and drives through his job conduct, and the administration attempts to maximize the quality of the individual's job conduct through providing varying levels of satisfaction for those needs and drives. The aims of both ought to be explicit and open. The individual brings order and meaning to his own world, and no one else can do it for him. Turning administration into a shell game can hardly be expected to win dignity for the individual.

Among those who seem to believe that it is more moral to cozen than to convince are the therapists in administration who advocate that people be "treated" into performing adequately. This school seems to feel that a Freudian explanation always underlies the behavior of the problem employee and that it is up to administration to doctor the pent-up hostilities which the deviant has been supposedly accumulating since infancy. No one can argue against the need for an understanding of the human situation by the administrator and his obligation to help the individual improve himself. But the extent to which administration can go in attempting to effect basic personality changes in the individual is limited by both economic and moral restrictions. Administration must first recognize the deviants as economic problems and measure the organizational costs of changing their ways against the economic returns to be gained from such change. The administrator is the steward of the enterprise and should be expected to use the resources of the enterprise for the purposes of the enterprise. He cannot be expected to assume any net expense on behalf of the enterprise in attempting to correct the accumulated deficiencies brought to a job by the individual from his home, school, church, and other social institutions. He must, of course, be sure the individual's experience with his organization does not add to such deficiencies. The moral restrictions are even more severe than the economic ones. Administration has no license to play God and to tamper with the individual's basic personality structure. People are psychologically put together in funny ways, and the part that is out of place may be just the part that is shoring up the rest of the personality structure. What is an obstruction to satisfactory organizational performance may be a load-bearing beam and to change it may cause the entire structure to topple. Administration has the right and the obligation to require that the individual make the grade, but it has no right to make him over. It is better for both the organization and the individual that the misfit be required to ship out if he cannot or will not voluntarily shape up. The real test of the administrator is not what he can do to people but rather what he can do with them.

The growing notion that the organization is a life-adjustment society has helped further the "whole man" concept of administrative responsibility. This concept lays all the individual's problems on the doorstep of the enterprise and asks that it be his keeper as well as provide his keep. Somewhere along the line there has been a misinterpretation of administration's legitimate interests in, and obligations toward, the many different needs that individuals have. This confusion can be clarified only if administration examines the moral issue involved in assuming responsibility for more than the job life of the individual. It may sound noble for the administrator to say he treats the individual as a whole person rather than as an employee, but if he actually does it, it can be both fatuous and insolent. The bargain between the individual and the enterprise relates only to the job, and the dignity of the individual is endangered when administration takes it further than that. The bargain gives administration no right to involve itself in the affairs of individuals beyond their job conduct. There is a difference between agreeing to give of one's self to the job and agreeing to give up one's self to the company. Nor does administration have the right to make the individual dependent upon the enterprise for any more than his job. A man's work is important to him, and administration must strive to keep it so, but his work still represents only a fraction of his time and his contacts. It is of no service to the enterprise or to the individual to have the employee's work become the whole meaning in his life. Both will be served better if the employee is asked to do his work well and helped to like it, but is left to find some of his meaning in his family, his church, and in his other pursuits off the job. The task of administration is to help the individual do his job well. If it restricts its efforts to that responsibility, it can then devote to it the sort of critical attention it deserves.

The "mother hen" sort of administration that goes along with the whole-man approach rests on some assumptions that can be seriously questioned. For instance, an unhappy home life does not necessarily mean the individual will have an unhappy work life. If there is a connection between the two, it could just as well mean that the individual will find in his job some of the satisfactions he is missing away from it. Or the fact that he is having problems with his children could be due to his great attention to his work and the consequent lack of attention to them. Worrying about what he can do for people rather than what he can do with them can also cause the administrator to work to keep people happy rather than to keep them constructive and productive. No commonplace is less proved than the belief that happy people are the most productive. People can be happy about any one of an unlimited number of different things, and most of these can seriously interfere with their job attendance and job performance. Getting fun out of life and working hard are not incompatible but neither do they always go together. In any event, the number and magnitude of things off the job that can affect people's happiness are such that it is impossible for the administrator to do anything meaningful toward controlling them.

There is also little evidence for the common belief that the individual's attitudes toward the company have a strong positive effect on the way he does his job. Liking the company and liking your particular job are two separate things. Neither does job satisfaction correlate closely with job performance. Liking to do something and liking to do it well are not the same thing. Liking to work hard is quite different from either of the others. The na-

ture of most jobs today is such that the individual does not need
to become emotionally involved with his work or with the company. So long as he feels he is worth his pay, he can do even a
superior job without making the job central to his life.

The great concern demonstrated over employee happiness and
satisfaction may be based to a large extent on a misapprehension.
We are prone to think that if something has a strong negative influence, its opposite will have an equally strong positive influence.
Thus, we have a tendency to think that if unhappy and dissatisfied employees are poor workers, then happy and satisfied employees should be good workers. This proposition suffers on two
counts. In the first place, it assumes an all-or-none quality for
happiness and satisfaction. People are not limited only to happiness or unhappiness, satisfaction or dissatisfaction, about things.
They can also be indifferent. The area of indifference is perhaps a
much larger one than the total of the two extremes. In most matters it probably makes little difference whether the individual is
happy so long as he is not very unhappy. In the second place, the
assumption relies on a *non sequitur*. Because I may not work hard
if I am dissatisfied, it does not follow that I will work hard if I am
satisfied. I may simply dislike hard work. Whatever connection
there is between good performance and satisfaction, it is likely
that satisfaction is the dependent variable and is the result, rather
than the cause, of good performance. An individual who gets
away with shoddy performance is likely to become an unhappy
and dissatisfied individual.

None of this is intended as an argument against the responsibility of administration to provide as much satisfaction for every job
as is consistent with acceptable performance by the individual
and with the resources of the enterprise. It merely argues that
being satisfied is not the final determinant of satisfactory performance. One does not have to be fully satisfied with an order to
fully execute it. He needs only to be satisfied that he has fully exhausted his capability to further influence it. The effects of satisfaction and dissatisfaction upon an individual's performance
cease at the point he believes he has maximized his influence and
has no room for further exercise of it. The better the opportunity
an individual sees to influence a situation, the more vigorously he
will assert himself and the more carefully he will survey the means
of doing so. The level of his dissatisfaction sets the level of his

interest in influencing a situation, but it does not set the level of his performance. It is the opportunity to influence situations, rather than the desire to do so, that ultimately determines what the individual does, and it is the indifference or indecision of administration that gives him such opportunity. The final determinant of whether a rule is followed is not the individual's satisfaction with it but his perception of how well it will be enforced.

The administrative fallout from overemphasis on the "friendly aid society" approach to administration can adversely affect the enterprise and the people in it in several ways. In his efforts to be helpful to people, the administrator can easily neglect his responsibilities to the enterprise and use its resources on "people" problems that are not related to the job and which do not affect job behavior. Also, there is often a difference between what is best for a problem and what is best for the people involved. Whenever conflict of any substantial significance occurs, the administrator needs to take the side of the enterprise if it is to have any side. Whether he fits a human relations model every time or not, the administrator is the agent of the enterprise and is employed to look at problems as being problems of the enterprise. Acting in the best interests of the total enterprise is the only way that the administrator can act in the best interests of all the members of the organization. Individual advantage can be given only at the expense of those who do not receive a similar advantage. Administrative actions are social bargains in that they involve the total membership of the organization, and this means that a fair bargain with the individual is a bargain that is fair to the whole.

Whether what is good for General Motors is good for the country might be debatable, but that the good of General Motors' employees depends upon the good of General Motors is not. Administration has a responsibility to maximize the opportunity for growth and development of all members of the organization, but it is doubtful that this can be met by placing more emphasis upon individual needs than upon organizational needs. The welfare of the individual is dependent upon the welfare of the enterprise, and the administrator's first responsibility is to the whole rather than its parts. In the long run that is the only way to assure the welfare of the parts.

Helping a person can often be a handicap, rather than a favor, to the person helped. It is probable that more people have been helped into mediocrity than have ever been driven there. This is because men grow stronger on workouts than on handouts. As Ralph Waldo Emerson put it: "Our chief want in life is someone who can make us do what we can do." People do not ordinarily do all they can do but rather what the situation demands they do. Saying that "necessity is the mother of invention" is a way of saying that necessity is the mother of effort. It is in the nature of people to wrestle with a challenge and to rest on a crutch. Said another way, what he can get people to do is the greatest thing the administrator can do for people. The failure of people to do things may often be more the fault of administration than of the individual. Organizational life is a contrived life, and the individual's work is cut out for him by others. He can do no more and no better than he is asked to do. The quantity and quality of his work is delegated, and he is not permitted to take over the work of others nor to spend the effort and resources of the enterprise in doing a better job than the enterprise wants done. He can only do what the administration has him do.

There are times when the individual really needs and deserves help, and the enterprise has legitimate reason to provide it. But even in these circumstances paternalism will provide little payoff for the enterprise. The great desire of man is to stand on his own, and his life is one great fight against dependency. Making the individual a ward of the organization will likely make him bitter instead of better. The Biblical axiom that it is more blessed to give than to receive refers to the rapture of the giver rather than that of the receiver. As Machiavelli put it, "Hatred is gained as much by good works as by evil." It is a fact of life that we are more attached to and interested in the people and organization that we help than in those that help us. Aside from the resentment that obligation kindles, people are prone to see an angle, rather than an angel, when the company does them a favor. This may mean that most people are too mature to believe that Santa Claus comes more than one day a year. Since paternalism seldom pays off in terms of better attitudes or performance, it may also mean that people understand some of the general laws under which they usually act and will act differently when someone tries to exploit those general laws.

Because obvious paternalism has produced so few door prizes for the enterprise, administration is being urged to practice its paternalism underground by working through the individual's subconscious, rather than his conscious, mind. If one reviews industrial relations history, there is irony in the manner in which psychological paternalism has replaced the material variety. Some of the strongest antagonists of material paternalism appear among the strongest advocates of the psychological kind. It is as if they were saying that administrative tranquilizers are less toxic if dispensed through the company psychologist than through the company store. It would seem that the psychological brands should be considered the most dangerous, for they aren't marked very well. The material sort is obvious and provides the individual with an open option to take or not to take. Although his ability to exercise the option might be restricted by his personal circumstances, his role as an individual is clear, in that he is a conscious party to the transaction. It is certain that the modern sort is the most insulting because it implies that the individual can be had for a few psychological crumbs from the administrative table top.

A spillover effect of the "hide the boss" movement is the rationale that authority wouldn't be such a bad thing if everyone had it. This "bottoms up" line of thought has led to much preoccupation with the concept of democratic administration. Admittedly, much can be said for a concept of participative management, but it is difficult to defend the idea that the sum of the thinking by all members of the organization is equal to the best thinking for the organization. If followed very far, this idea leads to administration by the lowest common denominator, under which the opinion of all comers is accepted as equally authoritative and knowledge and specialized experience can count for very little. Such dispersion of authority in equal parts to the members of the organization can in the long run lead only to the destruction of the values it is intended to secure. If the intent is to give every individual a voice, this cannot be done by stilling it in the noise of the crowd. If the individual is to be heard when he has something of value to say, then he must have a chance to stand out from the chorus and sing solo.

The impracticality of utilizing a theory that holds one man's opinion to be as valid or important as another's has almost restricted the practice of democratic management to the text books. However, it may have significantly affected the extent and manner of use of committees. This time-honored device for bringing to bear on a particular problem the best judgment of those best informed has become increasingly utilized as a homeopathic application of democratic administration and as an exercise in group therapy. Because it is being used as a means to let people sound off rather than as a means to let the administrator sound out, it has become in many instances a vehicle of expression for the most voluble rather than for the most valuable. It has also become an escape mechanism for those administrators who can't take the organizational heat and who resort to presiding in order to avoid the personal responsibility of deciding.

Participation in administrative decisions by those who have the facts and by those who have a significant stake in the particular decision is a must for effective administration. Such participation, however, does not relieve the administrator of the responsibility for the final determination. Administration is the thermostat, as well as the thermometer, for the organization, and its function is to regulate things as well as to record them. Huddling with his team is an effective means of communication, but the administrator still has to call the play and accept the responsibility for having called it.

Engrossment with the huddle approach to administration may be due in part to the extensive attention that has been directed toward group dynamics in recent years. It is doubtful if any subject has ever held as much fascination for behavioral scientists or engaged the research attention of so many of them. This enchantment has proven highly contagious for administrators, and many of them have come to use a group dynamics model in testing their policies and their supervisors. Some of the research has been both very solid and very exciting, and certain phenomena deserve all the attention that the behavioral scientists are giving them. But the findings have been misinterpreted and misused by some practicing administrators. Most of the research has been done with small, informal groups, since neither the methods nor the opportunities have been available for the study of complex and formal groups. These small, informal groups, however, have been looked upon by practicing administrators as counterparts of the structured and complex groups which make up formal organizations. Findings from motivational studies of such informal and inwardly controlled groups have been projected as characteristics of the outwardly controlled groups necessary in operating organizations. In a way, these administrators are saying they can see no difference organizationally between the role the individual plays in his Saturday night poker group and the role he plays on the production line at the factory.

In a free society, the individual's association with an operating enterprise is voluntary, but his participation is not. He may quit if he pleases, but he cannot do as he pleases. In its ultimate meaning, the purpose of administration is not a matter of cooperation but of corporation. The purpose is not joint participation but rather joined or unified endeavor. Cooperation, in the sense of being knowingly helpful, can have little meaning in large, complex organizations where people do not know each other's activities and mostly do not even know each other. Individuals do cooperate with each other on their individual assignments, but that is personal rather than organizational. The organization seeks coordination, and this is a function of administrative design rather than individual decision.

Among those who believe in "groupy" administration, the extremists advocate cuddling rather than huddling. The difference is that the boss is excluded from the cuddle. The notion seems to be that a behavioral contagion from the forces operating in a group can produce better individual performance than direct supervision by the organizational hierarchy can produce. The concept seems to be that the group is more responsible or wise than the supervisor. It is true that group influence is powerful and that efforts to make the individual deviate from the norms of his group are strongly resisted. Also, it is true that the individual needs the social interaction to be gained from acceptance by, and participation in, his work group. But before administration becomes too completely a servant of group methods, it needs to examine some of the hazards of an overemphasis on "groupiness." The most serious hazard lies in letting the group become the conscience of the individual. If administration is not sufficiently explicit and determined in setting out and maintaining the norms of performance it desires, the individual is left hostage to the norms of the group. The individual has no criteria for acceptable conduct other than what goes on around him, and if administration is willing to let group norms specify what is good and punish what is bad, the individual has little alternative but to go along with

them. The facts of organizational life make this so. Not only do
we find it easier to share the attitudes and habits of others than to
oppose them, but adjustment to the tempo and level of performance of one's work group is a requirement that is enforced by
organizational coordination.

Preoccupation with groupiness can lead to a "contented cow"
sort of administration in which harmony is used as a harness. The
idea has much appeal to the administrator because his world is a
problem-ridden world and much of his time is taken up by the
discontented. It is easy for him to see organizational problems as
the result of discontent rather than the cause of it and to see
harmony as the answer to his problems. While it is true that
harmony can keep his problems from showing, it can do this only
by hiding them. A group which is asleep isn't going to give the
administrator very much trouble, but neither is it going to give
him very much help. There is a difference between going to sleep
and going places. There is evidence to indicate that groups that
have been together a long time tend to perform less well as time
goes on because they develop a feeling of security. There is also
evidence that groups in which the individuals get along with each
other best may start spending more time getting along and less
time working. There is reason to believe that the most satisfied
are the most difficult to change. Still waters run deep, but they do
so because they are in a hole.

The yearning for "we" feeling in the organization is a strong
one for most administrators. In his own mind the administrator
believes that what he wants to do is best and that others would
be solidly with him if they could just understand. The notion that
understanding will produce agreement and support is valid, however, only in those situations where the interests of the organization are sufficiently identical with the interests of the members of
the organization. Because people often have different stakes in
organizational endeavors, the administrator cannot assume that
the interests of the members of the organization are always
identical with the interests of the organization. Such interests
have to be compatible and reasonably mutual, but it is asking too
much to assume that they are the same. Different results affect
different individuals differently, and such differences cannot be
"understood" out of existence. The notion that understanding
produces support assumes that the individual seeking support

holds the interests of the other party at least equal to his own. For the administrator, it also assumes that where two or more conflicting interests are involved, he can perform the neat acrobatic stunt of holding each of the two interests higher than the other at the same time. Administrators have faced the problem of choosing between conflicting interests too often to believe that understanding very often homogenizes significant differences into agreement. This does not mean that the administrator should not seek the understanding of those affected by his decisions. To the extent that understanding demonstrates that he believes he is acting rationally, it will help to reduce resistance. It does mean, however, that he should not expect any merit badges for his judgment from those who are adversely affected by his decisions. He should not be surprised when occasionally some of his best-laid plans are slipped an oversized mickey by those who are personal losers from those plans.

It is likely that the administrator wil have a much more rigid posture than other members of the organization on matters that affect the enterprise. The administrator represents the total enterprise and must uphold its party line. The direction of his thoughts and attitudes is in large part ready-made for him. To some extent his viewpoint is "store-bought" by the purposes and program of the enterprise rather than custom-tailored to his personal specifications. Often it is even made up of hand-me-downs of predecessors who set the cut of it years before when long term plans and programs were established. The lower the administrative position in the hierarchy, the more precut the policies the particular administrator must utilize; but strangely enough, the higher the administrative position, the less the freedom to make alterations on those stock sizes. The top administrator must fit his decisions both to the central purpose of the enterprise and to all segments of the organization. Policies that come in standard sizes, because they are standard, are apt to fit the greatest number of situations. This means the administrator's viewpoint is biased toward overall organizational goals rather than toward the goals of the parts of the organization. Because he is so strongly biased organizationally himself, he is likely to assume similar motivation on the part of other members of the organization. For this reason, it is necessary for him to remember that his bias for the total enterprise is usually shared by other members of the organization only in proportion to the level in the organization occupied by them. In fact this bias may not even be proportional because a similar sort of nationalism is developing in favor of departmental and subdepartmental goals all down the line. This means that the goals of different parts of an organization can never be identical with the goals of the total organization, and neither can the interests and ambitions of administrators of the parts be identical with those of the administrator of the whole. Such interests need not be at cross-purposes, but the difference in responsibilities of the administrators involved precludes the chance of their purposes ever being identical. Strong and aggressive departmental administrators should be expected to work vigorously toward the best possible performance by their own department. The sales manager cannot be expected to view the work of his salesman through the eyes of the credit manager. The production manager should be expected to resist some of the thinking of the industrial relations manager. Of necessity the chief administrator must see things a little differently from any one of his subordinates if he is going to see in common with all of them.

Some authorities on administration seem to believe that one of the most essential characteristics required of the administrator is an abiding affection for people per se; those who counsel and advise about administrative attributes often place much stress on this characteristic. Actually, the worth of this attribute as a criterion for success in administration may not be very great. This could be true for a couple of reasons. The first has to do with the fact that a general liking for people is one of the most universal attributes possessed by the human species, and therefore an evaluation of this quality is a relatively useless test for success. It's only the rare individual who would not pass the test with a margin to spare. The second has to do with the basis of the assumption. To be useful, relationships would have to be necessarily mutual, and the administrator's affection for others would have to cause them to have affection for him. It is true that we tend to oppose those who oppose us. But there is no established proof that relationships are necessarily mutual. One can have such feelings as affection, trust, and admiration for another person on a purely one-way basis. A good illustration of this fact is the strong affection and trust we develop for public heroes and leaders whom we never meet or see in person. Or, there is the fact that the patient trusts the doctor and bares his personal problems to him without the doctor's trusting in, or baring his own personal problems to, the patient. Perhaps a better illustration for most of us is the memory of the girls on whom we developed a crush and who responded only by scorning us. Even where our affection is returned, there is no certainty that it will be returned by high performance. While it is true that we are very reluctant to oppose those whom we like, it does not follow that we will go all out in performing for them. We generally give those we like their own way, but if we are not given to hard work, we will likely leave them with the difficulty of making their own way. It is often said that the spirit is willing but the flesh is weak. Put into organizational terms, this means that waltzing cheek-to-cheek is not the same as working shoulder-to-shoulder and that it can easily become the opposite if those around the administrator get the notion that a soft head goes with his soft heart.

The administrator cannot, of course, mistreat people and not expect to reap antagonism. There is more than a dictionary difference, however, between fair treatment and affection. We expect fair treatment and give no extra trading stamps when we receive it. We don't expect a person to have to love us in order to treat us fairly. It is much more necessary that the administrator like to deal with people than that he like them. The first is by far the more difficult. For instance, almost everybody seems to like children, but not too many individuals seem to like to work with them or even be around them for any long period of time. The problems of administration are largely the problems of people, and it is very easy to get tired of people if you do not like to work with their problems. Liking people will not assure that the administrator will like their problems, but liking problems can help keep him from disliking people.

The "loving each other" approach to administration can cause the administrator to get himself lost in his tunnel of love. The subordinate in dealing with the administrator is dealing with a social entity who also wants to be loved. To be loved by everybody can become such an overwhelming desire for the administrator that he will "fall" for the members of the organization who court his attention. The desire for personal acceptance is a very strong desire on the part of all normal people and a very important one for the administrator. His success depends upon how strongly the members of the organization second his motions, and most often their endorsement of his ideas depends largely upon their endorsement of him. If this desire for acceptance gets out of hand, however, it can damage his effectiveness in several ways. On the one hand, his efforts to be accepted can cause him to be a genial fellow who leans over backward to please. But the trouble with leaning over backward is that it marks him as an easy push-over and he soon becomes known as nothing more than the nice guy he wanted to be. On the other hand, the hunger for accept-ance can weaken, and even destroy, the integrity of the adminis-trator. It is paradoxical, but our conscience seems to be much more effectively silenced by the values everyone holds in high esteem than by those which are held to be evil. We seem to be willing to do almost anything to prove our loyalty, or to keep faith, or to protect someone. We violate the moral rules quickly, and almost eagerly, it seems, in order to keep the code of accept-ance. We don't hesitate to "break" the truth in order to prove that we are true to others. This sort of moral relativism may possibly have a place in the actions of the individual, but it is hard to find a place for it in the actions of the administrator. The administra-tor needs acceptance and ratification, but he must prescribe the ground rules by which he will seek the endorsement of those around him. If he doesn't do this, he is entrusting his administra-tive conscience and ultimate usefulness to those whom he is try-ing to please. He can hardly keep faith with himself while winking at his own rules.

Such esteemed feelings as sympathy and compassion can become more wayward than we think. They can easily get out of control and impair the administrator's judgment. The often-heard saying that "the way to hell is paved with good intentions" may be much more accurate than most of us believe. More lapses in integrity occur when we are trying to help people than when we are trying to hurt them. At such times we seduce our judgment with our most beautiful feelings, and under their spell we can be-come so broad-minded that we forget the difference between right and wrong. We have a tendency to react impulsively to touching situations and are apt to let them cause us to break pol-icy or make unwise commitments for reasons foreign to the inter-ests of the organization. We seem most susceptible in this connec-tion when the individuals concerned adopt a role of dependency or bewilderment and lay their burdens at our feet. We have a tendency to act similarly when someone places us in the role of expert, or appeals to our authority. Hardly an administrator lives who cannot recall more than several experiences of embarrassedly asking some colleague or department chief to break a policy rule in order to carry out a commitment the administrator made on the spur of being helpful. Being good to one another is a noble idea, but it can lead to the administrator's churning the milk of human kindness, at the organization's expense, to butter up his own feelings. Before he acts out of sympathy, the administrator should remind himself that administration is a function for the enterprise and not an outlet for the administrator.

Administration by the "soft touch" system has strong appeal at times to the administrator. It serves to balance his emotional diet. His position is wired into the operations in such a way that he hears very little of the melody from the busy hum of the workbench but gets the static from any discord that might be generated. Much of his day is devoted to the unpleasant task of denying the requests that come to him and in being the middleman in problems between others. Because he so often has to tie an administrative tin can to the ends sought by those around him, he feels a need to prove to himself as well as others that he really is like the nice man next door. But there is doubt that administration can always be a nice man's game. There are usually organizational wolves hanging around to take advantage of the administrator who lets his nice feelings show. In administration, the nicest men sometimes make the nicest chewing. For obvious reasons, one is far more tempted to walk through a flower bed than through a briar patch. The administrator has to get along with everybody, but he can do this only if everyone knows he is able and ready to handle anybody.

A winning way can be an asset to the administrator, but it can also be a liability to him and the enterprise. If the administrator leans too heavily on his winning ways, he will tend to ignore more difficult, but more permanent, ways of problem solving. He will be less likely to seek the facts and to develop a solution that can stand up by itself. Because it will be easier, and perhaps more entrancing, he will be tempted to "snow" the people who have the problems instead of helping them solve the problems. Also, the lack of opposition to the administrator, because of his winning ways, may represent a disservice to the enterprise. A good leader may not always be a good administrator. He may win followers, but these may not be the best individuals for the organization. The fact that he can get others to follow is no guarantee that he is going in the right direction. A little tugging with the opposition can sometimes serve a useful purpose by forcing one to examine more closely the path that he is taking. Too much "followship" by his subordinates can prevent appropriate roughhousing with the administrator's ideas and opinions.

There are other hazards for the administrator who practices more with his heart than with his head. The biggest hearted seem to get their feelings hurt the most often. This may be because the more they give, the more they expect; or it may be because they use more, they need more in return; or perhaps it is because they expose their feelings the most. In any event, feelings are easier to hurt than to heal, and the administrator is smart to keep his feelings out of the line of administrative fire. Crippled feelings are a handicap in the psychological race which he runs each day. They are too weak to carry their end of the mounting emotional load the administrator picks up throughout the day and have a tendency to cave in when the going gets rough.

The big-hearted administrator cannot expect any great capital gains on the investment of his generous feelings in the organization. What he purchases often has a very short life. It may be a reflection on the human race, but most people seem to tire quicker of saints than of sinners, and we are perhaps as upset by behavior that exceeds the average as by that which falls below it. The elements of satiation and boredom seem to keep close company with generosity and indulgence, since one can soon grow weary of too much of either. The effusive administrator is peculiarly vulnerable to having his excesses show through. He is required to spend most of his working day around many of the same people, and under such circumstances personalities are bound to rub each other. Under these close working conditions, the administrator who tries too hard to get into the hearts of those working with him may end up by only getting in their hair.

The great wave of broad-mindedness that is engulfing contemporary society is also having its effects on the modern administrator. In many ways, increased tolerance can serve to improve the effectiveness of administration and the lot of the individual. Both can be seriously impaired, however, if the tolerance is for the individual's conduct rather than for his condition. A "forgive them for they know not what they do" attitude can be destructive to the individual. A man's work fills important social and psychological needs, and these values can easily be tolerated out of existence. Forgiveness is a wonderful thing, but in the individual's work accountability is essential. The only way he can count for anything in life is to have what he does counted for and against him. He can't think he counts for much if any pattern of conduct seems equally acceptable. Easy forgiveness for his transgressions leaves him with no notion about what matters and no deterrent force to help him measure up to whatever does matter. It throws him back on his own in a way that is not in keeping with the realities of human nature and robs him of the psychological roughage he needs for self-sufficiency and self-reliance. A "blue plate special" of mercy does not fill the needs of a man who wants to keep growing, and holding onto the hand of the boss will not give him the feeling of security that he gets from toeing the line. The first makes him dependent, while the second makes him his own man.

The "friendlier than thou" practice of administration may follow a different course for those administrators who prefer to use fellowship rather than affection as a tool. These administrators seem to believe that if they join the gang, its members will automatically start working better for them. This represents an assumption that if you act like the other fellow, he will act as you want him to act. It is perhaps true that if the administrator becomes one of the boys, the boys will get to know him better, but how much it will improve their opinion of him depends upon how well he can stand their knowing him better. The administrator as a person may differ greatly from the administrator as an administrator. As an administrator his behavior is to a large extent structured, and he operates in a protected environment. On the job, his life is largely ordered by the role he is playing, and people accord him respect because they respect his position. When he lays aside his robes, he is on his own, but people will still partly see him as the administrator even though he sees himself as acting like a person. Also, if they learn to know him as a person, they will continue partly to see him as a person when he is on the job. Joining the gang can compromise the respect accorded him unless he is careful, and the administrator who works too hard at being one of the boys will sometimes find it quite difficult to be regarded as one of the men.

Another "palship" group in administration are the jolly rovers who apparently believe that people can be kidded into doing a good job. These administrators see a glad hand as being the same as a good hand and attempt to keep the members of the organization in line by having them trip the light fantastic all around the enterprise. The workday is so crowded with morale-building activities that it is hard for the personnel to find time for their coffee break, and the evenings are devoted to company-sponsored bowling leagues, little theater groups, and other pursuits that can't get scheduled during the day. Winning a softball game rates more raves in the company house organ than taking the red out of the operating statement, and prowess as the chef for the company barbecue gets one a quicker promotion than cooking up a new idea for the production line. No one can argue that people should not enjoy their work or that the enterprise should be an oversized mausoleum, but it is supposed to be a work place rather than a sideshow. The administrator doesn't need to lead a jamboree in order to make the enterprise an inviting place to work. The difference between a fiesta and a funeral is great enough so that the administrator can be lighthearted without being light-headed.

The protocol for being one of the boys most often involves repeated practice of the ritual of ordering a "double on the rocks." The administrator is not supposed to be an altar boy, and this chapter is aimed at his mind rather than his soul; but those rocks are dangerous shoals for the administrator's judgment. They are the rocks on which the careers of too many administrators have foundered. Used properly, alcohol may be a harmless source of pleasure. However, it can be a treacherous foe, and the smart man treats it as such. It can be a treacherous foe to good judgment because it attacks behind the glow of good fellowship. Also, it is deceptive in other ways. It affects the higher brain levels first and thus neutralizes the individual's ability to censor his own conduct. This is because the higher brain levels perform the critical functions and constitute the judgment center. The fact that our critical faculties are those dulled first by alcohol is one reason why we are never aware of the actual influence that it has on our judgment. Our inability to detect the influence of alcohol on our mental faculties is compounded by the fact that our motor abilities are controlled by the lower levels of our brain and are not affected at first.

Alcohol double-crosses the administrator's judgment because it stimulates by sedating. It increases his confidence by decreasing his standards, and thus places his judgment in double jeopardy. The extent to which his judgment is affected depends, of course, upon the amount of alcohol consumed. Even relatively small amounts can have an adverse effect. The effects are much longer lasting than the noonday drinker likes to think. After being absorbed, alcohol is eliminated from the body tissues of the average person at a rate of only ⅓ ounce per hour. The administrator confronted with important decisions must remember that long after the drink is over the malady lingers on. Admittedly, the administrator often finds it difficult to decline a drink when in a group of colleagues or acquaintances. It is not only that he doesn't want to be unsociable, but there is some unexplained quality of human nature that causes us to force a drink on another. We accept the other person's word when he tells us he doesn't care for a smoke, or for coffee, or for dessert, but we insist that he have another round of alcohol. There probably is no good answer to the problem of bending elbows with friends, but it is important that we recognize the effect of alcohol on judgment and that we place our judgment in escrow until the effect of alcohol has been spent.

One of the greatest perils of alcohol to the administrator is the effect it has on his tongue. At the time he should say the least, he is most likely to say the most, and the things he says are likely to be the most damaging. When we uncork the bottle, we seem to automatically unwind our tongues and proceed to vocalize every repressed opinion stored in our minds. The administrator doesn't need any special stimulant to talk too much. Talking too much is a common ailment of most administrators and is another of the occupational hazards to which his work exposes him. In many ways the administrator must live by himself and is insulated from much of the informal life of the organization. His desk calendar rules his day and chooses those with whom he spends most of his talking time. At the same time, he is likely to be more gregarious than the average person and to have more of a need for shared experiences. This is perhaps one of the reasons he gravitated into, and upward in, administration. In a way, the work of the administrator is at cross-purposes with some of the personal specifications by which he is chosen. He is supposed to like to talk with people, but if he talks very much he is bound to talk out of turn. It is dangerous for him to talk about the organization or things that are happening in the organization because such talk will be taken as official or be given undue meaning. His position leaves him little that he can talk about in terms of the things the other members of the organization are most interested in hearing. In a manner of speaking, the administrator is marooned in a crowd.

It is more than easy for the administrator to let his tongue trap his mind and outtalk his best judgment. Loose talk is one of the most common avenues to trouble for him. To begin with, much of what he needs to say is said in a loose context. The particular individual to whom the administrator talks at a particular time is only one of many individuals to whom the administrator will talk over a period of time. It is easy for the administrator to forget that others in the organization do not possess as much information on a problem as he possesses. This means the others have to do a good bit of inference drawing regarding what the administrator is talking about. It is also easy for the administrator to forget just whom he has talked to previously about a problem and to let a whole new circle into his confidence. Because other individuals seldom have the full story that the administrator possesses, they are likely to put a different meaning from his on things that he says and on plans that they only partially understand. For this reason the administrator must be careful that he does not talk too much while saying too little.

The loose talk that represents the greatest danger to the administrator, however, is the idle talking he does. This is the talk that does not concern the problem about which he is talking at the time or the individual with whom he is talking. The administrator has strong temptations for such gratuitous talking. He wants to be a part of the group around him and knows that one of the keys to membership is small talk. Being human, he also has the urge to gossip and the desire to be the first to tell something. For the same reason, he has his own needs to get things off his chest. He is forced to hoard irritations and worries from one interview to another but must finally unload them if he is going to hold his own personality together. All of this means that he is highly tempted to talk about the people and the problems of the organization when he finds a sympathetic ear. This is gratis talk, but it can represent a heavy cost to the administrator. Other people like to talk too, and the administrator can be sure that they will. The result can be resentment and misunderstandings from the individuals discussed and the premature disclosure of the administrator's thinking about problems. Loose talk is tempting to the administrator, but he is smart to remember that it is less difficult to hold his words than to stop them.

Overexpansiveness represents another vocal booby trap to the administrator's judgment. There is a euphoric quality about talking itself that causes us to get carried away with the situation and with our listeners. If our company is in any way pleasant, we seem to have a compulsion to say things that will please. We try to put things in a way our listeners will approve even if we are talking to strangers or speaking about matters of no direct importance to us. Under the glow of a friendly discussion, the administrator has a tendency to talk himself into a corner by overpromising and overcommitting. We always say that we let someone "talk" us into unwise actions, but usually it would be more accurate to say they "listened" us into trouble. Most of us can recall instances in which, under the intoxication of our own exuberance, we have caught ourselves trying to prove the other person's point for him and searching for justifications that will help excuse errors that he has committed. For reasons already mentioned, the administrator has strong temptations to practice a sort of "talk now think later" type of administration. The consequences of binding ourselves with our vocal cords, are such, however, that it is worth the effort to keep reminding ourselves that it is much easier to hold our promises down than to try to fulfill them later.

The administrator who uses his good feelings promiscuously runs the risk of having them used for hire. Courtesies provide an objective means with which to demonstrate affection and appreciation for another person. They represent a favorite food for goodwill, but they can also be used as engaging bait with which to trap the good judgment of the administrator. Such baiting is a constant risk to the administrator. Few people are willing to bait his ill will for their personal gain, but they do not seem to view the use of his goodwill the same way. Perhaps it is because goodwill is much easier to lead astray or so little finesse is required in its seduction. The job can be done with such bargain baits as gifts, entertainment, or the economy package of flattery. Whatever the temptations used, they represent a difficult problem for the administrator. It is not enough to say that honesty and ethics are adequate safeguards, since it is not easy to refuse a friendly gesture nor to decline a pleasant one. Also, cupidity is not always involved, and the dollar value may be small. Most individuals can't be bought by big favors, but they can be indentured by small ones. The bookkeeping for favors utilizes the unique rule that small favors can represent large obligations for the administrator. Administratively speaking, such bookkeeping can bankrupt the administrator before he realizes his judgment is being fixed and he is being used.

The extent to which they are influenced by friendship and kinship would probably surprise most administrators if they ever totaled it up. Patronage and nepotism are usually associated with governmental agencies, but they flourish with some vigor in a high percentage of all organizations. Some industries, such as fire and liability insurance, apparently secure a significant part of their business on a friendship basis. Most family-controlled enterprises, and many of the large publicly owned ones, practice a form of administrative featherbedding in which jobs are "found" in the company for friends and friends of friends. It may well be that prices are just as low from friends and that work performance is just as good from friends. The essential point is that the use of friendship as the primary specification in any transaction embalms the freedom of the administrator. He can't turn around when the need arises without turning on his friends unless he has left himself enough psychological distance in which to make his turn.

Good judgment depends as much upon controlling our respected emotions as upon controlling those usually held in disrespect. The emotions of goodwill can be as upsetting to the administrator's judgment as those of ill will. There is a place in administration for the use of both, but they should be controlled by the administrator instead of being allowed to control him. The problem for the administrator is to strike a balance rather than a gusher when he does permit his emotions to become involved in his work.

Success does not always come from succeeding

5 The winner's circle is the normal habitat of the successful administrator, but it is not always the ideal home in which to nurture and maintain the traits and characteristics required for a successful administrator. Constant success has the unfortunate proclivity of breeding some undesirable by-products that can ultimately damage the good judgment which helped produce the success. The fact that the administrator does not taste enough failure can lead to the overdevelopment of some of the qualities required in the successful practice of administration and can cause the administrator to make vices out of some of his best virtues. Continued success in administration does not always come from continuously succeeding. The successful administrator can unknowingly become a victim of his own excellence.

The literature of administration has been heavily spiked in recent years with the "leader" concept of the administrator. Under this concept the administrator is pictured as a sort of Moses who is endowed with attributes greatly superior to those of his followers. He supposedly maintains his following by becoming the father image for a group of lesser mortals who supposedly revert to something close to a state of childlike dependency the moment they punch the time clock. Actually, this classification of the managed as organizational thumb-suckers is not intended to glorify the administrator. On the contrary, those who advocate this concept of administration really have as their purpose the uplifting of the place of the managed. In terms of their semantics, they are saying that the manager, in reality, serves the managed and his success is a consequence of the manner in which he meets the needs of the managed. It would be difficult to find serious fault with that hypothesis. The fault lies rather in the rationale on which the proposition is based and the danger it represents to the outlook and attitudes of the administrator. The concern of this chapter is with some of the *grand homme* tendencies which affect the judgment and conduct of the administrator and which, without much encouragement, can lead him to think he deserves a place among the chosen. The concept of the administrator as the "great white father" can add rich fuel to these tendencies and cause him to forget that it is his function more than his personal superiorities that gives him his place and his following.

The nature of the administrator's work provides good grazing for any Jehovah complex the administrator may be harboring. If you are higher up on the ladder than others, your view of them is always one of looking down. It is easy from this position to start looking down one's nose at those below. This view is encouraged by the fact that the administrator more often sees his subordinates in their weaknesses than in their strengths. It is always easier to detect the lack of excellence than its presence. More important, when things are going best and those below appear at their strongest, the administrator hears least from and about them; the worse things are going, the more likely he is to be concerned with them and their work. If one mainly sees only another's weaknesses, it is difficult not to label him with his errors. Inferiority is further demonstrated to the administrator by the obvious answers to the problems his subordinates sometimes bring to him. It is hard for the administrator to remember that for a number of reasons the answers are easier for him. In the first place, his level in the hierarchy permits a better perspective from which to view the problem. In the second place, he is, to an extent, using hindsight,

since the other person's efforts have neither prevented nor corrected the problem and thus those particular efforts have already
been tested for the administrator. The element of second guessing
is extended by the fact that the original decision about whether a
problem really exists is often a product of the administrator's own
evaluation. Also, problems are brought to the administrator in
many instances solely for information or confirmation and not as
insolubles. The other person may know the best answer but feel
obligated to check it with the administrator before putting it into
use. Administrative decisions are not always based solely on
whether a thing can be done, but often must take into account
how much the administrator wants them done and how much
priority, with regard to resources and effort, he wants to give one
thing over other things that need to be done. Even when his
subordinates do not know the right answer, they sometimes give
the administrator a head start on the problem by asking the right
questions. The administrator must remember also that he writes
the book and that the chance to make up both the questions and
the answers is more than a passing advantage for him.

The evaluation of a subordinate's performance is always a difficult thing for the administrator. He knows that almost every decision, and the manner of its implementation, is in part a compromise between logical indications and social necessities. Some sort
of action is the ultimate purpose of a decision and this means it
must be usable. For this reason, a decision must be evaluated as a
social choice as well as a logical choice. The pull of the factors
affecting the social choice is often much stronger and more immediate than those affecting the logical choice. The social factors
become increasingly more powerful the closer one approaches
the firing line. Down where the work is done, people aren't so
impressed with mathematical formulas and sometimes get a chill
from cold logic. The subordinate is confronted with real, live people as he tries to implement a decision and under such circumstances is likely to worry as much about what can be done as
about what ought to be done. Also, he faces another hazard that
is present in all personal diplomacy. Face-to-face discussions of
problems do not always produce solutions that will fit back-to-
back with logic. Cold logic has a way of melting quickly from
either the warm glow of friendly palaver or the hot glare of determined opposition. The administrator, protected by a hierarchy

from the people below, can easily see simple solutions to complicated problems. In his sometimes splendid isolation he can overlook the fact that his subordinates often must find complicated
answers that will produce uncomplicated situations.

The administrator's illusions of superiority are not always
delusions. His judgment must have been proved right most of the
time, or he likely would not have obtained, or still be holding, his
position. However, success can breed an ingrown pride that can
easily turn into delusions. This pride can cause him to forget that
much of his success may be due to the circumstances of his situation rather than his personal superiority, and, given the same
facts and context, the chances are good that other individuals
would have achieved about the same results. Also, with many
problems there can be several different but satisfactory solutions.
Further, the administrator's solution may not have been completely his own but could have represented a product of those
around him. It is also a fact that many organizational problems are
self-correcting, and the answer is inherent in the situation itself. A
lag in one part of a process is often corrected by the pressure from
other parts of the process. Or, a recalcitrant individual may be
forced into line by the reactions and countermoves of his fellows.
It is an administrative fact of life that in every organization there
is an underlying organizational harmony that will provide a certain level of self-correction. There is also the fact that many inadequate solutions are never discovered, or are not of sufficient
consequence, to attract very much attention. And organizational
results, regardless of the type and purpose of the enterprise, are
most often composites made from numerous decisions, and there
is virtually no way to determine the precise value of any one act
or decision of the administrator. In administration there is a fairly
broad area of tolerance for management error on specific problems. Also, a good organization can sometimes tolerate a very
weak spot for relatively long periods of time. Likewise, the momentum of the organization will often override some important
temporary weaknesses.

It will help the administrator, both in taking credit and in at-
taching blame, to remember the phenomena of extemporaneous
consequences that attend all organizational activity. Most of the
results of such activity are in reality "outcomes" of the aggregate
of all influences rather than specific "derivatives" of particular de-

cisions. Decisions, as the product of intention, are steering devices and for the most part are corrective rather than creative in nature. Many of the forces that determine "outcomes" are beyond the control of a single enterprise and especially of a particular department of an enterprise. The situation can be compared to a sailboat on the river. While the skipper can take certain very meaningful steps, he can only go where the river leads and can only use the forces that are available to him. Most of the results that occur are consequences of his givens rather than his makings. In a complex organization and a dynamic environment the forces are great in number and to a large part interacting. This means that consequences are to a large extent self-generated and that once generated, themselves become forces that substantially influence succeeding consequences. In a very real way, administrative results are the product of "drift" as well as drive.

Often the administrator is the last person to learn of his own poor decisions. He looks more at the whole than at its parts, and it is the parts that are usually affected directly by his decisions. Because he is the boss, he will likely not have many open critics of his own work. Also, because it was the boss's idea, people under him will most likely work harder to make the idea work or tolerate it longer before making an issue of it. He is further insulated from his errors by his distance from the workplace where many of his decisions are tested. This doesn't mean that the administrator can survive a high percentage of failures. It just means that he may not be aware of all the failures he does have and thus may be judging the batting averages of others improperly by his own inflated average. This can result not only in his looking down at others but also in his developing a false confidence in his personal ability to lick all the problems the organization might face. This can become a special problem when it is extended to things in which he has little competence and which he assumes ought not to represent a problem to anyone else.

The fact that the administrator sits in judgment on himself can prejudice the trial in favor of his competence. Hearing his own case provides him with the unique opportunity to admit the favorable, and suppress the adverse, evidence. Despite our best efforts, we do not make good witnesses against ourselves. We are more eager to keep others, and ourselves, from learning about our errors than we are to learn from them. We sometimes search for ways to hide results that are likely to reflect adversely on us. In many instances the errors we make are less consequential than the efforts we make to hide them. We expend more effort in keeping our status in repair than in repairing our errors. Both unknowingly and knowingly, we disguise our faults in ways that keep even ourselves from recognizing them. We tend to disparage desirable skills and qualities that we do not possess and to paint as virtues the faults we cannot, or will not, correct. We are secretly pleased with the faults of others because we think they help excuse our own faults, and we are quick to condemn faults in others which we believe we do not possess. Admittedly, the administrator can't hang out all his dirty washing and expect to maintain the respect of those around him. It is an awful truth in administration that we are what other people think we are. We can't keep our own self-respect by constantly blushing at our deficiencies. The administrator must constantly remember, however, that a man who rests his case solely on his own evaluation rests on a very precarious perch.

The breath the administrator saves in not speaking about his faults is too often used to blow his own horn over his virtues. This can damage his effectiveness in several ways. In the first place, people get bored by the same old refrain and pretty soon no one is listening. In the second place, the administrator has such a gift of listening so well to himself that he may start believing that he is as good as he wants others to believe he is. Also, his efforts at self-glorification may cause the administrator to assume roles that make him painful to live with. To demonstrate his superiority, he may display undue concern over matters that demonstrate the inferiority of those working with him. He lets them know how good he is by showing them how poor they are. He reproves them to prove that he is free from their faults rather than to improve their performance. When he isn't searching for heads to climb on, he is looking for headlines to stand on. He lays claim to any and all accomplishments of the organization. Whatever succeeds comes under his administrative copyright. The administrator does, of course, have an extraordinary need to feel and look like a winner. Also, it is too much to expect a fellow who has caught a big fish to steal home through the alleys. At the same time, the administrator cannot both do things and always take credit for them. Aside from the fact that credit for excellence is the organizational medium of exchange, there are circumstances in which the administrator must stay out of sight. On some matters his interest will be held suspect and arouse opposition. On other matters his disinterest will be required in order to mediate solutions. Said in other words, the administrator must often stay out of the way if he is to have his way. This means that he must develop the ability to tolerate his own anonymity. While he cannot always act like a sidewalk superintendent, and still be effective, there are times when the administrator must keep his hand in but keep his name out.

It is easy enough for the administrator to assume competences that he does not possess. The chances are that he will have been around the organization for a long time and will have absorbed a great deal of factual knowledge about the enterprise and its problems. But even if he has been around for only a short time, his position at the crossroads of communication in the organization will provide him with a wide inventory of facts about the outfit. Because he is such a storehouse of organizational knowledge, others often will have to turn to him for information. Also, they will quite likely seek his opinion on matters regarding which an acquaintance with past practices might be of value. Aside from the fact that few things inflate a person's feeling of importance as much as having someone ask his opinion, the fact that he is highly informed about the enterprise can cause the administrator to believe that he is highly competent to direct all aspects of it. Such factual knowledge is important and occasionally essential to the administrator, but it is no assurance of administrative competence. Just as one may know where all the best fishing spots are but still be a very poor angler, so can an individual be a walking repository of facts about an enterprise and still be an ineffective administrator.

The assumption that knowledge spells competence in administration is encountered in connection with technical knowledge as well as with the folklore of the enterprise. Overreliance on technical knowledge is often found among administrators in those enterprises and departments whose processes and activities are characterized by complicated technology. It is true that most administration requires some technical knowledge and many administrative decisions cannot be made without a good bit of it, but such knowledge is only the background for administrative performance. Technical knowledge does not necessarily produce better reasoning. A mind filled with know-how may find it diffi-cult to admit enough light to see how. The evidence is strong that mastery of any specialized subject matter has little carry-over in improving general judgment. (The converse is true, and it is much more likely that good general judgment improves technical judgments.) Stated in another way, knowing what makes a missile work is quite different from knowing how to run a missile works.

Overconfidence in any form can cause the administrator not only to ignore his limitations but also to attempt to defy them. It can cause him to practice a "no hands on the handlebars" sort of daredevil administration that takes unreasonable chances with the enterprise's resources and reputation. Admittedly, all solutions are risk-tinged and administration consists of chance-taking. It is true that the effective administrator must take chances, but he tries to leave as little as possible to chance. Overconfidence can be self-feeding when the administrator is winning and can en-courage him to double the stakes rather than double-check the consequences. Like the novice in a crap game, he has an urge to keep betting the pot each time he wins. This means that when he finally does stumble, his run of luck only increases the size of his loss. Enchanted with himself, he is tempted not only to overly trust his luck but to overly push it. This problem would be less consequential to the administrator and the enterprise if he didn't have a tendency to keep betting on the same old horse. Repeated success tends to freeze the winner to the way he won and to close his eyes to new ways by which he might win "bigger" and more surely. In a sense, the overconfident administrator is not self-confident but "way confident." He will try any idea so long as it is one that he has successfully tried before. He likes high adven-ture so long as he can have it in a wheelchair.

It is that repeated success is an essential ingredient of high morale for the administrator and that repeated failure can seri-ously undermine morale. But repeated success can also overfan the torch of self-appreciation which the administrator must of necessity carry for himself if he is to have the sense of personal adequacy required in his work. Smugness can flourish in the warm bed of self-elation that accompanies repeated success. Aside from the fact that humility is more becoming than smugness, smugness imposes a number of incumbrances upon the administrator. Its quality of self-satisfaction can keep the administrator from being his own best critic. It can neutralize that small dash of anxiety needed to season every decision and action. Smugness also quarantines the sense of restlessness with which effective administrators must be infected in order to overcome organizational complacency and inertia. Perhaps most important, smugness provides an insulation between the administrator and the current of ideas originating around him. If he becomes entrenched behind a Maginot line of self-satisfaction, he can become invulnerable to the ideas and suggestions of those in the front lines who are in live contact with the problems confronting the organization. To reword an ancient crack regarding the alumni of a prominent university, "You can tell a smug administrator wherever you see him, but you can't tell him anything."

Intolerance is a twin of smugness. The administrator can learn to expect to have his way too often and with too much certainty. His need to get on with the show can cause him to overlook his need to get along with people. In his search for a solution he can't stop to take in everyone's washing and must at times move before he listens. Also, he soon learns that the administrator who tries to please everyone is never done. Effective administration often requires a high level of determination, and this means that he must be tough-minded. But, to those around him his tough-mindedness can look like tough-headedness. Unless the administrator is careful, that is what it can become. He can become so intent on pushing ahead that he starts pushing the ideas of others out of his way. He can become so sure of his step that he starts stepping on the feelings of those around him. His need to be single-minded can cause him to develop a one-track mind.

The successful administrator can get so used to having his own way that he is apt to forget that there can be any other way. When someone does challenge an idea, such administrators are prone to turn on the challenger rather than the challenge. They tend to act as if opposition on one idea means that the individual opposes them on all ideas. It seems to be a human tendency to classify people as either friends or enemies and to either cordially like or dislike individuals. Actually, it would be quite difficult for anyone to be all friend or all enemy. People have too much in common and at the same time have too many divergent interests to permit a simple division into friends or foes. It is an even greater error for the administrator to measure people organizationally in such a manner. Usually people are in an organization because they share more values with it than with any other organization available to them. They rarely share all the values, but they cannot be opposed to all of them. Actually, organizational conflict seldom is a matter of conflict of values. Members may have very consistent values but differ substantially with regard to means. It is the stepping-stones to goals, rather than the goals themselves, that most often represent stumbling blocks to organizational relationships. Such organizational divergencies as differing priorities of urgency, different responsibilities, and differing possession and interpretation of facts can cause members of the organization to advocate differing routes to the same destination.

The successful administrator has much to support his having his own way. It is difficult to argue with success. However, it is for that very reason that the successful administrator needs challenging. Success can get him set in his ways. Admittedly, he must take the present largely from the past, but his success with the past can cause him to try too hard to make the past into the present. The administrator needs a usable past and must serve as deputy for it. At the same time he must stand as proxy for the future unless he is to find that he is standing in his own way.

The proclivity we have to measure the worth of others by the way they get on with us increases the chances of the administrator's becoming set in his ways. First, this means he will tend to seek and to attract subordinates who see things his way. Second, his general success will leave his critics with little chance to be heard, and the evaluations that get through to him will be largely uncritical applause. Most likely he won't have many critics. This will be not only because of the desire on the part of the less courageous to keep out of trouble by keeping their noses clean and their mouths shut but because the atmosphere will also affect the more energetic and more courageous. They will say as little as they can in order to be heard as much as they can. They will know that it is better to be heard on occasion than to be banished to an administrative Coventry where no attention is ever paid to what they say. This means that the administrator must work hard at uncanning the candid in the organization. Getting others to speak out is the best way for the administrator to stand out.

The administrator must, of course, try to get those around him to like him, but this is quite different from evaluating them by how well he succeeds in winning their liking. The latter means he holds them responsible for his own failure. Even that, however, is not as unfair as the criteria we often employ in determining how well another individual does get on with us. If a person's friends don't like us, we are prone to think that the person himself dislikes us; and if we don't like his friends, we are likely to dislike him. Also, we want others to like those we like, and if they don't, we tend to dislike them or to think they dislike us. We expect those we like to hold the same conceptions of our enemies as we hold, and if they don't, we feel they are disloyal to us. In a real sense we ask our friends to make others over to fit our images.

Arrogance is another natural hazard for the administrator because it is only a half step away from self-confidence. As mentioned earlier, a highly developed sense of personal adequacy is an imperative if the administrator is to have faith in his own judgment. Many of his decisions are based on little more than faith, and this faith must at times be abiding and deep, since he may be wagering his reputation, and even his job, that he is right. Other members of the organization must use his faith if they are to believe in his decisions and confidently carry them out. This means he must not only have confidence in himself but also must exhibit it. He cannot expect others to have more confidence in him than he has in himself. One sure trait of the successful administrator is self-confidence, and he must work hard to possess it. The other side of the street is arrogance, however, and the dividing line between self-confidence and arrogance is needle thin.

The arrogant administrator impairs both his judgment and his relationships. He is prone to practice a "roughrider" kind of administration that disregards the ideas and the feelings of those around him. His decisions become arbitrary because he neither looks nor listens before he moves. He ignores the finesse and art of administration because he prefers to ride down the opposition rather than have it ride with him. He is likely to "ride over" the opposition rather than go to the bother of trying to put over the things he wants done. The most pronounced characteristic of the roughrider is the low sensitivity he has to others. Because he does not depend upon the skills of persuasion and inducement, he loses the art of cultivating people. Since he doesn't notice the feelings of others, he is unable to sense how they feel. We sometimes say of an administrator that he has a "feel" for situations or individuals. This is an excellent term, but it must be remembered that it serves as a verb as well as a noun and that one must first feel of a thing if he is to get a feel for it.

The impatience that his work grafts on the administrator can cause him to be oblivious to the feelings of others and even to trample them. The fact that the administrator travels a path where the dust hardly ever settles leaves him little time to pick his way psychologically through the organization. The veritable succession of deadlines which plague his day—or at least which he thinks plague his day—aren't conducive to his "waltzing with the egos" of those whom he holds partly responsible for the organizational hotfoot that keeps him scurrying. But pacing the floor isn't the same thing as pacing the organization. In the first place pressure-cooked solutions aren't likely to be very viable. They get cooked too fast to permit them to absorb all the factors that need to be included. Also, typically, the things we can do in a hurry are unimportant. The same usually can be said for the things we want to tackle on the spur of the moment. When we think we have little time, we shove aside larger problems and search for the little ones that we think can be handled on the run. This means that we often search for the unimportant and thus have increasingly less time for the important. But more significant in this discussion is the effect of impatience on the administrator's relationships with the people about him. When one emotion is aroused, another of a kindred nature is likely to be aroused with it. If I feel relaxed about my work, I will probably feel satisfied about your performance. On the other hand, if I feel harried and dissatisfied about my performance, it is probable that I will feel restless and critical about how you are performing. This is the reason the effective administrator has a sense of restlessness and dissatisfaction. He must have a strong feeling of wanting to get the job done well and done with, and those working with him must have his feeling visited upon them if the best job is to be done. The administrator can never expect anyone else to feel any more concern about the show than he demonstrates. He will seldom for any long period of time get more than he expects. But success can cause him to learn to expect too much and to expect it too universally. With each success his level of aspirations and expectations tends to move up. Because each higher level becomes increasingly difficult to achieve, he is prone to become increasingly dissatisfied with what others are doing. This can mean that the better people do, the more they are likely to be criticized by the administrator.

Handing out criticism is one of the most difficult tasks required of the administrator. Still, few things the administrator does are as essential as appropriate criticism. Without such feedback from the administrator the subordinate has no good way to know when to mind and how to mend his ways. But, if the administrator develops administrative hypochondria and indulges in too many complaints, the feedback becomes unintelligible to those below. The purpose of criticism is to establish boundaries for the individual, but if it is too much, and too much at random, criticism can obscure rather than secure the boundaries. The ultimate goal of criticism is not verbal punishment—not even just making people comprehend that an error or infraction has been made—but the reshaping and re-creation of people. It is supposed to result in an enduring change in attitude and knowledge. This means criticism must promote thought and feeling dissociable from any previous thought and feeling the individual might have had. Being put in the wrong is not enough. To achieve its purpose, criticism must serve to put the erring individual in the right. Knowing that you are lost doesn't tell you how to get where you are going, and neither does knowing where you are tell you how to get where you ought to be. It is certain, however, that you must always start from where you are. Properly practiced, criticism is a mediating process. It takes into account both what ought to be improved and what can be improved. Sometimes it is wiser for the administrator to change his instructions than to change the practice he is criticizing. This may be because at times it is easier and more feasible to do so, but it also may be because the practice is the better way. It may be hard for the administrator to accept the fact, but an infraction of his instructions can at times be saying something worth listening to. As a critic he must not only raise the sights of those around him but there are times when he must raise his own sights to the level of those he criticizes.

The techniques of criticizing compose another of those administrative subjects on which much has been written. At the drop of a postage-paid card, criticism cookbooks for supervisors and for those at other levels of administration are available from any number of sources and by any number of authors who have never had to stand eyeball to eyeball with willful and cantankerous people. Unfortunately, there are no foolproof mail-order recipes for dressing up an individual's performance without dressing him down. However done, criticism puts the other person in the wrong light, and no technique can be expected to make him glow happily under it. The purpose of criticism would be lost if such a glow did result. But it also would be lost if a slow burn resulted. The proper result occurs when the individual knows what is wrong about his performance and knows what to do about it. This means that criticism should be a matter of contrasting the individual's performance with what is expected of him. It also means that criticism should always be performance-oriented and never personal. Admittedly, it is difficult for the administrator to separate people from their performance. It is less than easy to treat performance in the abstract in a world that often seems marked by human cussedness. But, if the administrator is to raise performance rather than blood pressures, he will have to learn early to reason even with the unreasonable.

Administratively speaking, one of the most damaging aspects of arrogance is the disregard that it demonstrates. Few things can be as insulting to the individual and kindle his resentment as much as being disregarded or ignored. Men will oftentimes accept abuse and unfairness quicker than disregard. At times to do nothing may seem the most militant and menacing sort of action to the other person. Ignoring someone deliberately demonstrates the highest form of scorn and contempt. In an organization, one's "level of regard" is perhaps the major criterion by which status is determined. Who checks with whom provides a much more accurate picture of the importance of individuals in the organization than does the organization chart. One easily observable measure of the regard level in almost any organization is the manner in which the boss's secretary allocates time on the calendar. Titles mean little to the members of an organization unless they are validated by this pecking-order timetable. A 30-minute appointment has more than twice the significance of a 15-minute one. How long it takes to get an appointment with the

chief is likewise significant. The time of day of an appointment
and who gets in first to report to the boss each morning are also
important. Who waits for whom and how long they wait may be
the most revealing of all. Perhaps without knowing it, every
organization develops its own status system of promptness and
lateness. A tolerance range of lateness for appointments develops
according to the importance of different individuals, and to exceed it is considered a breach of organizational etiquette. Who
stays over his time is equally important, and the feelings of the
person who did the waiting in large part depend upon the status
of the person who did the overstaying. The way in which the en-
tering individual greets the departing individual is a pretty good
indication of the status of each. How we stand in line is generally
a pretty good indicator of how we stand in the organization.

Because we watch closely to see the regard level enjoyed by
each of those around us, we know that others are also closely observing the regard shown to us, and we become acutely sensitive
to any degree of slight. It is so important to us that we sometimes
oppose very sensible moves solely because we were not consulted.
Like the kid who prefers being paddled to being unnoticed when
company comes or the teen-age delinquent who breaks the law to
get the attention that is being denied him, people will at times
deliberately break company rules or sabotage the administrator's
plans if they are ignored. Most of us prefer a dirty look to no
look. We consider it a cardinal sin organizationally if someone
goes around us or goes over our head. On occasions we are even
more sensitive to what is not said than to what is said by those
whom we use to check our "affiliation score" in the organization.
Because we are so sensitive to being slighted, we are likely to see
a slight when it isn't there, or is not intended. For this reason
even the most considerate of administrators sometimes cannot
help hurting the feelings of those around him. With the arrogant
administrator, such hurt feelings are not always an accident, and
he usually leaves a legion of casualties in his wake as he fractures
his way unthoughtfully through the organization.

Much has been written in recent years about communications
in administration. Perhaps too much has been written, for it has
become a fashion in administration to bend the employees' ears
with a mass of canned information not worth the bending. Still,
failure to communicate represents one of the major sins of most

administrators. This failure in communications is not with the rank and file of the organization but with those who rank next to the administrator and get their cues directly from him. The failure is not due so much to inexperience as it is to experience. Because the risks in administration are personal risks, the work of the administrator accentuates the development in him of the personal characteristics of self-sufficiency and self-counsel. Always holding his cards close to his chest leaves little chance for him to be in close contact with those around him. His failure to make known the gaps in his knowledge means that his colleagues will have no way to help him fill them. Of greater importance, however, are the misapprehensions and threat felt by those around him. People always seem to fear that the most will happen. Gaps in communication usually are filled with fear and suspicion rather than with optimism and trust. The administrator must be self-reliant, but if he always keeps his thinking to himself, he can keep everyone else thinking the worst.

When the administrator does talk, he can't always be sure what he is really telling. What the administrator says is related to the whole organization, but what the other person hears is related to his personal corner of the organization. The listener scans a conversation looking for "local headlines." Listening is a personal, individual process producing unique meanings that differ according to time and circumstance. People hear according to their present attitudes toward the speaker and what he is talking about. What is said is mixed in with the listener's own thoughts and interpreted in terms of a momentary frame of mind. Since the other fellow's hearing depends upon his thinking, the administrator must listen before he really can know what he himself is saying. The administrator must know what sort of "thinking" he is talking to before he can know the sort of talking he needs to do. This means that the administrator must at times keep his own thinking under wraps until he can get the other individual to express his. Cloaking his thinking is not always an easy thing for the administrator to do. This is true not only because he is usually more eager to have others learn from him than he is to learn from them but because he is the boss and those under him will want to know his thinking before they disclose what they are thinking. Additionally, the more import a matter has to an individual, the more he will try to disguise his thoughts about it. For this reason we sometimes try to conceal our concern by using a deputy to speak our thoughts. We raise a topic by saying that "we heard," or that "someone said," a thing. Because of the reluctance of people to say what is on their mind, the administrator must often listen for what is not said. Stated another way, one of the administrator's most useful assets is his ability to hear the background music.

One problem of the self-reliant administrator is that he sometimes becomes a Lone Ranger. His self-reliance can prevent him from leaning on others and using their support. Unfortunately, the man who walks alone has no one to hold him up and thus he ends in the uncomfortable position of leaning on himself. Others can't help him even if they want to. They won't know what to do because they won't know what the administrator wants to do. They will not be able to see the relationship between their activities and his objectives. But it is unlikely that they will want to help because he probably will have alienated the loyalties they might otherwise have had. His lack of dependence on them will likely have been interpreted by his subordinates as a lack of confidence in them. Because he will have been running the show by himself, they will probably be pulling for him to hang himself. It is even more unlikely that they would be competent to give very much support if they did want to do so, inasmuch as a permanent level of mediocrity will most likely have developed around the administrator. He will have ridden down the strong, who could have stood up for him, because they had nerve and will to stand up to him. He will have only the passive and compliant left around him, and they will have survived only because they took refuge in the administrative "amen" corner.

Some of the personal traits and characteristics that cause individuals to gravitate into administration and become successful at it can cause the administrator to become a roughrider or to appear to be so. His own strength and the strength of his position can cause him to play rough without always realizing it. The effective administrator is usually aggressive by nature, and he has a strong tendency to grab the ball and run with it. He is also likely to be highly competitive and to look upon each encounter as a test of strength. Because he is action-oriented, he is tempted to overrun the opposition rather than to outrun it. Since others must be sure about what he wants done, he has to be decisive. He is ends-oriented and must be determined in his efforts to achieve the ends sought. This strong attention to ends can at times cause him to use less-considered means. These are all traits that contribute to the administrator's success. They can be overused and misunderstood, however. They can cause him to become a muscleman in administration who prefers to whip the opposition rather than to whip the problems that caused the opposition.

The muscleman in administration is likely to want to show his strength and work people over rather than work with them. The solutions he adopts may not be the best alternatives but those that drive the hardest bargain with whoever the opposition happens to be. Because he wants to show his full strength, he is given to massive retaliation and is prone to use his "Sunday punch" when a light jab would be more than sufficient. His reactions to opposition, imagined or real, are usually painful, not only to the objects of his attack but to those who witness it. For this reason, overretaliation can result in the administrator's winning a match but losing a following. Because he prefers to use his power over people rather than with them, the chances are that he will probably prefer fighting to finessing. This will sometimes require that he search for opposition, since it takes two to make a fight. In order to keep in fighting shape, he will likely maintain an inventory of axes to grind with individuals both inside and outside the organization. One of the big problems in going after the opposition is in knowing when to stop. If the aim is to prove one's strength rather than one's point, nothing short of unconditional surrender is satisfactory. The administrator who insists on always forcing the opposition to its knees runs several risks, however. First off, if he has a reputation for seeking to maim rather than to win, he can expect a much more determined fight from the opposition. The generals of the ancient Greek armies realized this fact and made it a point to never cut off their enemies' retreat because, when bottled up, the enemy would fight more desperately. More important, the opposition of today may be the allies the administrator needs tomorrow. Differences of opinion are not always differences of principle, and, in any event, the differences have a way of getting ironed out if they are not too deeply etched in. The surest way to deeply etch them in is for the administrator to force the opposition to cry "uncle." Most people can accept defeat but few can get over humiliation. For this reason, the administrator is wise to spare as much of the other fellow's face as possible by permitting him to retreat with dignity. It may at times be wise for the administrator to ask himself not whether he can win but how much does he want to win. The problem in pushing too far is that he may be pushing his supporters rather than the opposition. It is always a strong temptation to press the advantage in the areas most responsive to an idea. For this reason, good ideas are sometimes buried by supporters who were pushed into undertaking more than the situation warranted or their own strength would stand. He must bear in mind that the people he forces to crawl today won't be in a position to stand up for him tomorrow.

The administrator who goes after the opposition rather than the problem is likely to cease worrying about how he goes. The difference between what is good and bad, or between what is proper and improper, is often very subtle even for the best intentioned of administrators. And for those who are out to humble the opposition rather than handle the problem, all is grist that comes to the mill; the difference between what is good and bad is determined by which side they are on. Human nature being what it is, they are not always too hard put to justify what they do. All people are to some extent ambivalent and when passing judgment are prone to take into consideration whose bull is being gored. Actions that are considered immoral when practiced against us are considered moral when carried out against our opposition. What we might condone in our compatriots we condemn in our enemy. For these reasons, the administrator who gets preoccupied with getting the opposition can easily get out of bounds.

The administrator who practices a "vendetta" sort of administration does more than line up the opposition. He trains his own enemies and keeps them in superb fighting condition by forcing them to continuously defend themselves against his attacks. Through his example they are able to write their own guerrilla manuals. The equipment that they need for defending themselves is equally useful and readily available for attack, and the organizational framework provides excellent cover for the fighters who are forced in self-defense to oppose the administrator. Because of the varied personal goals and ambitions of all different members of an organization, some amount of organizational strife is inevitable and perhaps desirable. However, the effective administrator keeps this strife diffused and seeks to direct as much of it as possible into productive channels. He treats it somewhat as the experienced beekeeper handles a bee swarm, and takes care that he does not concentrate its attention on himself or the organizational goals. The strong-arm administrator has a tendency to do otherwise and to club his way into unnecessary organizational strife. This strife not only produces useless organizational scars but it means the administrator will have to carry an increasingly heavier club. His tough tactics usually have the unfortunate result of toughening up the opposition.

A sharp tongue most often goes along with the strong arm of the slugging administrator. There is always a danger that the administrator will be tactless without realizing it. The pressure of time often forces him to be forthright and direct. Also, most times he is speaking out of context. Those under him hear what he has to say rather than what led him to say it. Too, it is always more appealing to tell than to try to sell. But what are minor remarks to the administrator can represent verbal broadsides to his subordinates. Most individuals seem to watch much more closely for signs of disrespect than for signs of esteem. For this reason their self-esteem can be much more easily threatened than reinforced. When the administrator makes remarks in fun, the other person may think he is poking fun. Too often, the remarks may border on actual ridicule. The free-swinging administrator finds it easier to sharpen his tongue than to sharpen his wits. He gets a bigger kick out of stinging than out of pollinating. Much of what he says is intended to stick less in the mind than in the craw. When provoked, he is prone to use linguistic brass knuckles and cut others down to size. Such cutting may at times be indicated and necessary. He must remember, however, that every administrator stands on the shoulders of those below him and that his cutting remarks can cut their feet right out from under him.

One does not have to be arrogant to disregard others. Callousness can produce the same result. A thick skin can make one as insensitive as a big head can, and the administrator is peculiarly susceptible to both. A certain amount of callousness is necessary if he is to perform adequately. This is an essential part of his administrative maturity. We often speak of "mature judgment" and "seasoned judgment." This seasoning means the administrator has learned not to panic under fire nor to get buck fever when things get tight or nasty. He learns to live with the fact that he cannot please everyone and that he cannot solve all the problems. He discovers that old ideas are quite often resurrected by newcomers who do not recognize the toothmarks from thorough chewings that he and others gave the idea on previous occasions before it was discarded. He no longer drags out the big artillery every time someone cries wolf to him. He absorbs sufficient administrative geometry to recognize that there are at least two sides to every story. He amasses enough folklore about the people in the organization to know how much salt to take with each person's tale. He finds that the law of relativity also applies in administration and that the closer a person is to a problem, the bigger it appears and the fresher a problem is, the more difficult it seems.

Along with the psychological scar tissue that the administrator develops, there comes an attitude of skepticism toward what he sees and hears. To an extent this is a necessary attitude if he is to take the second look that guards him against impulsive action. It is a sign that he has become administratively sophisticated and has parted with the naïveté that marks the adolescent in administration. When properly controlled, this is a healthy trait and can prevent the administrator from going off half-cocked. However, if it is not properly controlled and carefully utilized, it can become insulting to those around him. There is a difference between seeking the full story and seeking the hole in it although they may sometimes add up to the same thing. This difference is demonstrated in the way one goes about finding the facts. The individual bringing the story cannot object to a full discussion of the matter. He would have reason to feel good over tactful questioning because it would demonstrate interest in his work and in himself on the part of the administrator. The picture is entirely different, however, if the administrator goes around or behind the individual, to check on him. To the individual concerned and to the organization, it is the difference between looking and spying. The effective administrator inevitably becomes a "doubting Thomas," but he must focus his doubts on the facts and their meaning rather than on individuals.

A fairly high amount of tolerance to problems and people is necessary if the administrator is to maintain his poise and survive emotionally. If he doesn't find this out for himself, it will be told him by the doctor who treats his first ulcer. The effective administrator has to learn to live with his problems, but he can learn to live too comfortably. His tolerance can be insulting to others because it puts them in the unenviable position of being tolerated. It can also grow into indifference and stifle the initiative and enthusiasm of those around him. It may become negligence and result in severe deterioration of the tone and performance of the organization. Somewhere between a stomach ulcer and a thick hide the administrator must find the proper combination of anxiety and diffidence.

Another form of disregard is practiced by the silent, strong types in administration who never say anything until they catch someone out in left field. These administrators pride themselves on delegating and boast that they never interfere. What they really mean is that they do not keep their subordinates informed because they get a red-blooded satisfaction from watching them hang themselves. They get a greater stimulation from pointing the finger than from pointing the way. Their major activity is correcting errors, and that is the only time subordinates hear anything from them. Delegation means having people act for you, but this can be done only if they know what they are supposed to do for you. It doesn't mean leading them by the hand, but it does mean giving them a road map. Lack of direction is perhaps more stultifying to initiative than overdirection. Moving around in the dark puts a premium upon caution and causes people to inch their way along. An unmarked crossroads discourages those who would assume responsibility and move in on a problem. Able men do not fear the road, but they do dislike ending up at the wrong destination. If the administrator is weak, his failure to provide direction can cost him his control of the organization. If he is rugged and fails to mark the trail, the organization will tend to wait on orders and develop into a dependent, rule-conscious bureaucracy. The able will have become disabled or displaced, and the only ones left who will stick their necks out are those who are looking out to see which way the wind is blowing.

Disdain is a close cousin of disregard and comes from the same family tree of ingrown pride. The difference is in the fact that disdain is demonstrated by what the administrator does rather than by what he does not do. It is more openly revealed because it is reflected in overt actions, and the recipient doesn't have to read between the lines to get the message as he does with disregard. The disdainful administrator not only feels that his associates and subordinates are inferior but he insists on proving that he feels that way by acting insultingly superior and in a patronizing way toward those around him. The condition is more prevalent among younger administrators and in their case could be described as "the administrative bends" because they came up too fast. Unfortunately, the condition isn't confined to the inexperienced administrators who can be expected to outgrow the problem, but it also can afflict the experienced administrator who doesn't protect himself against the effects of overexposure to success.

A patronizing attitude on the part of the administrator can be exhibited in a number of ways. The "forgive them for they know not what they do" attitude is one that is currently being urged upon him. Some of its popularity is due to the widespread support the doctrine has received from some of the doctrinaires who see an organization as a life-adjustment society rather than as a place where the individual can have a chance to show he can pull his own weight and earn his own keep. For most individuals, their work is about the only chance they have for proving their worth, and they won't have this chance unless they are treated as responsible adults instead of slightly backward children. It seems paradoxical to talk of increasing the dignity of the individual while belittling his accountability. A man can't count for anything unless a full count is kept on him. Aside from the outrage done to the concept of man as a responsible agent, there are logical reasons to argue that the practice of administration as a form of babysitting provides little payoff. During this period that this attitude has increasingly characterized administration, there has been increasing complaint by administration about the attitude and performance of personnel. Administrative pabulum has not produced a crop of roaring enthusiasts for hard work. Tying bibs on the personnel apparently is not a logical way to get them to do a grown man's work.

"People tinkering" administration is a growing pastime of some administrators who like to play psychological parlor games with other people's lives. These administrators want to "treat" people rather than deal with them. They aren't satisfied with running the organizational lives of their subordinates but attempt to intrude into their private lives. Because they apparently want people not only to work for the company but to belong to it, they equate the individual's job satisfaction with the level of satisfaction of his entire catalog of drives and needs. They insist upon "riding shotgun" over his marital, legal, social, and recreational life. For a mess of organizational pottage they attempt to indenture him to the company. They do not see the difference between claiming the individual's proper contribution to the company and claiming him personally.

The role of the administrator requires that he sit in a high place, and this does make it difficult for him to keep his feet on the ground. It also makes it easy for him to let his high position go to his head and to forget that administration is as much a test of character as of strength. Both his pants and his attitudes can get shiny from sitting on his throne. No other antidote for this seems as sure and as powerful as the sobering effect of occasional failure. The administrator must work to win, however, and cannot look to his failures to always hold him in line if he expects to succeed or remain in administration. He doesn't have to win all the time, but he has to win most of the time if he wants his judgment and his abilities to be respected. Neither can he practice a "Milquetoast" sort of administration that attracts opposition as an exposed street light attracts the kid with a rock in his hand. The major problem is to recognize the excesses and the deviations. Bad habits in anything always seem so much easier to develop than good ones. This makes it necessary that the administrator always watch his practices since bad habits can supersede good ones at any stage of his career. Unwittingly, his success can cause him to start behaving as if he is sitting in a high chair instead of on a throne.

The administrator's best skills sometimes become his greatest handicaps

6 Administration is an acquired skill. Because the implementation of the administrative process is an art, it can be improved with practice. Such improvement is not automatic, however. Many administrators never improve their performance, and some administrators become less, rather than more, able the more and longer they practice. There are many reasons for this deterioration in the administrator's ability, and some of these reasons have to do with his failure to maintain certain of the required skills. Either the particular position he occupies or his inattention to his own development may prevent the improvement of some skills necessary in a well-rounded administrator. The problem is not always one of underdevelopment, however, and the deterioration in administrative performance may occur because of overdevelopment of some of the administrator's most important and most used skills. Practice does sometimes make perfect, but being perfect doesn't always spell perfection in actual practice.

116

The effective administrator has not only a strong mind but also a skilled mind. Exercise is the cause of both. His strength and skill of mind are his greatest assets, but they can at times represent a liability. Like the athlete who may, through repeated use, overdevelop certain muscles and thus hamper his performance, the administrator may overdevelop certain mental skills through his repeated exercise of them. Just as the athlete is subject to muscle-boundness, the administrator can develop a sort of mental-boundness in carrying out his work. The nature of the administrator's work tends to cause him to cultivate, both consciously and unconsciously, certain mental skills which can significantly influence his judgment and performance. The fact that these skills are utilized so often by the administrator indicates that they are necessary and valuable to his work, but their value to the administrator lies in his use of them and not in their use of him. The mental-bound administrator is in a sense the victim of his own excellence, but he still is a victim. Too much can sometimes be more damaging than too little, and the commonly used term "too much of a good thing" is in this connection more literal than figurative. Just as the humble can become obsequious and the friendly can become unctuous, so can the administrator overuse his best skills.

It is quite probable that the unwitting overdevelopment and overuse of particular administrative talents are a part of the answer to the puzzle of the arrested career progress of some administrators. Every field of administration has had numerous and notable examples of highly promising younger administrators who petered out in mid-career. These men demonstrated unusual skills and talents and were definitely effective for a period of time, and it is likely they were written off as a "flash in the pan" when they fell back in their pace. This is a very inadequate answer because it doesn't explain what provided the flash and why it burned out before it became a steady flame. A careful study of the careers of these individuals would quite likely show that they did possess, in unusual amount and quality, some of the personal skills and characteristics that are at a premium in administration. Because these were the traits that gave them success and attracted attention to them in the first place, it is only natural that these traits would be utilized to the full. These administrators would be expected to employ their best traits even, in certain situations, as substitutes for more indicated skills. For instance, those with a high level of human relations skills, but short on conceptual skills, could be expected to use their "winning ways" as a substitute for logical justification in implementing an idea. Also, both their superiors and subordinates could be expected to call on such administrators' strengths, rather than their weaknesses, when making assignments or seeking assistance.

The high utilization, and consequent high development, of the administrators' best traits would be at the expense of their weaker traits. The weaker traits would suffer not only by comparison but also by neglect, and thus the disparity between the weaker and the best would be cumulative. We are all prone to put our best foot forward and to use our top skills the most. The same disparity in development of skills doubtlessly occurs, to some extent, with the average administrator as well as with the gifted. While it is true that certain administrative positions call for extensive use of particular traits and skills, this does not mean that the other and less-used skills must not be strong. While an administrator may be better than the job he has, his weakest skills must not be any weaker than those required for the level of administrative responsibility he occupies. In general, administrators move upward to positions of increasing difficulty when they do move. In most instances they are moved upward because of their best skills, but their performance in the new position will most likely be limited by their weakest skills. This could be one explanation of why so many administrators do not live up to their apparent abilities and potentialities.

The above could also help explain a number of other enigmas in the management selection and development programs that have been tried so extensively in recent years. Much time and effort have been expended in an effort to select men of promise and to hasten their development through special evaluation and training programs. Toward this end great stress has been placed on isolating the traits and skills commonly associated with administrative success. Validated tests have been developed for determining the level of certain of those skills and traits in individuals, and men in high positions have been urged to identify those characteristics and to coach their protégés in the development of them. But everyone is about ready to admit that the management development programs aren't much more successful in predicting or developing successful performance than the old method of survival of the fittest. The lack of better results in these organized programs could be due to the failure to examine the implications of unusually high scores made in these tests on certain traits and the failure to think in terms of rounded or balanced abilities. Perhaps a very high score on a few traits is a more adverse predictor than much lower scores on all traits. In this connection, the average of some very high and some very low scores is in no way the same as a fairly even balance between the highest and lowest possible scores on the various traits being measured. The attempt to "culture" administrators through planned rating and coaching programs could produce the same lack of balanced development. Because administration is a matter of getting things done, the primary attention of both the superior and subordinate is very likely to be beamed on improved performance in the subordinate's present job rather than on preparation for promotion. This means that the coacher is likely to devote attention to those traits and skills his particular administrative activity uses most often, and the budding administrator is likely to seek to press the development of those characteristics that he finds will most impress his coach. It is highly doubtful that the superior, who is primarily a practitioner rather than an experienced tutor, will really understand all the skills and traits that are the matrix for successful administration. The fact that he possesses them himself has little to do with his being able to isolate and understand them. True, if he is a successful administrator, he knows how to spot an effective assistant, but this doesn't mean he knows how he does it, and the chances are he does it in the round by observing the assistant's general performance. This way, he doesn't seek specifics and doesn't have to justify his evaluation precisely in terms of somebody else's criteria. He usually trains his assistants by letting them roast in the fire of general experience rather than overcooking them in spots. He is likely to work on their weaknesses to correct their shortcomings instead of exalting their strengths to prove he is an able teacher.

Whatever else the administrator is, he must be well balanced in judgment and in actions. Administration calls on the whole of a man's talent and not on certain particular skills alone. Also, his progress in administration depends upon a versatility of traits and skills. Jobs and organizations are so varied and changeable that the administrator cannot expect to find any two positions emphasizing essentially the same traits and abilities. It is hard for him to develop himself as a whole, however, because his work calls for him to use some abilities much more often than others. This not only leads to unbalance but at times leads to unwitting misuse of some of his abilities. The following discussion concerns some of the judgmental skills which are likely to be most highly developed in administrative practice and which may be misused because of their high development.

The most important set of skills used in administration are the conceptual skills. These are the skills that permit the administrator to put two and two together without being told the second two. This ability to conjure up the missing links is the most needed and most used ability in administration for a number of reasons. Most administrative problems are problems only because the full facts are not known. There are times when the administrator doesn't have access to all the facts and has no way of obtaining them. He must take the incomplete and inadequate information available and contrive a picture from it. In some instances he chooses to forego a portion of needed information because its value is marginal in terms of the cost of securing it. In other instances, there just isn't sufficient time to marshal all the needed information bearing on the problem to which he must give an immediate answer. On the other hand, there are times when he has a great number of facts available and must use a mental hacksaw and quickly cut them down to the few he considers critical and essential. The diversity of the facts at hand may at times require that he reduce the difficulty of evaluating them by reducing the sorts of facts he will consider; or a multiplicity of similar facts may force him to ignore many of them in order to get the number down to a size his mind can manage.

The historical nature of all facts requires the administrator to conceptualize information in terms of the past, but to be useful, the information must be projected into the future in light of the current situation which confronts the user. This means that judgment is a process of applying the past to present demands. At best, administrative vision comprehends events as they pass out of sight. The information he gets provides a background for the administrator, but it is only a background, and he must still call on his imagination for the picture he paints on it. This means that, in a way, the administrative use of facts is somewhat like viewing the future through a rearview mirror.

Using the past as a substitute for the present has a special appeal to the administrator. The usual scarcity of significant information causes him to hoard what he does get and to reuse it whenever he can. He hangs on to past conceptions in order to permit perceptual shortcuts. He arranges what he can take from his own experience and from his understanding of other people's experience, so that it has present meaning. Thus, the greater his experience, the more his mind becomes filled with preconceptions that he is prone to use in lieu of new considerations. The use of these warmed-over generalizations formed from past experiences makes administrative life more comfortable, as well as simpler, since the administrator doesn't have to face up to changing his notions. The administrator is like other individuals in wanting to stick with his notions—except more so. The thinking of a person is to a large extent a rerun of the impressions he developed yesterday. He interprets things he observes in the light of things he believes. This means that the stability of the individual's mind depends upon the stability of his beliefs. He can't afford any large-scale or rapid changes in his beliefs. For this reason, all human beings are constantly attempting to reinforce their assumptions, that is, to make their expectations come through, in order to make today's reality jibe with yesterday's impressions. This urge is so strong that we often try to reconfirm our beliefs by forcing events to fit things the way we believe they should fit. In ordinary life, this strong desire to continue to prove our beliefs may not directly affect anyone other than ourselves. The administrator's assumptions do directly affect the other members of the organization, however, and unless he is careful, he may let his preconceptions get in both his and their ways.

The tendency for the administrator to overgeneralize from his experience is a special hazard because of the unique nature of the judgment process. Judgment seems to be much more concerned with similarities than with differences, and one could describe it as a search for regularities. It appears to have a deep affinity for the familiar and to feel at home behind the fortifications of precedent. Good judgment, however, must be alert to the unique and respectful of the odd. The fact that an apparently familiar problem reoccurs should be evidence to the administrator that something new has been added to upset the previous solution. A particular setting may be repeated many times within the same organization or in the same administrator's experience, but it is highly doubtful that all the facts are ever completely duplicated. One can use the same frame for a variety of pictures. Also, one may get an accurate idea of the picture in a jigsaw puzzle even if a number of the pieces are missing, but the picture may be much distorted if one attempts to substitute pieces from a different puzzle. All of our actions are, of necessity, based on an assumption of similarity between ourselves and those around us. Unless we counted on the other fellow's thinking and acting as we do, the simplest sort of social environment would be so complex and demanding that life among other people would be impossible. If we had to stop and estimate a probable choice of behavior for each individual in each of the hundreds of contacts we have daily, we would scarcely get to work before the day was gone. We could hardly walk a block, much less drive on a busy street, unless we took for granted that everyone else was acting as we would act. By assuming similarity of response, we are able to ignore most of the events unfolding around us except those which directly concern us. We have very little other basis by which to anticipate the responses of individuals we do not know very well. When we do try to figure what sort of behavior to expect from another person, we define the circumstances and relate them to our own mode of thinking and acting. To a large extent, we figure the other fellow by adding in ourselves. By and large, this works satisfactorily. Human nature is baffling and diverse, but there are many basic human universals. However, casting others in our own image is a hazardous occupation in administration. In the first place, there is great dissimilarity between circumstances as viewed by the administrator and as viewed by any others involved. Where one stands has a lot to do with what one sees. Seldom can one find a mountain that looks the same from the bottom as from the top or from one side as from the other. Similarity of response has to assume similarity of stimuli. A second hazard is the double nature of any assumption of similarity. Given a point of disagreement, if I assume that because I do not want a blowup you do not want one either, I may push the point thinking you will back down. If I am correct in assuming such a similarity of thinking, a blowup is inevitable, since you will arrive at a similar conclusion that I will back down. This means that if I am going to read your mind by reading my own, I need to be sure to know the meaning of what I read in my own. Actually, it is highly unlikely that a person can ever fully know his own mind, but he can try to know how he uses it.

The sort of mind developed by experience in administration makes the administrator susceptible to a special brand of inference drawing. The trained mind in any profession is filled with preconceptions. These preconceptions consist, in part, of occupationally inspired attitudes. Because of these professionally transmitted turns of mind, individuals in the same profession see things to a large degree in the same light. We say a person thinks like an accountant or a lawyer or a minister. This means that each will infer certain specific things from situations that confront him. Each, according to his training, will overlook certain of the details that are present and supply certain other details that are not present. Because the administrator thinks like an administrator, he will see things in an administrative light. This can cause those in administration to mistakenly assume a similarity between their way of thinking and that of the other members of the organization. Unless the administrator allows for this professional equation, the conclusions he draws will be too heavily colored by the spare personality which his work has grafted on him. He must remember that because he is the administrator, his perspective is set apart even though he is a part of the organization.

A form of generalization quite often used by administrators is the stereotyping of individuals. The tendency to stereotype is stronger in connection with individuals than with situations because the administrator deals with people and is trained to see situations in terms of people. He is always looking for the human coefficient of problems and usually will attempt to personalize situations by projecting persons into them. He has learned that things are caused and therefore wants to insist that the personal responsibility for things be specified. Whereas the usual person is likely to depersonalize entire organizations by making them faceless entities such as "the government," "the law," "the church," etc., the administrator will insist on pinning faces to each activity within the organization. Although the administrator tends to look for the person in the situation, he does not have the same tendency to look for the individual in the person. Or better stated, he is more likely to see what the person does rather than what he is. This causes him to label individuals in terms of organizational performance, such as able, dependable, stable, cooperative, etc., or the reverse of these. Such labels are, of course, very necessary if the administrator is going to know whom he is depending upon and the degree to which he can depend upon each. At the higher administrative levels the administrator leads a secluded life—at least from the standpoint of most of the actual operations —and must depend upon others for both information and advice. This means that he has to decide what to believe as well as what to do about it. This doesn't mean that he can't trust those around him, but rather that he must do a job of interpreting. If he can label the sources, he knows the proof without testing the contents each time. The same problem or incident can come to him in several different wrappers, depending upon the personality of the individuals doing the wrapping. In one sense administration is a matter of making allowances. The administrator learns to discount for some individuals, such as the overanxious or the perfectionist, and he learns to add for other individuals, such as the restrained or the easygoing.

By classifying people, the administrator can save himself time and actually increase the validity of the information provided him by very honest people. By hanging images onto people, he simplifies their personalities into manageable entities and is able to "prediscount" the effects of their personal proclivities from the problems they bring to him. It sounds like double-talk, but the administrator catalogs people by their ambiguities in order to ignore their differences. The practice is a valuable one to the administrator if he controls it, because his life is much simpler if he can deal with stereotypes rather than with ambiguous characters. Tucking people into a mental pigeonhole is a hazardous occupation, however. It is easy to get them into the wrong hole, and it is hard to keep them in the right hole. People are difficult to classify properly and people won't stay put. Without attempting to examine the wonderful complexities of human behavior which horribly complicate the task of classifying individuals neatly, we should mention some practical difficulties of classification the administrator must keep in mind. If these are not considered, he can easily mislabel individuals and misuse an otherwise very valuable skill of administration. The administrator seldom gets a full view of individuals in the organization. He usually sees only their work side, and perhaps only a very cloudy view of that. Some of the time he sees individuals when they have problems and thus gets a troubled view. Often, he gets his image secondhand from others and thereafter looks more for confirming evidence than different evidence. We are apt to let a single incident fix our image of an individual, and the impression from such a single incident may be entirely fortuitous. It can leave a favorable impression because it was a pleasant circumstance or involved an easy problem to solve. On the other hand, it can leave an unfavorable impression because it arose in connection with a very unpleasant circumstance or a very difficult problem, both beyond the control of the individual. The hazard of this "one stop" sort of evaluation of individuals is greatly increased by the mental index system all of us use. We are prone to let a person's excellence in one thing carry over into our evaluation of all that he does. Similarly, a poor performance in one thing causes us to mark an individual as poor in everything. If we have no opportunity to see him perform, we tend to automatically index him as average. The conditions under which the administrator makes his contact with many of the people in the organization mean that he often has a low ceiling and poor visibility when getting his fix on the individuals around him.

One of the greatest hazards in stereotyping is the rigidity of images. The first impression is a persistent one, and we keep seeing people as we first saw them. This tenacity of images denies the fact that individuals can change and do change. Individuals are full of "living," and the administrator does not come to work with the same people each day. They may have the same names and the same faces, but they are never quite the same persons they were yesterday. The individual and his environment are in constant transactions with each other, and the drive of the individual is to maintain unity with his environment. The human capacity to make necessary adaptations is a strong one, and this capacity survives throughout most of an individual's life. For these reasons we cannot expect a man to relate to his environment without continuously assimilating part of it. This means that the administrator must keep his impressions of individuals up-to-date if he wants to use those impressions fairly and profitably.

One problem resulting from the administrator's stereotyping of people is that in so doing he may be describing himself. First, he most likely will be listing their specifications from his own index of values. More important, the traits he encounters in those working with him will have been stimulated in part by his own example and also in part by the experiences he has dished out. All effective supervision serves to produce uniformity of outlook and conduct between the supervisor and the supervised. Discrepancies are reduced by the pressures brought on the supervised to alter their observable characteristics in keeping with the expectations of the supervisor. In a large way, the traits the latter sees exhibited by those around him may be a reflection of his own handiwork and conduct.

The habit of precasting our opinion of individuals is aided and abetted by the disposition we have to expect individuals to act the way they look. This is easiest seen in the personal bias we show about particular ethnic groups. It can be demonstrated as operating just as strongly with regard to the individual's personality characteristics. This disposition has been given some scientific respectability by the "traitist school," which has developed varied tests for measuring certain of the traits of an individual. The traitist point of view is far too simple to be fully accepted by anyone who has spent very much time in administration, however. Traits are measured individually and as specifics, but individuals act, and react, as wholes. The important entity is neither the single trait nor the collection of traits but the totality of traits and their orientation. The mix of the traits, rather than the sum, is the greater determinant. It is likely that this mix is changing constantly as the environment sandpapers the individual's personality and wears down some of his more dominant traits while exposing some of his others to a greater extent. Individuals are characters rather than catalogs.

The initial question is how the individual uses his traits. How he responds to situations and how he works are the things that count to administration. Any sort of social behavior is affected by causes working simultaneously on many levels of the individual's personality, and these various levels differ at different times depending upon with whom and what the individual is dealing. A man may be one kind of man at one time or place and another at a different time or place. All of us have observed enough of ourselves and our colleagues to know that we are not the same per-

sons away from work as we are at work or the same at the bowling alley as we are at the PTA council. Individuals generally
attempt to employ their relationships with others to best advantage, and this means that they generally attempt the sort of behavior they think will provide the most productive relationships.
A man need not be basically kind or generous in order to act
kindly or generously if that is the way the situation demands that
he act. Most adults learn before they become adults that they
must act the way the social script says they are to act if they are to
get to do very much acting.

Saying that the individual cuts his suit not according to his
cloth but according to the way he thinks it is supposed to be cut
is in no way the same as saying that it will be cut the way administration wants it cut. It does say that the appraisal of people is
more a matter of judgment than of metric technique. What the
individual thinks he is supposed to do in a given circumstance
depends upon his own private image at that time of the way he
should respond, and this complex and changing image can hardly
be accurately measured and quantified. The life of the mind is a
private life, and the best of "head candling" will reveal very little
of what a man may have in his mind and even less of what he
may have in his heart. Self-determining individuals, reacting to
their own environments and filled with their own perceptions, can
be expected to have widely varying responses at different times.
Because one's frame of mind is a very variable thing, people do
"vary from themselves" from time to time. At best the act of the
individual can be predicted only in relationship to the particulars
of a situation. The most dishonest of men aren't too likely to steal
if they know they are being closely monitored, while the most
honest may succumb under certain circumstances when tempted
too strongly. The saliva response of Pavlov's dogs might have been
quite different if they had been seasick when he rang his bells.
Said in another way, what a man does may depend more upon
what situation he is in than upon what he is.

The actions of an individual have meaning only in relationship
to the whole of his environment. They are right or wrong, good or
bad, only in terms of consistency with the whole of which they
are a part. Unless this is true, there is no sense in the concept of
justice. There we insist on objectivity by demanding that the
judgment of the act be without reference to the individuality of

the actor. Actually, justice goes even further in recognizing the
role of context. It subordinates the part to the whole by recognizing extenuating circumstances. Men may be quite alike as human
beings but differ sharply in the way they attempt to solve their
problems. It is the qualities they demonstrate in live situations,
rather than the traits they have, that should concern administration. What the individual will do, rather than what he has the
ability to do, is the important thing. The administrative process
may not be able to change people, but it is designed to change
what they do. It is the function of the administrator to influence
how people act in spite of what they are.

Because the administrator is prone to focus his attention on
what the individual is, he has a tendency to confuse the effects
with the causes of the individual's performance. For instance, the
administrator often blames poor performance on the poor attitude that poor performers usually have and seeks to improve the
individual's attitude in the expectation that this will automatically
improve his performance. In a world that is so obsessed with
human relations it may be heresy to say this, but to suppose that
we need only to educate a man to what is right in order to have
him do it is largely wishful mist. The administrator will often get
much further by doctoring the performance than by treating the
attitudes. There is much reason to believe that poor performance
is the father of poor attitude rather than the reverse. A person's
attitude gradually shifts into line with his behavior; if he
works hard, his attitude toward hard work becomes more favorable, or if he does good quality work, he tends to become impatient with poor quality work done by himself or anyone else. How
hard he works and how well he does his job are not the product
of his attitude nearly so much as the product of his work environment. Attitudes are acquired and, as such, simply do not exist independently of their environment. They are the result of experiences or the lack of them. Attitudes are catching. Most people
seek to adjust to what is expected of them, and they determine
what is expected by constantly observing what goes on about
them. There is apparently a law of social gravity that pulls the
individual's level of effort toward the center. Both the poor and
the excellent will generally, over a period of time, gravitate in
their performance toward the average level of performance of

those around them. They think this is the level expected of them since this is what seems to satisfy the administration.

We have assumed that if we know an individual's state of mind, we have all that we need to predict his actions. Given an individual's inclinations in a particular case, we seem to believe that the conduct that will evolve is almost automatic. This has led us to assume that significant change can be obtained in a person's conduct if we can only change his mind. We have fallen heavily for the romantic notion that as a man thinks, so will he act. There is a sizable difference between thought and conduct, however. All of the individual's environment is a bonded guarantee that this is true. Man lives in and by a pattern of environmentally created restrictions, and his conduct is largely predicated upon these restrictions. He is imprisoned or enthroned within the system of his environmental imperatives. He seeks to do what he "wants" to do or "ought" to do, but this is always in part restricted by what a coercive environment tells him he "has" to do.

The administrator, of necessity, has to concentrate his attention on the separate acts of individuals, since it is only by their separate acts that he can determine their contribution to the performance of the enterprise. This means that he tends to judge, rather than understand, what goes on around him. The single act of the individual can be understood only in relationship to the total setting in which the individual committed it. Behavior that might be comprehended in its total setting may seem quite incomprehensible in an isolated setting. Specific and separate acts of an individual can be ambiguous and misleading to the administrator unless he evaluates them in a sequence and over a period of time. The administrator cannot always take each separate act at its face value, since the act can sometimes mean any one of several entirely different things. For instance, the credit manager, after being criticized over an increase in the total of accounts receivable, may send a nasty collection letter denying a discount to one of the firm's best customers who always pays on the fifteenth of the month rather than on the first as specified in the discount terms. It may look strongly as if he did so to get even with his superiors. But he may have been only trying to improve the collections or simply trying to follow what he thought was a new policy. His action could also have been due to a combination of two or more unrelated purposes, or it could have been done accidentally and entirely without purpose. Even if it were done maliciously, it may indicate nothing of his true attitude and such a demonstration may never be repeated.

The individual may have strong loyalties to the organization and simultaneously have strong feelings about the way it treats him. Or he can be indifferent about the cause he represents and still be greatly concerned about the way he represents it. All human beings seem to be capable of a great deal of ambivalence in their feelings, and within the same personality there is at times an active interplay of conflicting feelings. That there are such strong tendencies to both do and not do a given thing is demonstrated by the fact that we have "mixed feelings" about certain problems we face. At times we actually do things which run counter to each other, and we do them almost simultaneously. The fact that every person is a battleground for many tendencies has not been given sufficient recognition by those who have written the texts on motivation, and they have stressed our specific motives rather than our system of motives. Perhaps it is more a confusion of motives than a system, since it would be very difficult for an individual to maintain a fully organized and integrated set of motives. Aside from the question of conflicting motives, he has the problem of shifting goals. The reshuffling of goals that occurs continuously, all the way from the numberless and unrecognized smaller goals to the major and highly planned ones, leaves the individual with a multitude of mixed-up reasons for doing things at any given time. He can't change his motives as he can his socks. His motives are a part of his experience and never fully fade away. This means that the tag ends of earlier motives may fuse themselves onto the more current ones and cause the individual to operate with a mixture of hyphenated motives.

The assumption that people act logically causes the administrator sometimes to err about what people will do or to misjudge what they do do. Usually, people do not act either logically or illogically if they are deeply and personally involved in a situation. In such circumstances, they can be expected to act nonlogically. This is because they are human beings and apt to cut their acts from human fabric rather than the fabric of logic. This does not mean that people deliberately ignore logic or that they always act without logic. It means that their frame of reference is personal rather than logical. The behavior of a person represents his effort to satisfy the net balance of a number of interacting interests making claims on him at the same time. His effort may not be the correct one, but it is his own notion of the best way to satisfy as much of the net balance as possible. It is not a static balance, for the individual is in constant interaction with the environment. Neither is it ever fully satisfied. With most people it is a balance that grows through life, and with some people it becomes so heavy as to be unbearable. As someone has said, no man comes to work alone. He brings with him not only his own aspirations but his obligations to his family, his friends, and his union or profession, and all the many other entangling contacts that he has made along the way. Most individuals have so many interests with which to make peace that they have little room in which to try to make sense.

From an individual's viewpoint, his behavior usually does make sense to himself. Whether it looks rational or not depends upon who is doing the looking. The individual doing the behaving usually has little question in that regard, and if one understands an individual sufficiently, much of his behavior is predictable. Understanding permits others to take the individual's eccentricities into account. Such understanding, however, is in itself proof that more is needed in dealing with others than one's own system of logic. The eccentricity of another person is something that doesn't make sense to us. When we say we make allowances for the actions of another, we are really saying that we do not expect him to act as we would act. At the same time, we are in reality saying that we are making allowances for our own unique outlook. The practice of administration would be more effective if the administrator would remember the latter concept. The actions of others would be less confusing to him if he kept in mind that his own outlook is conditioned and that his reactions are shaped by that conditioning. To whatever extent possible, the administrator needs to be cognizant of his own biases and to allow for these biases in his evaluation of situations and the people who are involved in them. To the extent he can recognize and appreciate his own outlook, he will be better able to allow for the outlooks of others. He will never find it possible to see too clearly through the other fellow's outlook but he can try to keep himself out of his own line of vision.

The need to make allowances for the different outlook of another person does not mean that the administrator should reduce the "settle for" level and make allowances for a poor job performance. Sometimes he may have to do this, but it can represent a default in his responsibility to the individual concerned as well as to all individuals in the organization. Holding an individual responsible for his poor performance tends to produce responsible behavior on the part of all individuals in the enterprise as well as on the part of the particular individual involved. This is due in part to the fact that it serves as a notice that poor performance will not be tolerated. It is due more, however, to the fact that this is the most important way administration has for showing its opinion of the people in the organization. The sort of behavior we accept tells people what kind of people we think they are. Over a period of time this is the sort of people they will become. We make allowances for a person's difference in outlook in order to better perceive the difficulties which confront us in attempting to improve his behavior. The recognition of the nonlogical nature of human behavior is a way of improving, rather than excusing, poor performance.

Our interpretation of the conduct of other people is often confused by the idea that all their behavior is purposive. Much of our behavior is contextual, however, and its specific meaning cannot be pinned down. As administrators, we are concerned with specifics because situations are made up of specifics. The individual, however, has an imperfect awareness of the specific motives for most actions. Living is an everyday affair, and the circumstances of living call for choices and action even where there is no clear preference. When we do have motives, they are probably much more general than specific actions indicate. When conduct really is purposive, it may be quite misleading to the observer. The individual is not always able to know what conduct best fits his purpose, nor is he always able to act in the way that he believes is best for the purpose. Our actions often may result less from intent than from our inability to best express, or to maintain control of, our intent. Also, our lives are not confined to single purposes but are made up of many purposes. Even if we have major, dominating purposes, our general scheme of conduct is shaped more importantly by the much larger number and variety of lesser purposes. A difficulty in the evaluation of a person's behavior occurs when we confuse his immediate objectives with his purposes. The difference between the two is the matter of intent. An individual's behavior is often taken by us to mean one thing, when, in fact, it is only circumstantial to something else he has in mind. Such circumstantial behavior is conscious and deliberate, but in itself fulfills no final purpose for the individual. It is merely a means to some particular end. It does achieve an immediate objective, but that objective is consequential only as a step toward the purpose which the behavior is designed to help achieve. A simple illustration would be the act of a person crossing a street to purchase a package of cigarettes. The crossing of the street represents a conscious objective, but it has no ultimate purpose of its own and demonstrates little about the person crossing except that he is willing to cross a street in order to get a package of cigarettes. It will help the administrator in his efforts to figure out the other fellow to remember that much that people strive to do is not what they are striving after.

People often do things and say things simply because they think the situation dictates that they say or do those things. Group pressures of this sort on individuals are well documented. Similar pressures from within the individuals are perhaps even more controlling. Each of us has an image which we believe others have of us and which we feel we must maintain. We are likely to act tough because we feel we have a reputation for toughness. Or we will stay off the golf course if we have led others to believe that we are better golfers than we actually are. In many ways we attempt to shape and control the information about ourselves in order to maintain the impressions others have formed of us. One of the strongest forces felt by an individual is this desire to live up to his reputation. He may have gained the reputation fortuitously, but it is his trademark, and he is stuck with it. For this reason many of our acts represent *pro forma* conduct and do not mean what they seem to mean. The place that an individual occupies also influences his actions. All of us are constantly defining and redefining the role we feel we are playing, and we attempt to act as we think someone in our role is supposed to act. For instance, we yield to our superiors because we believe our role in the organization demands that we act that way. This fact can help explain the amazing metamorphosis that sometimes seems to occur when individuals previously considered timid are promoted and instantly start exhibiting aggressive leadership characteristics. Those who evaluate individuals only by the role they happen to be playing are using somewhat the same standards as those who buy a book because of its cover rather than its contents.

This notion that things are exactly the way we see them and hear them can be a deterrent to both tension draining and face saving in organizations. It can inhibit the sort of "double-talk" that serves as a verbal lubricant for organizational life. Because we insist on the literal meaning of the actions of others, we prevent them from saying and doing things, harmless to the organization, which relieve their feelings. We give full weight to actions taken at time of stress and attempt to make the individuals involved eat their deeds as well as their pride. An important thing about feelings is their need for expression. Banked-up feelings need to be spent before they can become a medium for hostility and antagonism to be used against the entire program. The surest way of spending feelings is to verbalize them, and the best time for the administrator to have disgruntlement expressed is as soon as possible.

The assumption that the facts speak for themselves is a common misconception. Facts can say only what they are permitted to say. The same facts may say different things to different people. To paraphrase Kant, we hear things not as they are but as we are. What a person hears depends to a great extent on where a person has been. The message he hears is in part a replay of the encounters he has had with his environment. Because of their conditioning, individuals, even with the best of intent, may honestly see and understand the same things differently. They are likely to project their past experiences and unknowingly read into situations what they expected to find in them. Also, they may read into situations a large portion of what they hoped to find in them or, if they are sufficiently apprehensive, what they were afraid they would find. The administrator always works with "used" people, and the facts are likely to speak the way those people are used to hearing them. The same facts may say different things to the same person at different times. We know the same individual reacts quite differently to similar situations at different times. Each of us reads into a situation much of what our mood tells us to read at a given time. Things that were funny one day seem serious on another. We appear to have a wonderful faculty for ignoring incidents on one occasion and ballooning their significance the next. To the administrator a complaining customer may be someone who needs help on one day and a person who just wants to be nasty the next. The facts may not change, but we do; or at least we change our psychological spectacles and succeed in changing our view of the facts. Said another way, things equal to each other aren't always equal to the same thing.

One reason the facts can't always speak for themselves is that we often try to tell them what to say. Under these circumstances we don't have to jump to conclusions—we start at the finish line. We are prone to ask the sort of questions that are most likely to yield the sort of facts that support our own notions. We turn to those individuals for information who are most apt to see the particular problem as we do and who are, therefore, most likely to voice our own opinions. Our preoccupation with the individuals involved in a situation can easily cause us to cut factual corners and obtain our facts right out of our emotional notebooks. Because we tend to listen to the people we like and ignore those we dislike, there is a strong chance that we will weigh the personalities involved rather than the facts. Often important decisions are made on the basis of who says what rather than on what is said. We also seem able to quickly develop a psychological deafness to facts that disagree with our preconceptions or that are inconsistent with our expressed opinions. At the same time we appear to have an automatic range finder for the facts that support our thinking. We will tend not to seek information if we think it will make a decision more difficult or painful. Because of the ever-present time pressure, or the fear of what he might find, the administrator may choose to bypass the facts and go all the way with only his personal opinion. Unless conscious effort is made by the administrator not to coach the facts in what to say, he may develop a sort of "echo" administration in which he uses the organizational acoustics for the purpose of listening only to himself. His colleagues are not always certain to provide sufficient protection from this hazard. Everyone likes to give answers that are used and appreciated. This means people usually think in terms of answers they think will fit the thinking of the asker. The administrator must lean upon his facts; but if they are going to provide him very much support, he must have facts that can stand up by themselves.

The administrator's world is largely verbal, and the imperfections inherent in the mechanics of talking and listening encourage administration by inferences. We can think about six or seven times as fast as we can talk. This means the listener has a great amount of spare thinking time at his disposal while the other person is talking. This spare time is a delightful invitation for inference making, since it permits the listener to anticipate what the speaker is going to say and never really hear what the speaker actually says, to add in ideas of his own and thus put words in the speaker's mouth, or to let his mind wander in and out and thus lose the full context of what was said. Our perception is always highly selective, and we have no difficulty in tuning out the unwanted and unpleasant. Because proper communication depends upon the fidelity of the receiver as much as upon that of the sender, any of these effects means that the chances for proper reception have been greatly decreased. It also means that unless the administrator carefully listens to others, he will in effect be listening to himself. This might be a very interesting monologue to the administrator, but it doesn't yield much to him in the way of combat intelligence.

The sort of mental shorthand that the administrator must, of necessity, practice causes him to have to take much for granted. He often has to transform one swallow into a summer. The hard-pressed administrator discovers very early in his career that unless he does take much for granted, he can never get very much done. He learns to pass over the routine as he looks for the deviations, and his attention is more marked by what it ignores than by what it notes. He sets up an organizational structure which is designed to screen narrowly the information he does get. Such selective perception enables the administrator to use his time and energy where they count most, but this habit can become overdeveloped at the expense of other necessary and competing qualities. Taking things too much for granted can disarm the sense of skepticism required in administration and lead to naïveté and an uncritical acceptance by the administrator of what he sees and hears. He can believe too much and believe it too strongly. Administration is a discipline of doubt, and the sort of questions the administrator asks helps determine the sort of administrator he is. One could argue that the greater function of the administrator is not to answer questions but to ask them. At least, the role of skepticism as a coefficient of good judgment makes it necessary for the administrator to learn enough administrative geometry to recognize that there are two sides to every question and that taking too much for granted can prevent him from taking enough with a grain of salt.

The need and urge to simplify problems and reach quick decisions can cause the administrator to let the decision become the thing and to forget that it must be implemented. The administrator must not only perceive what should be done but must also get it done, and whatever he gets done must be done through people. The way decisions are reached affects people's support of them for better or for worse. The process is often more important than the results. Wise decisions, as such, must be arrived at in a manner procedurally acceptable to those affected by them. Wisdom as an abstract quality simply does not exist in the minds of people. It must not only be used but must be seen being used. This is the reason the clandestine is suspected and the unilateral is resented. People want to see how the decision was reached and to know that sufficient consideration was given to the problem. The administrator must make good decisions, but he must also make them in a good way. Logic is not enough. The etiquette of decision making must be observed if the administrator's decisions are to be organizationally acceptable.

As someone has said, "Any fool can jump to conclusions—and usually does." Yet the nature of the administrator's work forces him to skip to conclusions even though he resists the temptation to jump. The enforced habit of working with partial information tends to develop highly the conceptual skills of the administrator, and his practice increasingly trains him to visualize the whole by seeing only a few of its parts. He is compelled to spend much of his time reading between the lines and in extrapolating from his experience. While such inference is a very essential skill, its use can be intoxicating to the administrator's judgment and can easily get out of hand. If not controlled and if used indiscriminately, it can lull the administrator into the habit of overgeneralizing and of making evaluations that are spurious and unfounded. The temptation for the administrator to depend too heavily on his conceptual skills, rather than grub for the facts, is very strong and insidious, and there is no ready answer to the question of how he can curb it. About the only answer is for him to be honest enough with himself to know that he does not usually possess or comprehend all the facts and that he is often called on to deal with what he does not understand. It will help his development if he keeps reminding himself that in the long run, digging for the facts can develop better administrative muscles than jumping to conclusions can.

The perfectionist in administration often reaps imperfection

7 Good judgment can be an everyday magic of the mind if given a sporting chance. It doesn't always get a sporting chance in administration, however, and at times its chances are wasted because of the administrator's insistence that it be perfect. Too rigid a search for perfection can get the administrator off course and lead him into an administrative thicket of imperfections. To desire perfection and to want to work toward it represent essential qualities for the administrator. It is certain that he will get no higher level of performance than he works hard to obtain. But desiring perfection and demanding it are two very different things. The first permits him to pursue excellence but still get the job done. The second may mean that he gets neither the ideal nor the feasible.

A demand for the perfect, instead of the accomplishable, can lead to an "all or none" sort of administration that adversely affects organizational performance in several ways. On the one extreme, it can mean that an improvement is never undertaken because the ideal solution isn't currently possible. Necessary changes will not be started because the opportunity for perfect solutions rarely comes along. Ultimately, it can lead to a form of "alibi" administration in which the administrator points to excuses rather than results. Major changes are always difficult to accomplish, and even the bravest and most energetic of administrators are sometimes tempted to rationalize their distaste for facing up to these difficulties by holding out for the perfect solution. This sort of thinking can become chronic and seriously impair the administrator's effectiveness. If he develops a habit of searching for difficulties, he will be sure to find them, since most problems are problems because they have already run into difficulty. If the administrator develops a negative attitude, he can easily pick any idea apart in terms of the difficulties it presents. The administrator who greets every idea for improvement with a carefully documented list of obstacles soon discourages even the most enthusiastic individuals in the organization. One of the greatest problems of the administrator is the resistance to change that besets all organizations. His task is to kindle enthusiasm for change and new ideas. A wet blanket can easily smother the brightest idea, and it is not very useful in kindling one.

The administrator can be a wet blanket without half trying. In fact, the likelihood of his being one without knowing it is so great that he needs to work consciously against accenting the negative. The competitive nature of day-to-day living causes our initial reaction to someone else's ideas to be negative, and we attempt to hold the ideas of others at bay until we see how they affect us personally. For the same competitive reasons, we also tend to play down the ideas of others. Often in conferences the criticisms of proposals seem aimed more at discrediting the individual than his idea, at convicting rather than convincing. Organizational etiquette won't permit us to attack the individual directly, so we attack his ideas. The amount of fault we find with his ideas seems to vary directly with the distance that separates his level in the hierarchy from our own—either upward or downward. The greater the status difference, the greater the support we give to the other person's ideas; and as the disparity of status decreases, the weaker this support becomes. We tend to measure the ideas of others by what they might do to us rather than by what they might do for the enterprise.

There are other than competitive reasons why we sometimes douse the ideas that ignite around us. One of these can be described as protective. We seem to believe that if we call attention to the weaknesses of an idea, we leave ourselves a verbal foxhole into which to crawl in case the idea backfires. We follow the notion that we can always point out the skepticism we expressed and shake off responsibility for the ideas that don't work by doing an "I told you so" routine. We anticipate, if the idea proves successful, that our initial criticisms will be forgotten or else classified as an astute effort in behalf of refining the idea. Having such a curtain of criticism to hide behind can be a comfort for the administrator, but it can also get him permanently hidden. He may find that it is quite difficult to get a fresh point of view from behind his wet blanket.

Even at best new ideas usually find the going pretty rough. They have to break into the lineup against severe odds. Old ideas have the advantage of having established themselves through use over a period of time. The new idea must win out against established ideas at a time when it is unproven and untested. It has to prove its worth before it gets a chance to show it. New ideas seldom come full-grown and developed right at the beginning. At the same time, they must pass a judicial review that by its nature is prejudiced against the novel and original. Evaluation is a critical process and criticism is a "past oriented" way of thinking. It has only the past as a guide by which to measure the new. The mind must link new material to old material in order to make it meaningful. This means that all new ideas have to prove themselves with the testimony of old ideas. They have no record of their own to offer in evidence, since they have no past. They must be taken partly on faith if they are ever to have a past to support them. This means a dilemma for the administrator. On the one hand, he must constantly exercise critical judgment, since this is the essence of decision making. He can properly pick among alternatives only after he has sufficiently picked them apart. His success depends upon the extent to which he can develop the ability to spot quickly and surely the infirmities in an idea. At the same time, however, that he is developing and exercising his power of critical thinking, he runs the risk of stifling in himself and in those around him the ability and willingness to think and act imaginatively. The two abilities are in conflict but both are very necessary. The administrator must somehow steer a wary course between the overdevelopment of critical thinking and the overdevelopment of imaginative thinking. In doing this, it will help him to learn to react to ideas before he judges them. If he first gets the feel for an idea, he can then take the idea apart without tearing it up.

New ideas have another sort of handicap working against them. Because the practice of administration is so heavily oriented toward problem solving, the administrator is likely to spend less time watching for breakthroughs than for breakdowns. He will be looking for ways to protect and maintain rather than change. The push of administrative life forces him to be more concerned with ameliorating than innovating. Genuinely new ideas, on the other hand, are seldom ameliorative in their effect. They tend to abet rather than abate the administrator's difficulties. This means that they are likely to receive scant consideration from the hard-pressed administrator. He will have an inclination to shun them because they are troublesome. But, unless they are troublesome, they don't accomplish very much for him. A new idea has value only to the extent that it produces change. Change always involves the loss of some present values. It also involves rearrangement and adjustments in the established order. If the administrator is to benefit from new ideas, he must develop a sympathy for the fact that the most valuable contribution of the creative ability is not in solving problems but in creating them.

Because the administrator is a persistent meliorist, the new ideas that attract his attention are likely to be those that help him solve current problems. For this reason, new ideas are largely measured by how well they sustain the old orthodoxy. They are judged by how well they can get along with old ideas rather than by how well they can do. When employed, they are likely to be used to conduct business as usual. This means that there is a danger that new ideas will be used to help the administrator spin his wheels rather than the wheels of fortune.

An important source of administrative "cold water" is the proclivity of people toward being more concerned with wrongness than rightness. We search harder for the wrongness in things, and we give wrongness a disproportionate weight over the goodness we do find. This accent on wrongness is probably due in part to the manner in which all evaluation must be done. We can establish the level of goodness of a thing only by determining the degree to which it is contaminated by badness. Badness has no counterpart to "pure" as an absolute for goodness so we have to start with purity and subtract the badness in order to determine how good a thing is. This means we tend to search for the bad rather than the good. The administrator is especially oriented toward emphasizing the wrongness of ideas because his work consists of problem solving and problem avoidance. Problems represent situations in which things went wrong, and the administrator has to identify the wrongness in order to remove it. If he can identify the wrongness in new ideas, he can avoid problems before they occur. However, if he becomes preoccupied with the wrongness, he can start spending more time finding fault than finding a way. He can also develop the notion in those around him that nothing should ever be done for the first time.

A preoccupation with wrongness can lead to the administrator's judging the quality, rather than the usefulness, of ideas presented to him. Scorning a solution because its slip is showing isn't always the smart thing for the administrator to do. Administrative choice more often involves choices between the good and good, or the bad and bad, than between the good and bad. There are times when the choice is not even between competing alternatives, but rather between doing a thing or doing nothing. For lack of a better way the administrator often must knowingly program problems. A poor way out in many instances may still be the best way out. How well a situation was handled can sometimes be more important for the administrator than how the situation came out.

Trying to identify every blemish on a solution can keep the administrator on a treadmill. If he feels compelled to always find every defect, he is not likely to be an efficient problem solver. Because the very last defect cannot be found until every fact is known, he will never know when to stop looking. Looking for the last possible fact in an administrative problem is like looking for a woman's last word. Too much concern with the "fine print" can get him lost in a wilderness of detail that has little meaning to the problem. As necessary as detail is, it represents a burden to the administrator's judgment in that each detail, to be of value, must be examined for its meaning. Too much concern about detail can result in the administrator's loss of confidence in his own judgment. He may begin to fear that something will be left out, or he may become uncertain as to the sort of detail he should have. This may cause him to seek refuge behind a study, a special committee, or an outside consultant. These have their places and can be valuable as adjuncts to the administrator's judgment but not as substitutes for it. Leaving no stone unturned is time-consuming and can cause the hesitant administrator to miss the boat so far as administrative timing is concerned. One problem of the reluctant perfectionist is that he is often forced to dash into a situation rather than deal with it. Because he spends so much time window-shopping for the ideal solution, he may almost miss the bus and have to grasp the first idea within reach as he makes a run for it. Every administrator is bothered by the tendency under trying circumstances to jump at the first solution that shows up, but the effective administrator learns to hold this tendency in check and not bolt in the face of difficulty. The tendency is accentuated in the perfectionist, however, because he is motivated by frustration as well as by desperation. Unable to find the ideal path, he is prone to panic and charge up a blind alley. Said another way, action taken in despair isn't likely to bring the administrator much distinction.

The administrator must recognize that there is a difference between what is ideal and what is real and that he seldom has either the time or resources to pursue the ideal. He must learn that the margin for error is often greater than the margin of time in which to decide and that most administrative action cannot await conclusive proof nor often spare the time to pay full attention to proof. The effective administrator knows that progress of any sort is usually sold by the inch and that, ordinarily, he is wise to stop his search for alternatives when he finds a workable one. He can do only what he can do, but he must get about the business of doing that. The fact that he must stop short of perfection is no excuse for stopping the performance.

The failure to recognize that administration is the art of the feasible may lead to the other extreme in which too much is undertaken too quickly. This may mean that an action which is undertaken is too radical and the organization will be subjected to useless turmoil and perhaps violent upheaval. Just as there are few perfectly good solutions, neither are there many perfectly wrong situations. Whenever a problem exists, one usually can be sure that there are some salvageable parts of the situation and that care must be taken to protect these from damage while making the necessary corrections. More important, the administrator must realize that there are always reasons why things are as they are. He must recognize these reasons even if he cannot fully or ultimately tolerate them. Problem solving is a matter of undoing history, and usually there is too much history to undo all at one time. The ways of an organization are reinforced by years of getting that way, and the effects of an organization's history seldom can be changed effectively except by more history. Also, the great trouble with history for the administrator is that it will repeat itself if the causes are not changed. This means that the administrator must take the time to change the whys before he can change the ways of an organization.

The rate of its speed is only one of the two aspects of change which the administrator must observe. The second is the extent of change. The extremist in administration most often will violate both if he violates either. One of the toughest aspects of problem solving is knowing how far to go. The cure can easily be more damaging than the condition we are trying to treat. For every solution we can expect some sort of pendulum reaction. Often the problem we are trying to cure represents a reaction from a previous overcorrection in the opposite direction. The hazards of overcorrection may be the reason for the adage that problems always come in pairs—the one we correct and the one we create in making the correction.

The proclivity of the perfectionist toward setting a single standard for all work increases the hazards of overcorrection. He is prone to give equal weight to major and minor problems and to demand a level of quality higher than that required in certain situations. Because his goal is perfection, he seeks it for its own sake. This can represent a waste of effort and resources. Solutions vary greatly in their importance to the enterprise, and each job needs to be done only as well as the particular situation requires. Most problems permit a fairly wide range of tolerance in their solution, and a margin for slack can be permitted in many administrative decisions. To a large extent administration is an averaging process, and the hardest efforts should be made where the largest results are required. Unless this is done, the administrator's work may well be marked by heavy efforts and light results.

In some instances the changes attempted may be ultimately

correct but not achievable at the time. Such moves ignore the necessity for administrative timing. The successful administrator must at times tolerate conditions of inefficiency rather than court failure by attempting to clear all the hurdles with one big jump. Every administrative decision must be weighed on the scales of feasibility. The effective administrator is sensitive to what can be done and tries to make decisions that can be carried out. This means that among his repertory of virtues the effective administrator must tuck a high frustration level. It is difficult to say this without implying that the administrator's standards are so fluid that they are constantly in danger of going down the drain, but the effective administrator seems to possess a sense of fatalism that permits him to accept the realities of life. This doesn't mean that he does not constantly and relentlessly stalk excellence. It means that he knows that few things in his life are the way we would like to have them and that he realizes that he must get along in situations that are not exactly what he thinks they should be. It also means that he is more interested in what he has than in what he lacks and that he has learned there are better uses for his head than wearing it out against a stone wall.

Because the administrator must carry out his function through people, he needs more than ordinary patience and tolerance. No matter how scientific his selection procedure is, it will not produce people with perfect specifications. People just aren't ever made that way. They come in their own sizes and not in those specified by the administrator. They come out of their past and not out of a catalog. The administrator always works with "used" individuals and never gets a brand new model built to his specifications. For this reason, he must accept men as they are rather than as he thinks they should be. This does not mean he should tolerate misconduct and misperformance. It means that the administrator should know his people, give due regard to their abilities, and attempt to gain his goals within their limitations. He must work toward improving them because that is the only way he has of improving his administration, but he must learn to accept people as people and not insist upon rapidly and completely remaking them. Even the rigid perfectionist must at times recognize that it is possible to achieve excellence in administration without trying to change the world by attempting to make

over the people in it. He will find it easier that way because any
other way is impossible.

The administrator needs to determine his goals and evaluate
the opposition to them. He can thus accept, and even select,
lesser results as progress toward larger goals. This permits him to
maintain constant pressure toward the desired ends without allowing the pressure to explode into an open break. It also allows
him, when necessary, to accept and attempt alternatives if they
lead toward the ultimate objective. Somewhere between the extremes of inertia and abortive change the effective administrator finds the path of consistent progress. By proceeding step-by-
step along that path, he can ultimately achieve his long-range
plans and at the same time secure the personal stimulation, so
necessary to his own morale, that comes from immediate accomplishments. He should not fret too much about taking a detour if
it will take him to the same destination. He must of course be
sure it is a detour and not the wrong road. This can be done if he
differentiates between an idea and its application. A compromise
on the idea may ruin it but a compromise on its application may
even improve it. A good idea can often be applied in a variety of
ways. It is an old saying, but there are several ways of skinning a
cat.

The "one best way" approach to administration suffers on a
number of counts. Too many unknowns are woven into any decision to allow that a one best way could ever be identified. Time
and circumstance make too much difference. The history of any
activity is to some extent a history of unanticipated events and
unintended consequences. Further, so many variables surround
every decision that it is impossible to support the notion that any
particular way is the one best way. The administrator must both
weigh possibilities and estimate significance in decision making.
The two considerations are quite different. The surest thing may
produce the least value. Kicking for the extra point after a
touchdown in the final seconds of a football game may offer the
best possibilities for scoring, but it may not offer the best value if
going for two points could gain a victory. The administrator must
also balance shifting ends and means. Neither are static and the
two are interdependent. Goals are commonly discussed as though
they were independent givens. They are probably the most de-

pendent variable cranked into a decision. Ends that do not realistically reflect means are administrative fantasies. Decision making is just as concerned with the job that might be done with the alternatives available as it is with different alternatives by which to do the job.

Reaching for only the best can cause the administrator to wind up with the least. This is because, with perfection, there is a difference between scale and degree. Like a diamond, a solution can vary both in quantity and quality. The administrator is forever confronted with the problem of trying to maintain the proper balance between the two dimensions in problem solving. Resources utilized on the one dimension are utilized at the expense of the other. For instance, given a limited budget for promoting a product, the administrator must decide between the scope of the promotion and the intensity of the promotion. The more perfectly he attempts to do the one, the less perfectly can he do the other. The more he goes all out for the one, the more he must leave out of the other. Said another way, his most pedestrian hopes will sometimes carry the administrator furthest down the road.

Compromise is such an important element of the art of administration that it deserves special respect and consideration from the administrator. This sort of regard is not always given it, however, and in some administrative circles it is even considered a bad word. Some of this disrepute is due to blame unfairly attached to compromise by associating it with appeasement. The administrative difference between the two is like that between fission and fusion—or, perhaps better stated, the difference between dispersion and integration. Appeasement scatters the administrator's aims and efforts while compromise serves to gather them. Through compromise, the administrator gathers as much as he can from a situation at a given time in favor of his program and proceeds to gain at least that advantage. He doesn't change direction; he only changes pace. He doesn't give ground to others but gives time to himself. The successful administrator has learned that even to put a modest number of ideas across requires a great deal of negotiation and selling and that much of his selling has to be on the installment plan.

The effective administrator knows that half a loaf is better than none in many ways. It not only keeps his program alive but it may prevent the administrative indigestion that comes from biting off too much at a given time. If he is smart, the administrator will never take more from a situation than the situation should give. The part that he takes beyond what the situation will support will probably do the administrator little good and most likely do him harm. Such excess can ruin an otherwise good solution by causing an organizational regurgitation of the workable along with the unworkable. The administrator needs solutions that will stay put and must remember that sticky solutions usually don't stick very long.

The suggestion that the administrator should stop when he is ahead does not mean that he can ever become satisfied and complacent. A sense of restlessness regarding the level of performance of the organization is an essential characteristic of the effective administrator. No matter how good the performance, he believes it can be improved and is constantly attempting to do so. He is chronically dissatisfied, but his is an enthusiastic dissatisfaction rather than a frustrated one. It is not the compulsive sort of urge that can cause the administrator to overtax the first opportunity for progress that comes along. The administrator's eyes can be bigger than the capacity of the organization, and he can take on more than the organization can tote off. The competitive disciplines within and without the organization require that the administrator's thinking be seasoned with restraint. He must be prepared sooner or later to have his program confronted by reality on the terms that the enterprise's resources make available. If he has overreached and overcommitted his resources, he will at that time learn the difference between the willingness to scrape a program and the necessity of having to scrap it.

Aside from the problem of overcommitment of resources, the administrator who takes too large a bite complicates the process of chewing. There is a natural tendency to broaden solutions and to attempt to have them settle several different problems simultaneously. Problems are interrelated, and the examination of one problem leads almost directly into another one. Also, the relationship between problems doesn't have to be too close to encourage someone else to use the occasion as a means of getting action on some of *his* more pressing difficulties. What started out as a fairly clear-cut problem can become unrecognizable and also unmanageable by the time everyone tacks his tangential issues onto it.

For this reason the administrator needs to define each problem as narrowly as possible and keep stripping off the administrative underbrush that can grow up so rapidly in problem-solving activities. This will not only keep the problem within manageable limits but it will expedite the solution by decreasing the number of bases that must be touched in developing and implementing the solution. The fewer interests involved, the less the delay that will be required for discussion and review. Also, the less will be the chance for opposition to develop, since there will be fewer individuals with a stake in the solution.

The all-or-none attitude of the perfectionist encourages another tendency which can importantly impair the administrator's judgment. This is the tendency to classify everything as black or white. The urge to use the "black or white" technique in sizing up situations and individuals is a strong one and can develop from several causes. The deficit of time which always plagues the administrator doubtlessly causes him to seek and to give quick answers. The "housekeeper" instinct to keep the desk clean leads to a desire to dispose of the file by quick off-the-cuff decisions. In other instances, emotional factors can cause the administrator to pick sides and thus eliminate the bother of looking at both sides. The proven advantage of decisiveness in administration may also be a strong force. The urge to simplify problems can be a strong one, and the ability to do so represents an important asset for the administrator if it is tempered with the knowledge of the dangers involved. However, oversimplification denies the fact that the administrator's task is to a large extent one of discrimination. Decision making is an effort to produce distinctions between very similar alternatives. The problems requiring the administrator's attention are rarely ever black or white in nature, but are usually of varying shades of gray. At least, if the administrator is fulfilling his proper role, only the gray problems will reach his desk and the clear-cut ones will be settled down the line where the facts are more abundant and better understood. At best, administration at each level is isolated from much of the information generally available at a lower level. Further, those problems which properly survive ascent up the diagnostic ladder are most likely to be many-factored and many-sided. This is especially true since the ascent of such a problem exposes it to the views of those at each administrative level and permits it to gather partisans as it moves upward.

A quick answer to a problem can sometimes be self-defeating even if it is the best answer. Problems which are properly screened up to the top level of the organization usually carry with them the troubled ponderings of those involved along the line of ascent. This means that questions permitted to reach the top level must be treated with respect, no matter how simple they may appear to the administrator. It may be possible for an individual to overestimate the importance of his problems with regard to their effect on the welfare of the total enterprise; it is impossible, however, for others to overestimate the importance of these problems to the individual personally. A cavalier treatment of a problem that appeared difficult and torturous to the other person can make the administrator look smart—but smart like an Aleck. It can also make the other person look foolish, and few people have any abiding love for those who pin the donkey's tail on them. If a quick decision represents a choice between conflicting views of two individuals, the loser is automatically justified in believing that his side did not get a full hearing. This can damage the organization's opinion of the administrator because people seem to always associate fullness with fairness and to appear to follow a sort of quantum theory of justice that says the amount of facts reviewed in considering a decision must be proportionate to the effects of the decision on the welfare of the individuals involved. It is not enough for the administrator to mean well. His decisions must look well.

No matter how simple the problem, there are times when the administrator must talk it through with the individuals involved. This not only demonstrates respect and concern on the part of the administrator but reveals to him both the facts and the feelings involved in the problem. Facts are a great deal like darning yarn in their tendency to become twisted, and their ends are even more difficult to find. The feelings often get entwined with the facts and can contribute more to the problem than do the facts. When a person is disturbed, fancy can be easily confused with facts, and the two must be carefully unraveled before a situation will be accepted by the individual concerned. Identifying the feelings is not always sufficient. Often it is as important for the

administrator to learn the reasons for the individual's feelings as
it is to know he has the feelings. The individual may appear irate
at one thing simply because he is angry about another thing.
Sometimes it is not so much a question of talking through a problem as it is of listening through an individual. When people are
upset or feel strongly about a thing, they need to verbalize it.
They do not seem to be able to accept or write off a loss until
they have had a chance to talk about it. Before they can overcome their feelings or learn to live with them, they need to ver-
bally reduce them. This means that the administrator must use his
office at times as a sort of verbal decompression chamber for
those around him. There is of course a limit to the time and
the punishment an administrator can take in empty listening.
Also, it will do people no favor for the administrator to become a
chronic crutch for their crippled feelings. There are times, however, when the administrator can get people to think straight only
by letting them talk in circles.

Giving a quick answer is at times like throwing an anchor to a
person who needs a life belt. The problem the individual brings
to the administrator is often only verbal boiler plate and may
be of minor consequence; it may even be manufactured. But
whether real or contrived, the problem may be intended only as a
calling card and the solution may not be the most important thing
sought. The individual is often seeking assurance and identity instead of a solution. The answer the individual seeks cannot be
stated directly in words by the administrator, but must be stated
indirectly in terms of the time and interest he is willing to devote
to the individual. Such need for reassurance appears to be a universal for all individuals and to vary only in degree. The administrator has the same need and can recognize it in his own behavior
in those instances in which he seeks out his colleagues and
wanders wide of the subject in discussions with them. Normal individuals do learn to keep the need for reassurance under control,
but the administrator must recognize that that need exists, and on
occasion must consciously listen the individual through even
though he knows the answer he is going to give almost as soon as
the conversation has started. This is admittedly a very difficult
assignment because answers are almost impossible to suppress;
and it is a strong human characteristic, whether in the kin-

dergarten or the administrator's office, to want to be the first to give the answer.

A fast brush-off of the other fellow's problem or idea reduces the administrator's opportunity to influence the other fellow's attitudes toward the administrator and the organization. Keeping people lined up in general support of his program is an eternal problem for the administrator. To do so requires some means of getting to the individual in a convincing way. Talking with a person is an important way of getting to him because it is a direct way and because it enables the administrator to put himself and his attitudes on view as a means of influencing the other person's attitudes. Most individuals will listen only if they are listened to, and this means the administrator sometimes can get to the other fellow only by letting the other fellow get to him. How a person views the world seems to largely depend upon how the world views him, and whatever control we have over how the other fellow acts thus becomes a function of how we act. Usually, a person will act toward others in a certain way only if he is convinced that others are acting that way toward him. I will be a good sport only if I think you are being a good sport. Rightly or wrongly, to the other fellow we are what we appear to be. To him we are what our behavior toward him indicates us to be. Paradoxically, in many instances our attitude toward another person actually does become what he thinks it to be. If he mistakenly thinks we are mad at him, he will get mad at us, and this will cause us to sure enough become mad at him. All of this means that some degree of visibility of the administrator is required if his own attitudes are to influence the attitudes of others.

The urge for symmetry that seems to affect all human beings can increase the administrator's tendencies to be a perfectionist. The need for order is apparently a compelling human need, and the lack of it can become an unbearable distraction to most individuals. People automatically rearrange things in a room or on a table if those things are not arranged in an orderly manner. We do this with our mental images too and insist on ordering our impressions and our understandings into neat mental arrangements. This tendency in the administrator is doubtlessly accentuated by his heavy dependence upon organization and his need for predictability. The proper arrangement of people, things, and events is a major function of the administrator, and he must always be concerned with the way he has them lined up. Concern for perfect order can be an important inhibition to effective administration, however. New ideas, when first hatched, are often unkempt, unfinished, and messy. They are likely to receive less than a hearty welcome by an administrator who can tolerate only the complete and the neat solution. Also, order depends upon rules, and an overemphasis on orderliness can foster an overdependence upon rules. The human desire for a stable environment causes most people to have a tendency for ready acceptance of rules and limitations. Most of us look for rules and will go so far as to make them up if we can't find them. A close examination of any activity or work situation will reveal numerous "common law" derived regulations which have no formal authenticity but which are as closely observed, and even as roundly cussed, by those who invented them as are the formal rules imposed by administration. We seem happiest when there are precise rules which set out in detail limitations on the way in which we can act. Such a fully structured environment appeals to the individual because it serves to relieve him of the onerous chore of having to use his personal judgment and eliminates any personal risk if he follows the rules faithfully.

A highly ordered organization has special appeal for the administrator. It helps solve his great problem of coordination by locking the parts of the organization into a solid-state condition. But unfortunately it is more confining for the administrator than it is for the organization. The great amount of red tape required to hold the parts in a steady state binds the administrator's hands when he tries to turn the direction, or to change the pace, of the organization. It helps him tie down the parts, but it can cause him to tie up the show. It also prevents the tension which goes along with uncertainty and which is necessary to prevent organizational indifference and to give a restless bounce to the organization. A well-regulated organization is essential to effective administration, but too much regulation can be an administrative straitjacket for both the organization and the administrator.

The penchant of the perfectionist for tying every thread in place can reduce or destroy the flexibility that he needs if he is to be effective. The administrator is continuously reminded of the wisdom of changing his mind and his policies as the world around him changes. Unless he is to fence himself in, his decisions need to be hedged and qualified so that some account may be taken of the contingencies that he can never fully see in advance. The impact of his own decisions can lead to a series of unsuspected changes, and one choice may force upon him an endless number of other choices. The more closely the administrator programs an operation, the more difficult he will find any later correction. This means that he must seek to keep open indefinitely as many as possible of the alternatives that he had at the time of the decision. Tight programs leave little room for the wheel of fortune to turn, and when it does turn against the administrator, his loss is much larger. The more precise the goals he sets, the more likely the deviations and the more costly the errors. Also, tight policies leave little elbowroom for the imagination and initiative of the administrator's subordinates. We speak of delegating authority, but, in reality, the only thing the administrator has to delegate is room.

Tight agreements are also binding on the administrator's relationships and can cause friction between the administrator and others, both inside and outside the organization. They more often mark the end, rather than the extension, of accord. They seldom ever work in the administrator's favor. If he tries to enforce them, he is blamed for being rigid and unreasonable. If they prove to be to the advantage of others and he seeks to change them, he is branded as untrustworthy and irresponsible.

The urge for specificity can prove to be a serious handicap in problem solving. People seem able and willing to discuss a problem much more objectively in the abstract, and there are fewer chances for individuals to disagree when problems and solutions are stated in general terms. As things become more precise, opinions begin to become more differentiated. Ordinarily, it is much easier to get people to agree on principle than to agree on method. For this reason, the administrator who attempts to spell out the last detail will find that he is producing more opposition than support. Too much specificity leaves too little room in which people can get together.

A collateral and important side influence of the perfectionist involves the adverse effects he can have on the professional growth of his subordinates. An unrealistic demand for perfection will impair the administrator's confidence in his associates because it will be impossible for them to meet his demands. This will not only distort his relationships with them but it will mean that he will be fearful of delegating responsibility to them. Professional growth in administration can be nurtured only by a consecutive series of experiences in meeting, facing, and solving problems. Administration is largely an art, and the skills required in its practice are not acquired out of a book or over a weekend in five easy lessons. Administrators cannot be successfully developed solely from the canned, warmed-over experiences of others. The habits of observation and judgment cannot be put on paper and passed along to others. Neither can administrators be well developed on only those assignments that they can handle perfectly. Efficient learning is largely a matter of discovering what not to do. A man cannot learn from experience unless he is reasonably free to make mistakes, and he does not ordinarily learn to choose good alternatives until he has chosen a few bad ones. Most of us don't seem able to recognize the hand of God until we have experienced the back of it a few times. But we must also learn to trust it. Struggling through the ordeal of his own errors will provide the necessary roughage for the developing administrator, but it can leave him permanently shaken and gun-shy if the demands are too exacting and the penalties for error are too heavy. These demands and penalties do not need to be overtly expressed and assessed by the boss in order to shatter the self-esteem and morale of his assistants. They can be self-generated in his assistants if the boss is a perfectionist. His own anxieties will likely be radiated to those around him, and the self-assaulting reactions on their part can be as strong as any verbal duress he might put upon them. The administrator's subordinates need a chance to make their own mistakes; but they need an equal chance to recover, and this is possible only if they assimilate their experiences with equanimity. Trial by fire is about the only way to season the developing administrator, but it can leave permanent scars if the boss is a perfectionist and attempts to hold the learner's feet too close to the fire.

The relationships of the perfectionist with his subordinates are likely to be worsened by his persistent efforts to make them over into his own overidealized image of what they should be. This is not likely to endear him to his subordinates for a number of reasons. He will probably see so much to correct that his corrections will be almost a constant process and will give his subordinates the notion that he is picking on them. His finicky outlook will cause him to be overly concerned about trifles and to exaggerate their value and importance. Because of anxiety about his subordinates' work, he will have an urge to watch over their shoulders and kibitz on every hand they play. When he gives instructions, he will tend to expand three sentences' worth of conversation into a two-page memo; and when he attempts to explain something, he will generally work overtime to make the obvious seem obscure. Because of his finicking and fussing, the subordinates will be reluctant to seek his counsel and advice when they do need and want it. They will keep their distance in order not to suffer from the infinite pains he takes.

The inability of the perfectionist to see things relatively will prevent him from properly evaluating the progress and performance of his subordinates. His use of a single, rigid standard denies the fact that relationships among different aspects of job performance may be small and that neither superiority nor inferiority are all-inclusive terms when applied to an individual's job performance. Absenteeism is not necessarily correlated with low performance when the person is on the job. Also, those who get to work late may do the best work or may be the ones who leave the job last. Responsibility to a job may not equate with a person's responsibility while on the job. The most honest employee may not be the hardest working, and it is quite doubtful that reliability and initiative are directly related. Very obviously, creativity and imagination are not necessarily virtues of the loyal and the trustworthy. The administrator who insists that his subordinates be paragons of excellence in all respects will seldom keep his assistants very long or maintain very much respect for them. This latter is important because the administrator's lack of respect will be communicated to the lower levels of the organization by his actions and his words. This will erode the effectiveness of his assistants because much of their influence on their own subordinates depends upon the influence the subordinates believe the assistants have with their superior.

The administrator who insists upon sandpapering every decision to a perfect fit will never get very much done. Decisions which take into account every factor and which always balance

them in a satisfying and compelling way are only something for
hard-pressed administrators to dream about. Even the best of
administrators must spend their waking hours working from
problem to problem and hoping that a respectable number of
their decisions will be validated to a reasonable degree. They are
forced to work for the percentage rather than for perfection and
must be more concerned about going the right way than in going
all the way. How far? How fast? and How well? are the questions
they ask in marking a route which may take them some distance
leeward of the ideal but which leads them to the achievable.
They can only steer a course between the known and the unknown, the perfect and the imperfect, while trying to reach the
feasible.

Perfection is a guide and not a destination, and the administrator should use it like the traveler who uses the North Star to show
him the way but who never develops the notion that the North
Star is where he is headed. It will help the administrator if he
keeps in mind that apparently ideal solutions are only estimates
and are subject to all the errors inherent in creating the foreseen
from the unforeseeable. In this sense, ideal solutions are only ap-
proximations and never absolutes. This being so, the most ideal
solutions should be those that most approximate the situation at
hand, and the ideal administrators should be those who make the
best decisions which can be carried out.

Administration is a matter of proportion

8 Among the adjectives most often used to describe good judgment, those related to symmetry lead all the rest. Terms like "even," "balanced," "consistent," and "stable" are bosom companions of the term "good judgment." The same terms are also used in describing the effective administrator. This demonstrates the close correlation between judgment and administration, but it also demonstrates more. It recognizes the fact that administration is an equilibrating or balancing process and that a good administrator, like a good chef, must observe proportion in all that he does. To say that administration is a balancing process indicates that there is always a lot of balancing to do in an organization and that doing it is difficult enough to represent special problems to the administrator. There is much in the nature of organizational activity and in the work of the administrator to produce disbalance and disproportion. This chapter will examine some of the unbalancing pressures and some of the personal tendencies that handicap the administrator in maintaining proportion.

159

Administration is a distracting business requiring the administrator to deal with many different things and to turn from one thing to another without much chance of giving consecutive thought to anything. His day is dictated by a calendar that usually propels him into a whirl of appointments, meetings, and memoranda. Under the pressures caused by diversity and inadequate time, it is easy for the administrator to bow to distractions and to confuse busyness with business. Distractions are not unwelcome to all administrators, and some seem to prefer to "hubbub" their way through the day. They get so addicted to distractions that they search for one if things start quieting down. They prefer flurry to routine and can rest only when they are being interrupted. These are likely to be the same administrators who boast of an open-door policy and fail to recognize that a hanging latchstring is an administrative snare and that doors were invented for the simple purpose of permitting discriminate entry. Unless the administrator exercises discrimination with regard to who gains entry, his time and attention will invariably be devoted to the problems of the more verbose and forward members of the organization rather than the more important and timely problems of less forward members. The demands on the time and the energies of the administrator make it necessary that he learn to put first things first. Administration is always a matter of selective attention and of recognizing the significant. This is so important that every administrator should preview his activities each day and allocate his time and interests to those problems and concerns with highest priority. When he finds that he is floundering in a calendar full of administrative potpourri, he should audit his time by reviewing with his secretary the calendar sheets for several months back. If he does not determine priorities, he cannot avoid practicing at random instead of by plan and becoming a troubleshooter who is forced to aim from the hip at whatever problems happen to come into view each day.

The problem of the trouble-shooting administrator is that he is always working under the gun. What he does must be done on the spur of the moment rather than by orderly schedule. This means he must practice a kind of makeshift administration in which he spends his time tying up the problems rather than tying into them. Because he never knows what he is going to do next, he is never ready and must catch at whatever straws are available in his attempt to mend the situation. Since he doesn't have time to properly study the problem and identify the best solution, he is forced to use a "pig in a poke" method of problem solving. Because of patchwork solutions, the work he does doesn't stay done and the succession of deadlines confronting him grows longer by the job. He really never can know when he is caught up since he never knows what is coming up.

Habitual shooting from the hip can cause the administrator to become trigger-happy and get too many things going at the same time. Administrative life can get to be a sort of free-for-all in which the administrator goes at all problems at once and shows a greater concern for extending his energies than for allocating them. It isn't very difficult for any administrator to have more going than he can "get with." Many of his problems just won't yield and keep on plaguing him as new problems keep accumulating. Other problems won't stay solved and keep coming back so often that he gets tired of their faces. From both frustration and boredom he turns for escape to new problems and new ideas. Also, good ideas have a rabbitlike propensity for multiplying, and the introduction of one idea leads to a whole medley of others. Yielding to the temptation to pursue every good idea that shows up, however, can get the administrator mixed up in an administrative mélange that keeps him from ever fully accomplishing anything. The effective administrator learns that he must renounce many appealing ideas in order to carry out a few and that he must decide which are the few which will really make a difference. He knows that in any organization, as in all of life, a few major efforts account for most of the accomplishments.

The trigger-happy administrator who fails to distinguish between the incidental and the essential is also likely to act impulsively and prematurely. There is much to be said for prompt action and for decisive action, but these must be coupled with administrative restraint and timing. This means the administrator must often keep walking around a problem until it is organizationally feasible to grab hold of it. Also, there is a difference between taking chances and leaving things to chance. The introduction of a new idea is supposed to have consequences, and it is the responsibility of the administrator to recognize and weigh them. Unless he predicts and provides for the consequences of his actions, he can soon find that both he and the organization are in over their heads. Administrative "bends" can be as damaging as administrative lag, and the administrator at times must walk a fine line between them. This is not a matter of timidity or of dread but one of wariness and concern. It requires a sufficient tinge of administrative uneasiness to cause the administrator to look before he leaps. The competent administrator takes many risks, but he also takes many precautions that the less competent might neglect.

The administrator in a hurry is likely to develop a fast draw rather than an accurate draw and to confuse fast thinking with clear thinking. Even under the best of circumstances the administrator seldom has time to fully consider any problem and is often forced to act as much from reflex as from plan. Patiently defining and narrowing a problem can be both trying and boring. It is much more appealing, and very much easier, for the administrator to ad-lib his policies as he "*ad hocs*" his way through the organization. Because the administrator is results-oriented, he has a tendency to become fretful with investigation, testing, and other nonproductive activities that should accompany the introduction of new ideas. The fact that he must keep the show moving causes him to be impatient with uncertainty and to seek quick answers even to complex problems. There is much about his job to cause him to become a dash man rather than a miler and to practice a sort of stopwatch administration. But there is more to administration than firing off a hurried memo, and the administrator who moves too fast may find that he is finished before he arrives.

The speed demon in administration exhibits a strong desire to stop the clock and start over when he runs into obstacles. His first thought is to wipe out the problem rather than work it out. This urge to radically revamp the organization and to erase people and policies when trouble occurs is in part because of the human tendency to assign a single utility to each object and a single purpose to every arrangement. The human mind runs toward specialization of articles and of effort. This special-purpose outlook makes us unlikely to look for ways to fit a new idea into an existing arrangement or to put an existing arrangement to a new or improved use. The desire to wipe the slate clean is increased by the fact that administration is largely a matter of observing and treating exceptions. The attention of administration is, of necessity, devoted to the variations from the planned or expected, and little attention is given to, or required for, those things that work well. Because administration is largely concerned with disorders and malfunctions, the administrator is likely to assume that an entire arrangement is defective when there is a defect in one of its parts. There are, of course, times when a full sweep is indicated, and the administrator must reach for a clean broom. But the trouble with a clean broom is that it leaves little in the way of continuity and consistency of operations. Sweeping changes in policy can blur the image of an organization. Policies are the pedigree of an enterprise, and if they are shifted too radically, any special character of the enterprise is proportionately diminished. The administrator who acts too drastically can throw out the baby with the bath water and lose the values that might be preserved by an adjustment rather than a replacement.

The "organizational clearance" approach to problem solving can lead to administrative bulldozing in which vigorous attack is confused with accomplishment. Being energetic is a necessity in administration, but it is not always the same as being effective. Plowing boldly into a problem will unquestionably produce results, but they may not be the desired results. In a very large sense, administration is the art of the compatible. Influencing others is a way of life to the administrator, and to do this he must avoid extremes of any sort. He must look for the amenable, rather than the abortive, if he is to unify the efforts of the diverse interests with which he contends. He can hardly expect to create and maintain a strong organizational rhythm by constantly bowling over the band. Organizational relationships are not natural and derived but are synthetic and contrived. This means that there is always an element of organizational uneasiness and instability and that such relationships can be easily jarred. Said in other words, acting like a bull in a china shop is no way to walk on psychological eggs.

The problem with shortcuts in administration is that they usually take the form of uppercuts. Most individuals have a tendency to overreact and to go to excess, even in minor matters, when they become involved in something. This tendency toward overcompensation and overcommitment is magnified in administration because of the way the administrator works. He works from problem to problem, and his perspective of the enterprise is more sequential than panoramic. Most organizational problems are local in nature, and this means the administrator seldom works on the organization in general. Because he is preoccupied with the problems of a particular part, he is prone to go overboard in correcting those problems and to slight the problems of other parts until a breakdown forces them to his attention. For these reasons, the administrator has a tendency to go for broke, rather than for balance, when he gets going on a problem.

Balanced attention in administration does not mean equal time, however. The administration can get out of balance as much by giving equal attention to all problems as by overmagnifying particular problems. Both time and resources can be wasted if they are distributed on a share-and-share-alike basis to all problems. Such allocation of attention will mean that the more important problems are only partially attended to, while the less important are overattended. It is somewhat the same as feeding the same amount of oats to a pony as to a draft horse. Both suffer from the practice. Administration is, in a sense, a process of allocating scarce resources. The administrator is in this sense a differentiator, and if he is to perform appropriately, he must react differently to different situations.

The habit of going too fast or too far is exhibited in several different ways by administrators. There are the empire builders, who equate size with status and seem more concerned with fighting for larger budgets than with making the most effective use of the ones they have. These administrators use every problem as an excuse for adding more people rather than as a justification for paring off the excess that tends to accrete to every operation. They do not recognize the value of leanness as a device for determining significance or the fact that if people are given more work to do, the less important work will most likely drop by the side. Somewhat related to the empire builders are the swashbucklers, who get their "kicks" from grandeur. They insist on a chauffeur-driven brougham to drive them to the company plane which stands in readiness to fly them to and from meetings at the most exclusive watering places. The enterprise can afford such grand-standers much better than it can the "monument makers," however. These are the administrators who are unhappy unless they "skin an elephant" every day. They find it difficult to properly distribute their enthusiasm and energies and have interest only for big projects and big deals. With such individuals their interests in even the big deals is short-lived, and those too soon suffer from inattention. They confuse a big start with a good ending and seldom taste the joy of winning because they seldom go to the trouble of finishing.

Lack of proportion in administration is manifested by some administrators in a manner best described by the old expression "making a mountain out of a molehill." This consists in over-emphasizing incidents and problems that have little consequence to the enterprise. Such a practice not only wastes the energies and attention of both the administrator and the organization but it diminishes the administrator's influence on matters that are important. Members of the organization easily develop organizational callouses from administrative riding, and for this reason both the whip and the sugar should be used sparingly and only when circumstances warrant. Making much ado about nothing can leave the administrator with much to be undone when there is something to be done.

One way to make a mountain out of a molehill is to build it out of minutiae. Piling up such a mountain can become a favorite pastime of the administrator for several reasons. For the inadequate it gives something to hide behind, and for the uncertain it provides something concrete to do. There is, of course, a necessary amount of detail that must be observed in every organizational effort in order to provide direction and to assure conformity and consistency in operations. Detail represents a powerful cohesive force that binds tasks, jobs, and systems together. The necessity of observing detail forces an individual to stay in step and to stay in line, but a guideline can very easily become red tape if the administrator should become too great a stickler for detail.

How far administration can go in giving people their own way is always a perplexing problem. Aside from the insecurity on the part of subordinates that vagueness in direction creates, the failure of the administrator in a high position to be sufficiently specific or explicit can create an administrative "no man's land" of unassigned or unaccepted responsibilities. Uncovered areas of responsibility exist to some extent in practically every organization. There are several reasons why this is true. The higher administrator often is "in on the problem" from its origin and by the time it reaches the decision phase he has become so closely identified with the solution that lower administrators are likely to anticipate that he will make the necessary assignments. He, in turn, has become so familiar with the problem and the solution that he doesn't see it as falling outside ordinary channels or being entirely in his own hands, and takes it for granted that those at lower levels know as much about it as he does. This state of affairs is compounded if his involvement extends several levels down in the hierarchy, since there will have been no opportunity to consolidate information at a logical action level. This will not only leave the subordinate uncertain about what to do but it will leave him without the authority to do anything. The exercise of authority is dependent upon the possession of information, and the extent of an individual's authority in a situation can never be any greater than the scope of information he possesses about it. The lines of authority in an organization are, in actuality, lines of communication; and when an individual is placed in a position of authority, he is placed astride these lines. The point at which he is placed determines the level of the communications he can get, and this determines the level of information by which he can act. Before a person can know what to do, he must know what is going on. Said another way, the subordinate can play his own hand only after it has been dealt to him.

The functional specialization of activities in an organization inhibits balanced and comprehensive administration. Horizontal gaps in jurisdiction occur between administrative equals at each level of the hierarchy because it is impossible to always fit responsibilities sufficiently close, without overlapping them, to prevent organizational gaps. The administrator is more aware of overlapping than gapping because overlapping is more structurally visible. Also, overlapping occurs only from positive action, which gives the administrator an opportunity to observe what he has done, whereas gaps represent something he has failed to do and thus are likely to go unnoticed. There is also a built-in alarm for jurisdictional overlaps because of the interests of subordinates in protecting their domains. Getting crowded into an organizational corner usually produces an outcry, but an organizational vacuum is regarded as an opportunity to be exploited rather than advertised.

A similar problem of misfit quite often occurs between vertical levels of the organization. This is due to the mistaken notion that the bottom of each level of the hierarchy is best shaped as a straightedge rather than as a serrated line and that the higher executive must delegate everything below his position at exactly the same level. This ignores the fact that the abilities of the superior and those of the subordinate do not match or join neatly and also that every administrative unit has functions of differing degrees of importance. The "square bottom" concept of delegation prevents the high executive from handling certain functions of the level below him even though such functions might be very crucial and their mishandling could seriously maim the total enterprise. Likewise, this concept forces him to take over all functions above that level even though the subordinate, because of special experiences and abilities, might be much more able to handle certain of those functions. Expressed in administrative terms, the abilities of individual administrators and the requirements for different functions of individual administrative units seldom fit exactly.

The idea that the line of demarcation between different levels of the administrative hierarchy should be notched, rather than squared, does not mean it should not be clear cut. A fence that turns a corner is just as effective as one that runs on a straight line. The problem is one of respecting and maintaining the fence. Too often, an administrative wilderness is created by the failure of the administrator to observe the organizational land grants that he has given. The inability to resist poaching on areas he has assigned to subordinates leads to unattended or, even worse, loosely attended sections. If a superior becomes directly involved in a problem of a subordinate, or goes around him, a cloud is formed over the subordinate's grant of authority, and an area of administrative uncertainty results. Honoring his own organizational chart is always a difficult thing for the administrator to do. Either impatience with the progress being made or worry over the importance of a problem can cause the administrator to want to grab the ball and carry it himself. Also, it is natural for the administrator to have a strong yen to put his hand into work with which he is familiar, or in which he is especially expert and adept, or which he likes to do. This is especially true with regard to the areas from which he has been promoted. The strangeness of the new assignment and the sense of inadequacy that he is, on occasion, bound to feel can give a strong attraction to the old and familiar neighborhood and make the administrative apron strings of former assignments hard to cut.

Paradoxically, a clean-cut observance of organizational lines can serve to create gaps in the administrative intelligence system. This has to do with the manner in which the concept of delegation has developed. It has become an established principle that an individual must have authority commensurate with the responsibility assigned to him. This in turn has been interpreted to mean that the individual should not be held accountable for things over which he has no authority. Such an interpretation represents a confusion between responsibility and accountability. Responsibility is a matter of the particular, whereas accountability is a matter of the general. The individual is delegated responsibility for specific things, and these are defined in order for everyone to know that this particular individual is supposed to get them done. Similarly, he is delegated authority to do specific things, and this is defined in order for everyone to know he has a right to do them. Both responsibility and authority are specifically conferred and therefore must be specifically circumscribed. Accountability, on the other hand, is imposed on the individual generally and therefore cannot be specifically circumscribed. This means that the individual is accountable for anything that he might know anything about. His accountability is not restricted to things for which he has been delegated responsibility and authority. Administrators at all levels are accountable for reporting and giving recommendations concerning anything they might observe, or be supposed to observe, at any point or level of the enterprise. A simple example would be an administrator's accountability for reporting theft or other wrongdoing he might observe in someone else's department. Accountability in that sort of instance is usually recognized. Accountability is less well recognized, but no less real, regarding the reporting of all observations and ideas that might be of value to any part of the enterprise. The purpose of organizational lines is not to mark off a private part of the enterprise for the individual administrator, but rather to tie each individual administrator into the whole.

"Organizational hangover" from past operations is another common cause of unbalance and is found to some extent in almost every enterprise. The gravy stains of outdated policies and outmoded practices are difficult to remove because they become

so deeply imbedded in the organizational fabric; for this reason
the administrator is tempted to leave them be. Because of the
time and trouble involved in such removal, he sometimes suc-
cumbs to administrative indolence or dread and attempts to
launch new plans without terminating the old. This is illustrated
by the addition of new functions that compete and conflict with
existing ones and by the creation of new positions and titles without redefinition or elimination of previously established ones.
Such actions can produce several difficulties. One of these is an
administrative version of "musical chairs" in which everyone is
more interested in scrapping for position than in scrapping the
obsolete and outdated. Another is the interference with the implementation of new policies and practices that occurs if the old
ones are not clearly and fully abrogated. Successful innovation is
often more a matter of recognizing and discarding the obsolete
than of adopting the new. In order to accomplish desired change
most effectively, the administrator must have the foresight and
courage to jettison the administrative debris that accumulates on
the organizational decks over a period of time.

One reason the administrator loses direction is that he doesn't
always look where he is going. The great urge to look after
present necessities can keep the administrator so occupied with
the here and now that he doesn't take time to look up. Also, his
role as problem solver causes him to work from problem to
problem, and this serves to direct his attention to the next problem
rather than to the road ahead. The fact that the enterprise is a
real place with issues and problems of concern to real people
means the administrator is judged largely on a day-to-day basis
and his attention is likely to be much more taken up by present
than by future things. It also means that he is apt to favor the
most highly visible projects rather than the most highly valuable.

The pressure for immediate solutions can cause the administrator to become much more concerned with symptoms than with
causes. There is much in his work that gives him a tendency to
focus on symptoms. Since the objective of administration is to get
things done, it is primarily concerned with results and only sec-
ondarily with causes. Causes are important to administration only
because they influence results, and they are likely to become of
real interest to administration only when the results are unsatis-
factory. Also, the precipitating factors of a thing are not always

treatable and the administrator can only treat the symptoms. This is especially true with regard to actions of labor, unions, governmental regulatory bodies, and similar outside agencies possessing the power to enforce arbitrary and unilateral decisions. Also, there can be an upsetting seepage of uncontrollable and unpredictable causes into almost anything the administration attempts, and the best that can be done when this occurs is to treat the results. There is no alternative but to chase the horses when they escape from the barn. There are, however, many causes that can be treated and controlled, and the administrator is much smarter to put a lock on the barn than to be always chasing the horses.

The romantics in administration prefer wishful thinking to locking the barn. They seem to look upon administration as a form of black magic and to believe that a wish is the same as a fact. It is difficult for them to realize that facts refuse to alter themselves to suit one's desires and that the administrator must harness his decisions to the stern requirements of reality. Because romantic administrators live in an administrative dreamworld, they usually gaze at the future through rose-colored glasses and seldom reckon on a storm. In their search for administrative ecstasy, they are prone to bypass the dull and difficult and to attend to the easy and enjoyable. However, administration is not a smorgasbord from which the administrator can choose the problems that best suit his taste and disposition. It is more like the boardinghouse table, and the problems that he shoves aside one day are fairly sure to show up as leftovers the next. The impulse to reach for the more agreeable problems is a strong one with most administrators. It is never easy to tackle the important instead of the pleasant, and forced attention is always the most exhausting. But the distaste the administrator feels for taking on certain of his problems can be a valuable warning signal to him. The temptation to turn away from a problem is usually almost tantamount to the problem's having a high priority tag.

The appeal of administrative moonbeams is not restricted to the wishful thinkers. The playboys in administration also find the daily routine flat and uninteresting unless they can mix jive with the job. This is accomplished in such ways as making passes at the company blonde or passing the work day at the country club. Their big moments are reached in the small hours at the better known nightclubs, and going out of town is synonymous with going out on the town—at the company's expense. Admittedly, administration can at times be a boring and drab affair, and all work and no play does make Jack a dull boy. But relaxation is supposed to be used as a spice and not as a pasta. The judgment of the administrator is constantly on trial, and he can't kick up his heels without kicking his own dignity and damaging the regard others have for him. He is not required to be a sombre individual, but he is expected to behave like a sober one. His "visibility" to the organization is such that his feelings and conduct must always be tempered by restraint. Administration is not supposed to be a chronic fiesta, and for the administrator who habitually attempts to make it into one it can turn into a fiasco.

Fadism and cultism are increasingly causing administration to get out of proportion. The rapid emergence of the professional administrator and the great desire of this new professional to have a science and technology of his own has caused some administrators to be an easy mark for almost any plausible notion about administration that might come down the turnpike. Such administrative hitchhiking has involved the full spectrum between the extremes of administration by rigid mathematical formulas and administration by formless assent. Some of the new ideas have represented real advances, and perhaps many of them possess elements of value if utilized appropriately. The tendency, however, has been to go overboard and to overuse and overemphasize the ideas that happen to be popular and stylish at a particular time. This has meant that in many instances administrators have gotten on the bandwagon before they knew the direction and the distance it was taking them. The willingness to accept the new and to continuously adapt the organization to it is a very necessary quality of the effective administrator. He must be progressive and farseeing if he is to meet the demands of a constantly shifting environment, but he must also remember that men of broad vision must be careful that they don't become wide-eyed.

The danger of riding off in the wrong direction is not confined to those who jump aboard every bandwagon that passes. Some administrators demonstrate that they get lost with equal facility by riding their hobbyhorses. The temptation to give undue attention and support to pet ideas and projects is a natural and strong one for the administrator. It is a very effective means for achieving leadership in his field. Simply being good in general is not

enough, and the individual needs to be outstanding in some specific field in order to develop the necessary visibility for recognition as a leader. More important than leadership aspirations is the
universal desire to demonstrate one's uniqueness. It is only by
establishing his uniqueness that the individual can differentiate
himself from others and establish his own identity. For this
reason desire for uniqueness is a laudable motive in the administrator if properly directed. It is not always properly directed,
however, and some administrators seem more in quest of a character than of excellence. They attempt a shortcut to recognition by
seeking the eccentric rather than the excellent. Others use creativity as a device for securing easy ego satisfactions while avoiding
the hard and tedious everyday effort for improvement. There are
no shortcuts and easy paths for the imaginative in administration,
however. By its nature, imagination increases the difficulty and
complexity of the administrator's task. This is because it creates a
wider frame of reference for him to examine and more alternatives from which he must choose. It forces him to be more discriminating, since it produces added testimony both for and
against a given decision. It increases the risks of failure, since it
extends the options beyond the safeguards of the tried and
proven. For these reasons, only the successful innovations are
classified as imaginative. The ones that don't work are called
follies. This doesn't mean that the administrator should never
venture off the beaten path. The urge on the part of the administrator to be creative can be highly beneficial to the enterprise if it
is seasoned with operational concern and is not gratified at the
expense of the overall welfare of the enterprise. However, unless
the administrator remembers and honors his responsibilities to
the enterprise, his efforts to be creative can result in creating
mostly confusion and dismay.

The fact that the administrator possesses special knowledge or
has special competency in a particular aspect of administration or
in a particular function of the enterprise can result in the overall
program's becoming misshapen. Distortion is always a hazard of
expertness. People feel most secure in doing those things they can
do well and are prone to shy away from undertaking the things in
which they are least competent. Also, most normal people have
a compulsion to impress others by exhibiting their superior or

best skills. This is indicated by the things we talk about. Even
with strangers, we maneuver the conversation around to topics on
which we have special knowledge or which permit us to relate incidents that demonstrate special prowess on our part. For these
reasons, the administrator is apt to devote extra effort and attention to areas in which he has expertise and to neglect those areas
where he is least knowledgeable and skillful. Even when he tries
to properly distribute his interest, he is handicapped by the gun-
barrel vision that accompanies expertness. If an individual is
trained to look only for certain things, it is likely that he will see
mostly those things. The chief executive who comes up through
production is more likely to keep his eyes on costs than on sales.
One can recognize a thing only if he knows what it is. Likewise,
the chief executive who comes up through finance is not likely to
maintain a close watch on product engineering. Because administrators usually work their way up through specialized divisions,
they develop specialized knowledge and interests that can warp
their attention unless they keep strongly in mind the fact that
they are consumers of their own past.

Another cause of disproportion are the drumbeaters who see
administration more as a crusade than as a function. Their number has been increased in recent years by the gospelizing that has
occurred concerning the social mission of administration. This has
sent many administrators scurrying in search of a soapbox on
which to stand, and some of these have shown a willingness to
follow almost any righteous-sounding standard that someone
might raise in front of them. These administrators prefer to save
the world rather than to serve it and would rather uphold a cause
than support the organization's objectives. Their names are often
found at the top of controversial petitions, and their fingers are
commonly discovered deep in the most complex social issues.
Admittedly, every administrator needs to rise above the press of
circumstances and to make the enterprise a force for good in the
community. It is doubtful that he has a right, however, to use the
enterprise to force his notion of good onto the community. Even
if the administrator feels that a cause deserves sacrifice, it is not
his privilege to sacrifice the enterprise. The enterprise has a responsibility to do right by the world, but it is asking too much to
require it to do the world over. If the enterprise is to have the

strength to stand up and be counted on its own actions, it cannot
be burdened with issues irrelevant to its purpose and over which
it has no control.

The administrators who insist on being in the middle of everything are a common cause of disproportion in administration.
There are several varieties of these administrators. One sort are
the perfectionists who stand guard to see that the picayune is
given great significance and that the trivial is accomplished with
exact precision. Another kind are the jacks-of-all-trades who believe that they excel at everything and are willing to bungle up
anything to prove it. These are related to the do-it-yourself types
who never learn to depend on others. The administrator chooses
the things he tries to do. Unless he establishes priorities for the
things he is to do himself, he will not be able ever to properly
delegate a part of his work to others because he will never know
what to delegate. This might demonstrate that he is able to carry
a heavy load, but it will also prove that he is not smart enough to
share it. The uncertainty that is bound to accompany the failure
to exercise selective attention about what they do may be the reason that some administrators never quit worrying about things
that do get done. The problem of the administrator is to know
what is going on without taking over, and this means he must be
able to put his nose in but keep his hands out.

Keeping the hands of others out of his work is an equally difficult problem for the administrator. This is because there is an
abiding desire on the part of people around him to tell him what
he ought to do and a natural temptation on his part to ask them.
The supply of advice always more than equals the demand; and
the more complex the issues, the greater the supply seems to become. There are many reasons why the administrator is a willing
customer. For one thing, the administrative process is in great
part a matter of gathering and interpreting information. It represents a constant search for informed opinion from both inside and
outside the organization, and the organization is supposed to be
structured to best expedite the reception of such opinion. But the
inclination of the administrator is to go beyond the limits of the
informed. This inclination is encouraged by the fact that the
administrator doesn't work for any one person or organizational
activity in particular, but is supposed to work for the enterprise in
general. For this reason, he has a tendency to seek the broadest,

rather than the best, opinion. The fact that most of us are inclined to trust our judgment only if it is in the majority is another reason we want a poll before we can believe ourselves. We often give in because our idea is outnumbered rather than because it is outpointed. This desire to validate our ideas by having them confirmed by others sometimes causes us to give weight to the opinion of strangers. Too much advice can damage the coherence of administrative thought and administrative policy. The purpose of seeking advice is to obtain the advantages of different perspectives and different insights. If this purpose is served, the administrator is very likely to get differing and sometimes conflicting recommendations. This should represent no problem if all the advice is considered at the same time and before a decision is reached. But getting the advice of different people at different times can impair the continuity of the administrator's thinking and cause him to act inconsistently. For this reason, the administrator should be hesitant about receiving advice after he has committed himself. He must also be careful about whom he receives advice from. Receiving advice tends to obligate the administrator because it creates a sort of social obligation to defer to it. Ideas are often promoted by individuals who stand to gain personally from the idea and thus are quick to proffer advice in favor of it. Also, there are individuals who have a great need to be heard and will press loudly for any idea that gives them a chance to be heard. Since these individuals usually do not occupy an organizational platform, their advice is unseasoned by operational responsibility and they find it easy to support abstract notions. Still other individuals are exceptionally articulate, and this gives their counsel the advantage of being well presented. These latter have special appeal for the administrator because he is prone to be impatient with the obscure and to rate an idea by the ease with which he understands it. There is a difference between pretty words and wise words, however, and the administrator must learn to distinguish between them if he is to turn for advice to the most valuable, rather than to the most voluble, sources.

Administration is largely a matter of using the minds of others, and this means the administrator, to an extent, survives on the advice that he gets. This also means that he can be incapacitated by the advice he receives if he isn't careful how he uses it. Advice should be used as a dictionary rather than as a Bible and should provide explanations, rather than solutions, for the administrator. The final decision is not as much a right of the administrator as it is a duty. Aside from the requirements of continuity that necessitate consistency in decision making, the obligations of organizational integrity demand that the administrator make up his own mind on those decisions that are going to wear the makeup of his office. This does not mean that he cannot delegate or that he should not seek the best advice he can get. It does mean that he needs an open mind rather than an empty one easily filled with the conclusions of others. He needs to be more interested in other people's definitions and evaluations than in their personal solutions of the problems which are brought to him. Problems which properly come to his desk should be those which require his unique and singular perspective. The solutions should bear the distinguishing mark of his own way of thinking if he is to personally influence the direction and character of the enterprise. Simply reading out loud the thoughts of others is an unlikely way for the administrator to develop his voice in the organization.

Retaining the distinct color and shade of his own turn of mind is very difficult for the administrator. There is a strong tendency for him to become culture-bound and lose the distinguishing features of his own way of thinking in the organizational milieu. The decisions of the administrator, in the long run, must be validated by the actions of his subordinates, and this causes him to look down, rather than up, for sanction. Since he can influence his group only through being influenced by it, he faces the problem of recognizing and observing the values of others without assimilating them. This means that because of the demands of his position, the administrator is continuously faced with the hazard of having his personal identity captured by his own followers. This chauvinism inherent in the administrative process is accentuated by the strong desire for friendship and the need to be liked exhibited by almost all individuals. Because we want to be liked, we tend to shape our thinking to appeal to as many of those around us as possible. Because the administrator has so many people around him and these have such varied views and interests, he cannot develop a way of thinking common to all of them. For this reason, he is more prone to temper his outlook than to recast it. This manner of accommodation follows the principle that the more passive one's outlook is, the greater the number of people who will fit into it; and the more ambiguous it is, the less the number who will be offended by it. The trouble with such a recipe is that it can produce a "patty-cake" type of administration that has little influence on the organization. Being liked is wonderful for the administrator, but having an impact is essential. The role of the administrator is to provide flavor and character to the administration and not to neutralize it.

How to take advice and not become an administrative advice addict represents a very difficult problem for the administrator. Leaning on the advice of others can easily become habit forming and cost the administrator his confidence in his own judgment. The better the advice he gets, the more damaging it can be to his sense of self-value. Dependency is a self-feeding characteristic in that it encourages more dependency, rather than less, as time goes on. People who do not work out their problems for themselves miss the only exercise that can lead to self-improvement and self-confidence. The development of mind and will, like getting a suntan, is something that no one else can do for the individual, and it occurs only when the individual exposes himself. Similarly, the more the administrator is exposed to the tensions around him, the greater the exposure he can tolerate on subsequent occasions. Admittedly, a person can become sunburned by overexposure, and the administrator is foolish not to prepare himself with the best information and counsel he can get before venturing into the middle of a situation. His problem is to observe the difference between acquiring advice and acquiescing to it. Or to carry the suntan analogy to a conclusion, he should use advice as a lotion rather than as an umbrella.

The administrator who attempts to practice what everyone tells him pretty soon runs out of any room in which to practice. Most administrative problems are people problems, and the decisions the administrator makes often represent choices between people. Trying to do what everyone says is bound to result in a collision of the policies and practices that are adopted. The administrator's efforts to avoid getting caught between his own conflicting decisions can lead to an ambidextrous sort of administration in which the administrator starts dealing with both hands. Aside from the effects that such dealer's option has on continuity and consistency of policy, it is likely to give the administrator a reputation for double-dealing.

It is easy for the administrator to get off course if he doesn't have one. Getting his decisions from a grab bag is likely to confuse the administrator as much as those around him. Much is said about policies as a control of others, but it may be that they perform an equally important function in controlling the administrator. Stated policies represent an impersonal force which serves to reduce the dependence of the enterprise on the whims of the administrator and to protect the administrator from the pressures of others. Once he has clearly and openly enunciated a policy, the administrator pretty well locks himself on course. A declared policy is a heavy encumbrance on the administrator's freedom of action since it represents a precommitment to others. It provides a public sign post declaring the course the administrator should take and organizationally embarrasses him if he ignores or misses it. Because he must justify his deviations from established policies, he is more likely to try to observe them. Also, others will recognize that the course is well defined and will be less likely to try to lead the administrator away from it. Admittedly, a course that is well defined by policies is hard to change even when there are legitimate reasons for the administrator to change it. But unless he has set up policies to mark the course for both himself and the organization, the administrator will find it difficult to keep on course. It will be impossible for him to ever really know where he is going unless he knows the way he is taking to get there.

The administrator with a one-track mind is as likely to get off course as the administrator who doesn't know his own mind. In some ways the former represents a greater hazard. Jolting experiences are likely to teach the indiscriminate administrator that he can't go in all directions at the same time and thus cause him to improve his ways. But, since successful executives must be somewhat resolute with rather narrowly focused aims, successful experience can cause them to become too single-minded. This can lead to the administrator's using a "single means" approach to administration in which he is both unable and unwilling to recognize alternatives. This sort of practice not only decreases the chance that the best solution will be adopted but it increases the risk of decision making by putting all the eggs in one basket. This represents an unwise and imprudent move for a couple of important reasons. The failure to examine and set up alternatives means that the administrator has provided no escape hatch if the backwash from the decision is too violent. More important, it makes no allowances for the fact that the one sure thing in administration is that all conditions are subject to change. For this reason, solutions are ever in need of repair, and one characteristic of a good solution is a built-in provision for correction.

Misplaced people are perhaps the greatest single cause of unbalance in administration. The administration is made up of people, and these people must fit their administrative niches if the administration is to be trim and shapely. The choosing and promoting of subordinates is an important test of the administrator's judgment. This fact has been widely recognized, and administrators have sought help from any and all quarters in developing an infallible method by which to select their assistants. In recent years, considerable effort has been devoted to the problem of describing the traits of the effective administrator. Successful administrators have been cross-sectioned at work, at home, and at play in an effort to ascertain the common traits possessed by those who have demonstrated competence. As one reviews these efforts, he is impressed with the similarity of the traits listed for the effective administrator and those usually ascribed to the average good citizen. Certainly, the effective administrator must be honest and loyal, possess integrity and enthusiasm, and love his fellow men if he is going to be allowed to run loose in society and not be avoided by his own secretary. It is very doubtful, however, that he can parlay those virtues alone into a successful career as an administrator. Possession of the proper traits is not in itself sufficient. It is their appropriate use that determines the degree of administrative success. From the same piece of steel one may fashion a lock or a burglar's tool for breaking the lock. Administrative effectiveness cannot be predicted by the segmented attributes of the individual but rather by his total actions and reactions. Administration is practiced in situations and is also the practice of creating situations. It is what the administrator does or does not do that produces an effect on the organization. Said in other words, it is the sum of his behavior that determines the sort of influences the administrator will have on the organization.

Despite all the research that has been done and all the tests that have flowed from it, the administrator is still largely on his own in choosing his team. He still has no infallible way to select his people. The tests can indicate intelligence and aptitude, but they can't measure talent and attitude. Capability is quite different from accomplishment, and in administration it is the latter that counts. This means that past performance continues to be the major criterion available to administration in the selection process. But, for a number of reasons, administration does not always use wisely the evidence available from that source. We are prone to rate a person's qualifications for a higher position by the way he served us in his present position rather than by the way he would serve us in the new position. We forget that the tactics that got him into the foremanship of the supply room may not be the ones that should make him the head of the procurement department. Also, we tend to equate interests and abilities. Because an individual has a high interest in sales, we are likely to think he also has a high ability in that work. Or, conversely, we may think that high ability in sales means that he will have a high interest. While it is probably true that people will, over a period of time, come to dislike doing things that they can't do well, there is little evidence that they will necessarily work hard at things they can do well. Further, we have a tendency to use the selection process as a means of creating an administrative sanctuary. Promotions are made and individuals are retained because of their loyalty and out of deference to their long service. Also, we give preference to the charmers by confusing the affable and cooperative with the competent and the effective. Similarly, we are prone to become blinded by a glaring trait and let it transcend all the rest. If the individual is especially strong or especially weak in a particular trait, we tend to let it overshadow all the rest and rate him high or low mostly on the basis of that one. Too, we let our first impressions become fixed, and, to a large extent, we continue to evaluate a person by his initial success or failure. This means that those who make the best first impression usually become better because they increasingly garner our attention and support. Conversely, those who make the poorest initial impression become poorer because of increasing lack of attention and even hostility on our part. To often we overlook the fact that people are dynamic and change because of countless influences in and out of their work. This often keeps us from noticing deteriorating performance until it is so far advanced that radical steps are necessary. In the other direction, it prevents us from recognizing latent and emerging qualities that would change our assessment of an individual. Finally, because administrators live in the here and now and must get the job done today, we are apt to prefer experience to potential. This desire to be sure the job is handled adequately today is one of the reasons that the potential of individuals in the administrative group is rarely developed to its fullest. It also means that the fullest potential of the enterprise is never realized, since we are utilizing criteria that minimize the probability of failure rather than criteria that maximize the likelihood of success.

The administrator must
be adept at adapting

9 Administration is a constant center of change. In a real sense, the most important thing the administrator administers is change. Administration can be defined as the constant reconciliation of the enterprise to a constantly shifting environment. Effective administration is custom-tailored to fit the enterprise and its environment. This tailoring is a continuous task, since neither the enterprise nor the environment will stay put. No enterprise or organization is exempt from change, even over short periods of time. This means that administration is a continuous "tape measure" process. Fitted administration, however, requires a willingness and ability on the part of the administrator to adapt to, as well as to recognize, changing circumstances. Unless he possesses the necessary degree of flexibility, he cannot expect to accommodate to the shifting circumstances which constantly confront him and the organization.

Administrative accommodation is always a difficult thing. First, there is the problem of morality—what is right or wrong. At what

point does administrative flexibility begin to equate with amoral-
ity and represent an unconcern with right and wrong? There is,
of course, no absolute answer except at the extremes. Most situations faced by the administrator cannot be answered for him by
an administrative catechism or by the Ten Commandments. At
best, these provide him only with general rules. They point the
general direction he should go, but they do not work out the
specific trail for him; and he is, to a large extent, on his own as he
tries to cut an administrative path without cutting moral corners.
The administrator is confronted often by crossroads which are
barren of ethical signposts. The push of the organization behind
him and the heavy traffic created by the environment around him
will not let him stop and hope that Heaven will send someone
along to show him the right way. This means that he must develop his own set of personal convictions regarding goodness and
badness so he can have a built-in moral compass available at each
turn of the road.

Without a set of established convictions the administrator can
be so flexible and broad-minded that he doesn't know the difference between right and wrong. The problem with convictions,
however, is that they are what the individual believes and not
necessarily what he ought to believe. They are dangerously like
prejudices, and the individual who has them usually can't tell the
difference. Both prejudices and convictions in a way represent
frozen beliefs, and the one is as difficult to change as the other.
The administrator needs the strength of his convictions, but he
needs also to occasionally check their continuing validity if he is
going to be sure that he really is standing up for his convictions
rather than leaning on his prejudices.

The administrator who lives by his prejudices believes in
change, but he usually wants to change everything except himself.
He is prone to always be right in his own mind and to uphold the
idea that the king can do no wrong. He is apt to practice a sort of
self-communion and insist on taking his text from the scriptures
according to the administrator. The big trouble with the high-
minded is that they can easily become high-handed and unknowingly adopt an attitude that says the ends they seek justify any
means they choose. They sometimes develop a special brand of
intolerance and seek to suppress the opposition with strong appli-
cations of righteous wrath and moral indignation. They see them-

selves as men of high principles but do not always realize that they may have the wrong principles or that there is a chance that they may be misapplying the right ones.

The tendency to develop a single-value concept handicaps the ability of some administrators to adjust to changing situations. These administrators cannot adjust because they cannot compromise. They do not see that almost all good is accomplished at the expense of other good and that choices are usually between varying values. Also, they cannot recognize that gains are seldom made that do not require some kind of sacrifice. They forget that there are few choices where the gain is absolute and that usually one must take a little of the bad in order to get some of the good. For example, those of us who believe strongly in free enterprise may be smart to accept, and even seek, government intervention on problems which cannot be handled privately but which, if left unsolved, may endanger large areas that are being successfully managed under private means. It is the largest total value to be derived, rather than the largest single value, that should control the administrator's decisions. A number of smaller values may far outweigh a single value, no matter how large the single value may be. Decisions may be partly right and partly wrong at the same time in the sense that they may both help and hurt. If administration is, in fact, a matter of risk taking, this must mean that certain desired values are often jeopardized.

The administrator can be locked into his own mistakes by worshipping precedent. The origin of certain policies and practices in an organization may be so ancient as to be unknown, but their continuing wisdom goes unquestioned. They are perpetuated because they have become organizational dogma, and anyone who questions them is classed as an organizational agnostic. Like the lighthouse that now burns its light so bravely several miles inland because of a shifted shoreline, certain administrative policies may have saved the corporate ship in days gone by. Most administrative policies lack the picturesque appeal of old lighthouses, however, and to outsiders they may seem more like continuing to cook on a kerosene stove. The fact that a thing once worked well, or even that it still works, should not entitle it to an administrative "pass." The kerosene stove probably works better today than it did in grandma's time—but this isn't grandma's time. The outmoded policies and practices that still do work probably represent a greater hazard to the administrator than those that don't. They are like a concealed leak in a water main that reduces the vitality and strength of the stream without being detected. The effective administrator looks to the past for guidance, but he does not let it become an idol he worships. Company tradition and company symbolism can permanently embalm the organizational vigor of the company. Walking about in high-button shoes is no way to demonstrate vitality.

The worship of precedent isn't the only cult with which administrators sometimes affiliate. Almost every administrator joins the "sacred cow" sect at times and puts certain policies and practices off limits to reconsideration or discussion. They are sacred cows because they are so closely identified with the administrator. They are his brain child, and he feels that he must defend his mental offsprings even after they have, through organizational trial, been proven delinquent. It is in this connection that the administrator is victimized by one of the proven universals of human nature. This is the urge all human beings demonstrate to defend, fully and blindly, whatever they own or author. The fact that the most casual of circumstances may have prompted an individual to purchase a particular suit of clothes will not prevent a deep feeling of resentment over a slight criticism of it. We respond the same way when someone criticizes one of our ideas, no matter how off-the-cuff or how old it might be. The strength of this urge to be eternally justifying anything that has been closely identified with us makes it necessary that the administrator be careful what he puts his administrative brand on. He can stay off the defensive more often if he guards against committing himself too early and too strongly to courses of action that are in the discussion stage. But even where he does have a great idea, he can't keep it great by canonizing it.

The pull of personal affiliation and association is a powerful force in favor of the *status quo*. Just as we often defend the *status quo* because we helped create it, or think that we did, we also defend it simply because we are associated with it. It is a sort of virtue by association that causes us to praise and defend things merely because we are linked to them. The administrator is, of course, ultimately responsible for the policies and practices in the organization and naturally feels that an attack on any policy is an attack on his administration and on him personally. If he isn't careful, however, he may find himself going to great length to explain and justify practices in the organization which he really knows little about and which subsequent investigation may show are actually contrary to policy. If he is too quick to defend, he may find himself sanctifying someone else's error. It is true that one cannot disassociate himself from his own herd, but this does not mean that the administrator must play Sitting Bull and refuse to budge. It is no reflection on him or the other members of the organization if he recognizes that the grass has become greener on the next hill. Change does not necessarily mean that things have been done wrong in the past, but the failure to make needed change is a guarantee that they will be done wrong in the future. Few successful administrators have ever gained their status in the *status quo*.

The *status quo* seems to have an ideological appeal to administrators, and one can safely say that the usual administrator is a conservative. The nature of his work tends to make him that way. The maintenance of organizational stability is a prime function of the administrator, and his effectiveness (and often his administrative life) depends upon his protecting that stability. He can afford only as much change as he can reconcile with organizational stability, and thus he tends to seek change in small-size packages and on the installment plan. Organizational control is another of his major goals, and this requires a high degree of conformity unless different members and parts of the organization are to go off in all directions at the same time. Innovation is a natural enemy of conformity, and the administrator must hold innovation within digestible limits unless he is to lose control and become simply the figurehead for a freewheeling organization. The need for conformity not only affects the willingness of the administrator to recognize and cater to a changed environment but tends to make him suspicious and distrustful of other members of the organization who attempt to introduce change. The role of continuity in operating efficiency is also apt to prejudice the administrator against novelty. Operational smoothness depends upon a well-charted course of action and upon a well-trained organization. The familiarity that comes with continuity of policies and practices is the means to both. Like the unexpected rain on a Los Angeles expressway, the new and strange may bring operations to a slow and jerking pace with an occasional organizational pileup. Because the advantages of stability and continuity are so well recognized, they can tend to make the administrator more concerned with shaking down the organization than with shaking it up.

All organized effort is, by definition, structured effort. By the same definition it is also conditioned effort. The administrator soon learns to be cautious about tinkering with either the structure or the conditioning and, for this reason, is tempted to practice a "don't rock the boat" sort of administration. His chief concern becomes one of keeping the organization in the groove. The effective administrator learns, however, that there is a significant difference between being in the groove and being in a rut. It is the difference between holding the organization steady and holding it down. His willingness to make appropriate concessions to a constantly changing environment will determine whether he actually functions as an administrator or simply takes over the role of organizational caretaker. This does not mean the administrator must give up his conservative outlook. The consequences of his actions are usually of such importance to the enterprise that he must look before he leaps. The fact that he represents the last checkpoint at which ideas may be examined dictates that he act with restraint and with caution. None of these factors, however, justify his failure to continuously reorient the organization to an altering environment. A conservative driver doesn't drive on the wrong side of the road and doesn't exceed the speed limit. But neither does he park in the middle of a busy highway. There is a difference between being conservatively progressive and becoming progressively conservative.

Besides being conservative, the effective administrator is likely to be determined in his goals. He knows how easy it is for a program to become sidetracked by either inattention or opposition. He also knows the value of momentum and realizes that even a modest change in direction can in itself produce a strong braking action. He learns that he cannot deal simultaneously with all his problems and that there are some which he has to dog tenaciously one at a time. He also learns that there is a danger of the tractable being detracted and that an open mind can become a drafty hollow that represents an inviting entrance for interference. All of these things mean that the administrator must develop a certain level of stubborn purposefulness if his objectives are to be accomplished instead of mothballed. This level is difficult to maintain, however, and the purposeful can too easily become the obstinate. Steadfastness can be an appealing disguise for mulishness, but acting like a mule won't pass for long as horse sense.

The need to institutionalize policies and procedures encourages organizational sclerosis. In his efforts to prevent random behavior within the organization, the administrator ties tasks and activities into systems. Being a part of systematized effort has appeal to individual employees because of the yearning everyone has for a fixed environment. Personnel learn to think in terms of the system of which they are a part rather than in terms of the whole organization. Administration likewise has a tendency to evaluate the whole by evaluating the manner in which each of the systems is performing. Under such circumstances, following the system may become more important, to personnel and administration alike, than final results. The system then becomes an end in itself, and the effort is to protect the system rather than change it.

The tendency to confuse practices with purposes sometimes prevents the administrator from acclimating the organization to emerging circumstances. The administrator should be goal-oriented and should fix the policies and practices of the organization to fit its goals. It is the policies and practices, however, that make up the operations, since goals are ends and not means. The administrator thus attains the goals by implementing policies and practices. This means that his attention and interest become centered on the functioning rather than on the function, and he worries more about how things are done than about what is done. Whatever concern he has about change tends to involve better ways of doing things instead of better things to do. This is sort of like working to improve the old ferry service instead of building a bridge across the river, or perhaps like the professor who works hard on better answers to questions that no one is asking any more. Smoothness and efficiency of operation are, of course, important concerns for the administrator, but they are not his only concerns. He can become so engrossed in how things are done that he fails to keep the enterprise in tune with the changes that are taking place around it. The administrator must remember that doing things well does not always mean that he is doing the best things.

A "middle-age spread" in administration is a hazard to all successful organizations. Because things are going well, the administration is prone to let well enough alone and rest comfortably on
its laurels. It grows tolerant of its environment and reacts to the
forces being generated by the environment only to the extent
necessary to remain comfortable. It quits "running scared" and,
like the hare racing the tortoise, develops a disdain for its competition. It thinks it has the resources and the ability to outrun
the opposition, so it ignores the progress that the opposition is
making. Under such circumstances, the administration can begin
to spend more time polishing the organization's image than planning the organization's destiny. The thinking seems to be that the
organization has reached the top, and the administration wants to
make a great to-do about it rather than to do a great deal about
it. For those enterprises at the top, life would be wonderful if life
stood still. The problem is that life won't stand still, and this
problem is greater for those outfits on top than for those below. It
is easier to be shaken off the top than off the bottom, and those at
the top are always more exposed than those at the lower levels.
The top is never an ideal spot on which to coast or to ignore the
road signs that signal sharp turns ahead. It is hard to keep awake
on a full stomach, and the administrative complacency that may
come with success can wreck the organization on its own excellence.

Administrative slumber may be due to the inability of the administrator to recognize changes in the environment. It is not too
difficult for him to detect changes after they have occurred and
the results have kicked him in his administrative shins. It is a
much more difficult matter to identify changes while they are taking shape. The drift into organizational ineffectiveness can be
gradual and unnoticed unless the administration maintains a
sharp lookout. Changes in the environment are often subtle and
obscure, and if the administrator waits for their backfire to
awaken him he may sleep through the time when adjustment is
easiest, or even still possible. The administrative siesta can sometimes go undisturbed for long periods of time because the organization may make its own adjustments if the administration fails to
do so. The one sure thing about organizations is that they will always change. Usually, most of this unplanned change is a natural
adjustment made in the general direction of the goals of the en-

terprise. It represents spontaneous responses on the part of the different individuals and segments of the organization to the problems and situations constantly confronting them and their activities. Up to a point, such informal responses are essential at each level in the organization if the work is to be accomplished smoothly and promptly. The alternative would be an impossible spelling out of every eventuality. This in turn would create an untenable amount of red tape. And if individuals were forced to follow such minutely prescribed policies and procedures, the effects on the initiative and morale of the members of the organization would be devastating. For these reasons, effective administration draws only the formal outline and depends upon the informal responses at the point of contact with the environment to paint in the detail. These responses provide a means for the various parts of the organization to maintain a flexible position and suitably accommodate to the contour of the shifting environment. Natural adjustments by segments of the organization at the point of contact with the environment can keep the total enterprise on general course for a time somewhat in the manner of a blindfolded person feeling and bumping his way across a room. But sooner or later, the changing landscape becomes too unfamiliar, and the enterprise playing blindman's buff with its environment ends up in the rough or up against a stone wall. After this happens, the failure of the administration to make the necessary changes in the general course of the enterprise can no longer be obscured, and radical adjustments become the order of the day. The hibernating administrator can seldom count on a gentle awakening from his administrative slumber.

Recognizing change while it is going on is not enough to prevent the enterprise from being bushwhacked by change. The administrator has to anticipate change and take steps to nullify or exploit its effects even before he knows what it is going to be or when it is going to occur. He has to be prepared to point the unknown in a useful direction when it becomes known. This means that he must plan for future eventualities at the same time he is wrestling with today's actualities. Admittedly, the administrator can never be certain, but through planning, he can know when he should be uncertain. Proper planning can provide him with an administrative road map which will help him identify events as they unfold around him. Since by planning he will have taken the offensive toward change, he can at least use a pitcher's stance, instead of a catcher's, in his workout with the future.

With all of its virtues, planning is not a synonym for adapting, however. It is only a part of the story, and for a number of reasons it sometimes may not be the best part. Planning is only as good as its implementation, and the failure to implement a plan, or faulty implementation, can negate the best of planning. Not only do the best laid schemes of mice and men "gang aft a-gley," they also grow out of date, and the rigid following of yesterday's plans can keep the enterprise hitched to programs as outdated as yesterday's timetable. The most monumental plan can, with a change in circumstances, become a tombstone for the administrator. There is a great difference between using planning for a sense of direction and using it for a rigid determination of destination. The effective administrator never knows too exactly and finally where he is taking the enterprise. Much must be left to administrative opportunism as the future becomes the present. He must, of course, have goals, but these are never ultimates and never static, and they should change, even as he is trying to achieve them. This means that planning is not so much a matter of setting future goals as it is a matter of being prepared for them.

Unless the administrator understands the role and limitations of planning, his actions can vitiate the purpose planning is supposed to serve. The existence of a plan can soothe that needed tug of anxiety that must be the eternal companion of effective administration. The human urge to want to feel safe is so strong that we are tempted to seek an antidote for our fears rather than a treatment for the hazards that prompt them. Planning cannot remove the uncertainties of the future. Its purpose is to increase the inventory of possibilities for handling future eventualities. Contrary to some of the things that one reads about planning, it is not so much a prediction process as it is an action process. This overemphasis on prediction is perhaps the reason that it is most often treated as a staff function and held in something less than high esteem by the line officers. Proper planning means both thinking ahead and doing ahead. While it is an exercise in time, it must depend upon present action for whatever influence it is to have on future consequences. It looks to the future, but seeks to provide for it in the present. This is necessarily true because we shape our future by the way we solve today's problems. In a real sense, we prepare for the future by staying out of the way of it. Each decision needs to provide for contingencies so that account can be taken of impacts that only the future will disclose. This can be done only by leaving as many alternatives as possible indefinitely open. Unless the administrator is to be more involved in undoing decisions than in making them, he must live simultaneously in the present and the future. Effective planning is not so much an attempt to predict the future as it is an effort to protect it.

Going down a one-way street doesn't give the administrator much opportunity for turning about. It seems to be a human characteristic to risk too much on absolutes. Often decisions are made and actions are taken with no provision for necessary corrections. Once a decision is in motion, its trajectory is unchangeable. Like a high-wire artist, a decision proves either good or dead. A good decision is seldom characterized by a point of no return. It is marked by built-in switching devices that provide both for safety and for increased opportunity. Keeping on course doesn't always mean keeping on a beeline. Effectiveness in administration doesn't lie solely in knowing the right solution but perhaps more in knowing how long to perpetuate a solution.

Adaptability isn't always simply a matter of change. The administrator can get the enterprise off the main drive and into a cul-de-sac as easily by turning too quickly as by turning too late. Adaptability is more a matter of fitting than of changing. Taking the first suit off the rack is a poor way to assure a fit. There are important reasons why the administrator is tempted to cash in his trading stamps too quickly, however. When things are going badly, any change is appealing. At such times the administrator is likely not to be half as critical of the cure as he is of the ailment. Another reason for quick change is the delay in the notice that the administrator receives when a problem exists. Most problems can be figured only by the past. They show up more often in the results than in the process. Most problem solving is actually troubleshooting, and the administrator is usually working under the gun. The essence is time rather than timing. Said another way, most organizational adjustments are mothered by necessity rather than by design. As Benjamin Franklin said, "Necessity never made a good bargain." Such *ad hoc* administration seldom assures anything except more problems. One adjustment always calls for another. Admittedly, this is true of all change. Planned change, however, leaves the way prepared for subsequent change, but impromptu change only leaves the way for anything. Sometimes it is better for the administrator to sleep on what he wants done than to stay awake over what he has done.

Administrative changes may be delayed or never attempted because such change often involves the administrator's changing his mind, and this is never an easy thing for him to do. Aside from the emotional problems faced by all individuals in admitting they were wrong, the nature of the administrator's work can place serious difficulties in the way of his changing his mind. Because of the need for the administrator to demonstrate decisiveness when he moves, he has a tendency to act too positively and to overcommit himself. Similarly, because he is action-oriented, he seeks the strongest support possible for each idea he attempts to implement and thus has a tendency to overconvince and to oversell others. Both of these tendencies can delimit the area of administrative maneuverability needed if the administrator is to make any necessary adjustments because of changing circumstances. All decisions take on the meaning of contracts. They are in the nature of treaties with the different parties affected, and those affected have a right to depend upon the decision and to plan accordingly. This makes it exceedingly difficult for the administrator to change things when they need to be changed, and if he has promised too much or sold others too strongly on his decision, his difficulties are multiplied when he has to change course. To those adversely affected it appears that the administrator is reneging on a promise, implied if not explicit. The inevitability of change invests every decision with some degree of contingency, and this means that every decision must be endowed with an equal degree of hedging room.

Closely related to the above problem is the importance that administrators necessarily attach to loyalty. Since they need many hands to do the job, they need the loyalty of many people. No one knows better than the administrator the compelling role of organizational loyalty. It is an adhesive that helps hold the organization together, and disloyalty is appropriately considered a cardinal sin organizationally, and one which cannot be tolerated if the organization is to function effectively. The administrator also knows that loyalty can be purchased only by trading in kind and that he gets back only the loyalty that he gives. Further, by some kind of moral alchemy, loyalty supersedes almost all other values in the minds of most people, and the administrator is expected to do outrage to other values for the sake of loyalty. Because the administrator cannot totally ignore the bonds that loyalty sometimes imposes upon him, he does not always have a free hand in making needed changes. While there is no complete answer to this problem, the administrator has to keep in mind the fact that the freedom of administrative action is at best an indentured freedom and that he must guard closely the number and sorts of loyalties that can place claims on him.

The administrator can mortgage his freedom of action even more heavily by practicing a sort of *quid pro quo* administration that places him under obligations to others, both inside and outside the organization. One aspect of this practice is the administrator's acceptance of favors and gifts from those who seek to buy his influence. Such administrators finally have no influence because they come to be recognized as panhandlers rather than problem handlers. Another aspect is the conflict-of-interest situations, which have been widely publicized in recent years and which the administrator creates by attempting to serve two masters at the same time. More subtle and much more common to the usual administrator are the alliances that naturally encrust administration. Administration depends for its success upon the actions of others and is, in a sense, always trading for support. This trading takes many forms (including wages, working conditions, and other tangible and intangible benefits), but it essentially means providing as many inducements to the individual as are consistent with the behavior desired and the welfare of the enterprise. At higher organizational levels it often becomes a matter of "I'll scratch your back if you'll scratch mine." This means, in effect, that the administrator creates over a period of time a number of back-scratching alliances that restrict his freedom and inhibit change. Things often cannot be done because they will disturb the support necessary for the doing of other things. Admittedly, some reciprocal back scratching is required in the administrator's recruitment of effective support, but he must recognize the infirmities of the obligated administrator. Unwise trading on current problems can make him into an administrative broker with little left in the way of "futures."

The efforts of the administrator to introduce change into the organization can be blockaded by alignments among others as well as by his own mutual-aid alliances. Over a period of time the aggressive administrator steps on enough toes to stimulate the formation of mutual-protection pacts among various individuals and activities in the organization. These compacts usually do not call for rebellion but rather for a sort of passive resistance to new ideas and ways. This type of resistance is usually expressed through the sudden support one or more departments start giving to the threatened practices and methods of another department or to the seemingly unending number of potential problems that other departments suggest when change in one department is being discussed. At times this passive resistance may be unknowing and unintended and can come from individuals who ordinarily are the strongest supporters of the administrator. Also, such resistance may represent a discrete incident each time and have no general significance. It does demonstrate that horizontal obligations develop among colleagues in an organization and that these can sometimes be as controlling as the vertical ones that develop up and down the administrative hierarchy. They can be more frustrating than the vertical ones to the administrator because he is not a party to them and cannot be sure of their scope and intensity. He cannot, of course, ignore such collateral resistance, but he may be wise not to respect it too strongly unless he can specifically identify the interests of the recalcitrants that might be adversely affected by a particular change. Human nature being the ambivalent thing it is, we can act one way and feel the opposite; or, we can support something for one reason and hope we lose for another. Individuals may feel obligated to attempt to block a change but be relieved if they fail.

The desire to be a "nice guy" may deter the administrator from making indicated changes in the organization. The hankering all of us have to be known as a good fellow has been considerably enlarged in the administrator during recent years by the "friendlier than thou" philosophy of administration which has been preached so strongly to him. It is very difficult, however, to always serve up administrative change with a human relations dressing. Change can be painful and unpopular, and it often involves applying real pressure to real people. The administrator must remember, however, that he is competing for excellence rather than popularity and that he must cater to a changing environment before he can cater to congeniality. Needed change can be as effectively smothered by brotherhood as it can be by the administrator's worst enemies.

Perhaps the "apple a day to keep tension away" philosophy helps account for the reluctance that some administrators have to attempt change. They have been told that people resent and fear change. It would be difficult to show that this generalization has ever been proved. In fact, as a general rule, the opposite would appear to be true. All advertising studies show the power of the word "new," and one only has to review the advertisements to see that more emphasis is given to change than to any other characteristic. An interesting and convincing example of the readiness of people to change is the almost universal and radical change in the styling of automobiles and clothes that occurs every year. One can hardly argue that change is stoutly resisted when he recalls the unbelievable switch to the chemise frock that occurred a few years back. Reaction to change always seems to be specific and individual. The psychological factors involved are neutral and are just as likely to facilitate change as to retard it. Whether they facilitate or retard change apparently depends upon the particular change and the consequences as seen by each person affected. There is nothing psychopathic about a person who resists something that could leave him worse off. It isn't that he is afraid of change, but rather that he is anxious about what it might do to him. This means that people want to have some notion of what the change involves so that they can measure its personal implications. The fact that they understand the change will not guarantee their approval of it, however. If it is not appropriate to their personal interests, they can hardly be expected to applaud it warmly. Resistance to change can be expected at times because change will at times adversely affect some of those involved. Resistance is not an appropriate excuse for administrative default, however.

Resistance can be expected to prevent some changes and to slow the pace of others. There is often a difference or a lag in what the administrator would like to do and what the real world around him will allow. But the real world around him can be changed despite its resistance. This is proved by the fact that it does continuously change, and it is just such change that requires the administrator to attempt compensating changes. The problem of administration is how to appropriately engineer the desired change. This means setting realistic goals for change and packaging it in such a way that it is most acceptable. If people are as smart as they are supposed to be, we can expect them to question change in terms of its appropriateness to themselves, their group, and the organization as they see it. This means that for change to be acceptable, the goals need to be visible and obtainable, and the change attempted must offer improvement and appear worth the trouble. Because change implies criticism, an effort must be made to save the faces of those involved in the change. No one likes to be told his petticoat is showing, even though he wants to know if it does show. It may be that people often do not change because they are fenced in. In some instances they feel they must act a certain way because they are expected to act that way. There are times when people would like to change their ways if they could find an excuse to do so. The administrator must remember that organizations operate as a totality and that individuals and activities are locked in general step with the whole. Often one change is dependent upon or compelled by another. It is difficult to change one's socks without first removing one's shoes.

Making the right turn requires that one have a good view of the road. The administrator sometimes misses the turn because he gets in his own way. He gets so used to the road that he stops watching it and starts going by what he knows rather than by what is happening. This is a natural sort of habit to develop. As a result of our experience, all of us tend to develop blind spots which make it hard to observe events that stare us in the face. We see what we know and very little of what we are looking at. Some of our most important ideas come when we finally see what we have been looking at but not noticing. Experience is an invaluable ally of the administrator, but it has to be used with caution. Too much dependence on it can lead to a process of self-imitation. We tend to interpret our experience to fit what we already know and to read into it what we have learned to expect. If we leave it too much up to our experiences to feed us, we soon can become self-impoverished. Our experience does have a story to tell, and an important one, but unless we keep quiet we will never get to hear it.

One of the products of experience is that it causes us to get set in our ways. It is easy for the administrator to become institutionalized as he becomes experienced. Experience fixes a pattern as he continues the successful ways and discontinues the unsuccessful ones. This means that the administrator increasingly utilizes only the proven and traditional and thus is more oriented toward the repetitive than the innovative. This trained-in preference for old ways over better ways ties him in an administrative straitjacket. Adaptability calls for getting rid of the old as well as for instituting the new. If the administrator always insists on sticking with the proven, he has little chance of ever changing for the better.

Changing his mind is perhaps the most difficult and complicated mental process an individual can undertake. As a cultural being he is not completely the master of his beliefs. His beliefs are molded to the greatest extent by environmental coercions he never recognizes and therefore can never question. Unwittingly, broad bands of outlooks are developed and adopted small bits at a time. We speak of a "closed" mind, and this is what it is. It is closed, and often apt to remain so, because it requires thousands of keys to unlock it. The locks that hold it closed are fabricated from literally thousands of unknown and unsuspected observations that must be disproved and removed before the mind can be opened. Reasoning can help identify the keys required to open the individual's mind, but it is not always a willing helper. Reasoning is used most often to support traditional views and oppose the novel. Usually, we say "it stands to reason" when we wish to stand pat. There is no easy answer to the problem of how the administrator can unlock his mind. It will help him, however, to be as careful as possible about what goes in and to remember that it may some time have to come out.

Change is usually difficult and can require much administrative energy and time. An overburdened administrator has little of either to spare. If he doesn't have the time to implement required changes, he probably doesn't have the time to see that they are necessary. Change presupposes evaluation and planning, and these are the least exciting activities of administration. Such evaluation doesn't compare with the excitement of wrestling with live, jumping problems. The difference between the two is sort of like the difference between the fun of fishing and the drudgery of cleaning the catch. It is not only lack of excitement, however, that keeps the administrator from getting around to taking stock. Problems do keep coming one after the other, and the administrator can become so involved that, like a kid jumping rope, he can't look up. Like the journals that one puts aside to read in his free time, evaluation and planning are likely to be put on the shelf until the pace lets up. But also like the journals that never get read, the postponed evaluation and planning never get done because administrators simply never have any free time unless they consciously make it.

Because administration is essentially a matter of adjustment and adaptation, neither change nor the evaluation and planning which must precede it are free-time activities. They represent a high-priority claim on the time of the administration, and the failure to honor this claim can eventually spell administrative bankruptcy. If the daily obligations are so heavy as to preclude adequate time for keeping the organization in step with its environment, the administrator should audit his time and that of his colleagues. The interest he doesn't pay to the changing environment is cumulative, and when he finally has to settle, he will find that the unpaid interest has compounded. Attending to changing circumstances, both internal and external, is a command performance for the administrator, and he cannot ignore the R.S.V.P. attached to each changing circumstance.

Administration is not a numbers game

10 The image of the administrator as a thinking man standing behind his judgment has been replaced in some circles by that of a "data addict" kneeling before a programmed prayer wheel. In this transistorized version of administration, linear programming and operations research have become passwords, and the computer has become the symbol of the administrative fraternity. The administrative world is pictured as a sort of mathematical preserve inhabited by sterile tape handlers who are afraid to venture a decision until they are sure right down to the nth digit after the decimal point. Apparently, the only contingencies the electronic-age administrator is supposed to encounter will come from his stubbing his electronic toe on the square roots of overgrown mathematical formulas.

There is nothing wrong with the administrator's trying to be sure. Being sure is a good way to be in administration—if one can be sure. The wrong comes from the excesses to which the administrator may go in trying to be sure and the damage which he can

200

inflict on his own judgment if he falls too hard for the extreme rationalism being advocated by those who apparently see administration as a sort of numbers game. There is much about administration to encourage the administrator to confuse exactness with excellence and to equate scientific methods with thoughtful practice. This chapter examines some of the reasons why this is true and why all the wondrous ways of processing data can never replace personal judgment in the practice of administration. What is said is not intended to deny the usefulness of mathematical techniques and data-processing hardware for the administrator. These can represent important aids in helping the administrator gather and organize the facts. But they are only added tools, and like all tools, their usefulness depends upon the manner of their use. Making them into something more than tools will succeed in making the administrator into nothing more than the keeper of the records.

The psychological safety promised by slide-rule administration should have great attraction to men who spend their lives trying to guess right. A mathematized approach to problem solving has much appeal to individuals who must develop and adopt answers without proof and who must bet their reputations and, at times, their jobs on propositions that can be tested only in the unfolding and uncertain future. In decision making, history must be written before it is made, and in a sense the administrator is always buying his reputation on credit. The notion that one can remove the uncertainties in his decision making by using certified recipes from a mathematical cookbook is enough to cause even the most confident of administrators to go numbers-happy. The desire to hide behind a statistical model goes beyond the administrator's search for personal cover and security, however. Administration is a matter of dealing with people, and both human and moral considerations often weigh heavily on the administrator's mind. For this reason, the opportunity to trade ethical concerns for a statistical justifier has quite an appeal to the administrator. He could live with himself more easily if he could place his ethical doubts in electronic escrow and let a mechanical conscience be his guide.

The fact that mathematics is a selfless thing presents an alluring thought to the administrator. It would be wonderful if he could depersonalize his decisions by clothing them in the formal dressings of mathematical methodology. The administrator occupies a position but acts as a person, and those affected by his actions find it difficult to take him positionally rather than personally. Actually, much of what the administrator does is selfless and results from the position he occupies. But, whether his actions are volitional or involuntary, the people on the receiving end of his decisions see his handwriting rather than the seal of his office. For this reason, the idea of organizationally disassociating himself from his actions by deputizing a machine to take the blame is likely to be quite captivating to the administrator. Pushing a button is an attractive alternative to pushing people, but hiding behind an electronic curtain is no way to develop the visibility needed to head the show. Trading the pesonal equation for a mathematical one can cost the administrator his personal identity and result in his becoming recognized as little more than a glorified caddy for a batch of punch cards.

Part of the administrator's fascination with quantifying techniques and hardware comes from the fact that the practice of administration is an art. It is a diffuse and formless art that is highly personal with each individual practitioner. To some extent this is true of all professions, but few other professions depend so much on an art rather than on a specific body of knowledge. Because the practice of administration is so subjective in nature, the administrator is likely to give a large place to methodology and form. Since those are tangible and objective, they provide concrete proof to all concerned, and especially to himself, that he is working with more than the seat of his pants. Because people tend to be suspicious of judgments that spring from a person's individuality, most of us try to make everything we do look objective. We go to great lengths to find data to support conclusions that we have already reached and to carefully explain the manner in which we reached those conclusions. We seem to prefer that our score be kept in terms of the methods we use rather than the judgment we demonstrate. In our efforts to appear objective, we sometimes disguise the subjective contributions of rich experience and tested insights by weak facts and marginal evidence. Admittedly, the process by which the administrator reaches a decision is an important factor in its acceptance, but this doesn't mean that he has to act as if his undocumented feeling on a problem were deceptive and unreal. A strong feeling often can be more acceptable and convincing to the other person than weak evidence.

In any event, it is doubtful that the administrator can make a poor decision look better by dressing it in a lot of facts.

The concept of a disinterested administrator sitting on his Olympian seat and arriving at important new truths by impartially reviewing the facts as they march past is a logical contradiction. The administrator must choose sides on an idea if he is to properly examine it. Choice is necessary intellectually if he is to understand the possibilities confronting him. It is only by taking one side or the other that one can examine a proposition. As in viewing a mountain, one cannot meaningfully see both sides of a proposition at the same time. By and in themselves facts mean nothing. Facts require some sort of assumption for their interpretation. They have meaning only as evidence for or against ideas. In this sense, an idea is an apparatus for explaining the meaning of facts. Unless the idea is set up, there is no means of testing the facts. In a manner of speaking, the administrator must create an answer before he can ask the questions.

Ideas are very subjective things. They represent a personal arrangement of the facts. The individual supporting an idea, or going against it, had to set up the facts to build a "case" for the position he holds. Because facts are used as building blocks, they cannot be selected impartially. In attempting to build a case, the builder must seek facts that will fit what he is building, and thus he must search for the facts he needs. A search for the facts is not a random search. It is a search for the "wanted." The specifications of the facts sought must be fairly well defined before the administrator starts looking. Unless he knows what he is looking for, he has no way of knowing when he has found it. He can be critical in the selection and use of the facts only if he knows what he wants them to do. If he is wise, he will only use "good" facts, and he will reject the entire idea if he cannot find the necessary good facts to build a valid case in support of it. If he does that, he need not worry about the fact that he chose the material with which to build the case. The material the administrator uses can never have any more value than the use he makes of it, anyway.

We like to think of decisions as springing self-induced from the facts at hand. The decision maker supposedly serves as a midwife who delivers whatever decisions the facts have conceived. The conception is supposed to occur without involvement of the decision maker—*in vacuo*, so to speak. This notion is no more than fiction. Decisions are always biased because the decision maker knows the consequences he desires from the decision. He uses the desired consequences to evaluate alternative decisions that might be made. Only after he has determined what he wants from a decision can he choose the facts that must be used in making the decision. One does not usually mix the ingredients for a cake without first establishing what sort of cake one wants to bake.

Too much has been written in administration of objectivity as if the administrator belonged to the neuter gender and was neither one thing nor another. The notion seems to be that he should straddle the fence while keeping an ear to the ground on both sides. While this would represent quite an acrobatic feat, it would be an administrative absurdity. The effective administrator is a position taker. This is necessary politically if he is to persuade others to action. He must make his position known if he expects others to know and support it. This does not mean that he should commit himself prematurely or that he should be dogmatically unyielding in his position. There are times when he needs to be ambiguous and oblique, however. He cannot expect to remain forever unimplicated and uncommitted. If he expects to have a hand in what is done, he must expect to show his hand. There is no purely nonpartisan way open to the administrator. The only way he can get into the game is to venture out of the locker room. If the administrator wants to keep on top, he cannot forever keep under cover.

One result of our distrust of subjectivity is an urge to quantify. We seem to attach the greatest validity to those things that can be counted and to pay least respect to those that cannot be put through an adding machine. The assignment of numerical values to things greatly assists the administrator in organizing and examining them and in determining their relative rank and relevance. It also serves to help impersonalize the influence of things on the administrator and the evaluations other people make of his use of things. Because numbers do greatly simplify his task and his relationships, the administrator tends to develop a predisposition to quantify. This predisposition is a mark of the effective administrator, but he has to be careful not to let the aura of his numbers blind his judgment. The deification of numbers can cause the administrator to favor those facts that can be measured and to push aside intangibles that may greatly exceed them in importance. He may forget that facts that cannot be quantified are still facts and must be dealt with. Dealing with unquantifiable intangibles is a particular responsibility of the administrator. The concrete and definable tangibles should be acted upon at the organizational level where they first appear if the organization is functioning properly and if the administrator is spending his time appropriately. The administrator ordinarily needs to become involved only when the facts outrun the organizational language and require high-level translation. Serving as the interpreter is not the only concern the administrator has with the "indefinables." The messages they bring may be the most crucial ones he receives. This is because his most important problems often are an inextricable scramble of value characteristics which defy distinct definition and discrete analysis. The sort of problems that are amenable to logic and yield to the rule of methods seldom possess great consequence for the administrator. It is the problems of people that are likely to affect the enterprise most significantly. These are the problems that most stubbornly resist logical reduction because they are so interwoven with the nonlogical values of individuals. It is the things which defy accurate description that should have first claim on the time and interest of the administrator. The things which can be reduced to machine language rarely represent a problem in organizational linguistics.

The ultimate concern of the administrator is with human action, and the particulars which affect human action often depend for their influence more on the way they are joined than on the way they are separated. The precision of the line by which the administrator can measure the meaning of each particular in a problem separately is severely restricted. Most particulars of human action become practically meaningless when viewed separately and outside the situation which they jointly constitute. This means that the administrator cannot look only for the particulars in a situation but must also consider their relationships to each other. He must look for the common thread that binds a set of particulars into a specific situation. The heavy emphasis given by employees last year to a demand for an increase in group life coverage may have come immediately after the sudden death of a fellow worker who left eight young children. Or, the new salary schedule for supervisory personnel that was so well received two months ago may look just the opposite when the new bonus ar-

rangement for top management is announced. Unlike the physicist or chemist who deals with inert values, the administrator
deals with feelings. The physicist and chemist can, with high
accuracy, work with the particulars in a compound, but the best
the administrator usually can do is size up the situation. If he
were required to work with precise particulars, he could seldom
do anything.

In the world of the animate, reasonably accurate predictions
are very hard to make. The administrator who overlooks the fact
that he is dealing with ever-shifting qualities runs the danger of
slipping on an administrative banana peel. People won't stay put.
They adapt quickly to other people's moves. In a way, life can be
described as a matter of continuous countervailing. It may be
that most of the things we do are to offset interferences rather
than to implement opportunities. This defensive quality of people
would not represent such a disadvantage to the administrator if
he were always dealing with people who were equally as informed and sophisticated as he. But like the expert bridge player
whose game is upset when he bases his play on the actions of
novice opponents, the administrator is at a serious disadvantage if
he attempts to anticipate too rationally and precisely the countermoves of others. He must not only consider their rational coun-
termeasures but he must allow for their irrational responses and
countertendencies. The "game theorists" from the mathematical
side of the house have blurred this fact in their efforts to apply
their methodology to administrative decision making. Administration may be a sort of game, but it is not the sort where there are
only two sides or where all those on the "other" side have similar
objectives. The worker at the bench and the salesman on the road
aren't basing their moves on a match with the boss. They are engaged in a match with their personal world, and their moves are
dictated by that larger opponent. The boss is a part of that personal world but he is only a part. He should not be surprised to
find that his strategies don't always fit the game the other fellow
is playing.

The scientific climate that prevails today is causing some administrators to suffer increasingly from delusions of accuracy in
decision making. The fact that the new mental hardware permits
the computation of the consequences of technical processes right
down to the last quiver of a decimal point is causing them to look

to their machines for similar accuracy in predicting the consequences of administrative acts. Unfortunately for these dreams of
electronically certified decisions, the world of the animate differs
from the world of the material, and our power to control nature
will always exceed our power to control man. Unlike physical reactions of materials, human reactions cannot be stopped with
timetable precision. Each action feeds a chain of reactions that
extends far beyond the initial action. For this reason, no administrative action ever has a single result. Along with the planned
consequences, the administrator gets unintended extras in the
form of collateral consequences. These may not always be unwanted and sometimes are highly valuable. Their occurrence is
sufficiently predictable, however, to rule out any notion of mathematical accuracy in decision making. The ability of the
administrator to compute possibilities precisely is also affected by
the spin of events outside the orbit of the enterprise. Even a single capricious occurrence can produce profound results. A single
crazed individual can upset the department-store sales or the
stock market of a nation by assassinating the President. The
administrator acts on a precarious balance and can never expect
to accurately comprehend all the possibilities. This does not mean
that he should ever rest his case on less than sufficient evidence. It
does mean that he must use reasonableness, rather than exactness,
as a guide.

The administrator can be misled by the illusion of exactness
that numbers give. Numbers are actually very ambiguous sym-
bols and most times provide only a glimpse of the reality they are
supposed to represent. They are bits and pieces that have been
abstracted out of the total reality to simplify it. To be useful to
administration, they must be reduced to totals and totals of totals.
This means that most of the figures the administrator uses represent averages rather than specifics and are general rather than
exact. Because they are reductions of the total reality, they are
likely to be anemic representatives of the story they are trying to
tell the administrator. Also, in expressing an array as a sum, there
is a risk of concealing the most meaningful and consequential elements. The purpose of numbers is to eliminate the individual
characteristics of things by standardizing them, and thus numbers
have meaning only when they represent a common property. This
means that when we utilize numbers, we assume that the unique-

ness of the things being numbered is not important. Certainly, numbers constitute an invaluable language. The scientist would be helpless without such a language, and the work of the administrator would be both primitive and clumsy. But numbers are not magic. They only represent a narrow, specialized language that permits the administrator to deal concisely with things where "number" can be used to denote a common property. This conciseness can be purchased only at the cost of ignoring the identity of other properties. In many instances such loss of identity of any other characteristics of things is not important, and in other instances such loss is justified because of the clumsiness that would result in using everyday language to deal with those things; but in most things with which the administrator is concerned the quantifiable characteristics are least important. The administrator's job is to determine values, and quantity is only one of the dimensions with which he is concerned. Numbers can efficiently express quantity, but they can seldom ever effectively express worth.

The preoccupation with being exact has started another trend in administration. This is the trend toward excessive documentation. The notion seems to be that engulfing the administrator in a morass of detail will somehow give him a better view of the situation. It is doubtful if a sheer mass of data can assure anything—except confusion. The wisecrack "don't confuse me with the facts" may be wiser than it is cracked up to be. In the first place, it is literally impossible for the administrator to deal with all the facts relating to any important problem. The number of facts involved in even a simple incident is countless. One only needs to try to describe a football play to a person who has never seen a game to realize the number of facts involved. Such an explanation still would touch only a few of the total facts connected with the play. An idea of the number can be had if one images an inhabitant of Mars trying to explain the entire setting of a football play to another Martian who had never seen a human being or a game. Fortunately, such detail is never required because of the great amount of shared information among all people with a common environment. In administration, relatively little detail is required even for major problems, since those working on a problem are usually well informed regarding its context. Additional information is required only for the purpose of filling the gaps.

Ordinarily, the administrator needs only to be briefed on a problem in order to sufficiently understand it. Increasing the amount of documentation can blur, as much as it can brighten, the administrator's vision. Massive facts may perhaps greatly enlarge the chance of perception, but they vastly complicate response. Understanding is always the simplest common denominator of a situation. We simplify our view of the situation until it becomes understandable. Some detail is essential, but the less essential details must be rejected if there is to be clear thinking. Making up one's mind is as much a matter of clearing one's mind as it is of adding more information.

The increasing complexity of modern enterprise has ushered into the administrative lineup an array of report producers who are adding considerably to the contents of the administrator's briefcase. Because of the great diversity of technical knowledge required to properly plan and evaluate the activities of the usual enterprise, it has been necessary to add a variety of staff specialists to supplement and extend the knowledge, time, and energies of the line officers. The need for these specialists in methods, marketing, finance, etc., is unquestioned. The "general practitioner" in administration will continue to know less and less about more and more, and must therefore seek the expertise of a specialist in many areas of his work. But what the administrator gets is too often a handicap rather than a help. "Reportmanship" has become a self-justifying activity intended to show what the expert knows rather than what the administrator needs to know. In some instances the prestige of the expert seems to depend on the size, rather than on the sense, of his report. The obvious and the frivolous are given the same treatment as the crucial and the relevant. If the administrator doesn't get lost in boredom early on the way, he may be able to separate the useful from the useless and extract what he needs to know. Wearisomeness is not always his greatest problem, however. Most likely the reports, even the better ones, will be written in the jargon of the specialist and will be fairly unintelligible to anyone not an initiate. The administrator needs the help of the staff specialist, but what he more often needs is a lot less report and a lot more thought. Wading through a sea of obscure information is not apt to be the best way for the administrator to locate meaningful ramifications.

The great emphasis given to communications in recent years

has caused some administrators to regard the transmission of information as almost a thing in itself. More detail going to more people has become a mission, rather than a means, for these administrators. Every advance in duplicating and transmission equipment is seen as a challenge to create new and superfluous items to be fed into the company's communications channels. An interest in improved communications is, of course, a very proper concern of the administrator. How to provide better information at all levels of the organization is a perpetual problem for him. Getting things done depends upon keeping people informed about what should be done. However, the purpose of administration is not the transmission of information but the influencing of behavior. Drowning problems in an ocean of information is not the same as solving them.

Facts are probably the administrator's best friend. Certainly, he can't do very much without their support. They suggest all his ideas and they measure all his results. But it is an unfortunate truth of life that our best friends have their weaknesses, and if we don't recognize those weaknesses they can lead us into difficulties. Our sticking too close to the facts can allow them to influence us too heavily and can permit their weak characteristics to affect our judgment. One of these weaknesses is that facts are essentially negative in character. Accumulated knowledge tends to oppose new ideas because it invokes established and traditional values. An imaginative idea, by definition, has to go beyond the known and transcend the established order of things. Accepted ideas have a built-in proof, factually determined by use, but new ideas seldom come with their proof packaged in with them. The way facts are used in the decision process helps give them a negative character. Decision making is a process of choosing among alternatives. Facts are used to rule out different possibilities in order to make a final selection, and for this reason they are more identified with the possibility of destruction than with the creation of new possibilities. Facts and fresh ideas don't always go steady for another important reason. All facts are empirical, since a thing can't be a fact until it has happened. This means that facts are past oriented and look backward more than forward. The novel and untried, on the other hand, are altogether future oriented and must use a path that facts can never fully mark. The only way to increase knowledge is to recruit new knowledge from the unknown. Where truly creative advance is concerned, there is no past; the mind must jump the gap in knowledge represented by the advance. It could be that a mind heavily loaded down with facts is in poor condition to make a very good leap forward.

Facts have other weaknesses to which the administrator must accommodate if facts are to be his best friend. They are much better on defense than offense. They show up only after things have happened, and thus their main value is likely to be corrective. Even when they are projected into the future, they are more likely to serve a preventive, than a creative role. Like mountain guides, they tell the administrator how to keep out of trouble by keeping him on previously explored trails. Also, they are one-sided by nature. They show what has happened but never show what could have happened. Looking at the facts is like walking in a circle in a forest. One never gets a chance to see how the trees look from the other side. The usefulness of most facts is not very enduring, and staleness is a besetting weakness. This is especially true of the sort of facts with which the administrator is most concerned. He is primarily concerned with change, and most times the usefulness of facts that reflect change can be expected to keep like a fish. Keeping facts in an electronic deepfreeze won't help them keep their meaning.

Some facts are really very whimsical things. They don't change, but, like a chameleon, their appearance does. They are quite accommodating and are willing to mean anything an individual believes them to mean. The recess bell can mean regimentation or freedom depending upon how the individual student interprets it. Information can never have any meaning outside the comprehension of the individual receiving it. The role of the receiver in forming and shaping his own interpretation of facts simply cannot be denied. Any idea that information can be understood impersonally cannot stand before an explanation of the nature of understanding. Information is no more useful or meaningful than the coefficient of the individual receiver's understanding allows it to be. Understanding is an individual, personal matter because it is compounded out of the fallout of an individual's prior experiences. Understanding of new information is an extension of the existing understandings of an individual. The new fact is mixed in with all the previous experiences and is understood as a part of the total comprehension rather than as a specific by itself. The value of a franc or the length of a meter can be understood by an individual only if it can be "comprehended" into his prior understandings. There can be no such thing as understanding in the abstract—as something separate and distinct from an individual's other understandings. But, even a precisely understood fact conveys no precise meaning. A meaning is a personal interpretation and reflects a person at the particular time he registers the meaning. The administrator may be quite unconcerned about the operating report of a department presented on one morning but be quite disturbed by the same report on another morning if it is presented following some unrelated disturbing incident. It could be said that in looking at the facts, the administrator tends to look for himself.

Facts are very seductive things. There is something about them that lulls our anxieties. Having facts is like having someone with us in the dark, and we feel a sense of security simply by possessing the facts. Because they do relieve our anxiety and concern, they dull our sense of skepticism. We think we have the facts and fail to ask the questions we ought to ask. Being full of facts, even facts not worth knowing, fulfills our need to be informed. It also dulls our sense of responsibility. We tend to assume that somehow we have fulfilled our responsibility toward a thing by coming into possession of a wealth of information about it. Our sense of guilt seems to be more concerned with not knowing than with not acting. We feel less duty to act upon information than to acquire it. Also, we feel less responsible for doing than for telling. We believe we pass the buck when we pass information.

To complete this obloquy on the administrator's best friend, it should be pointed out that facts are very dependent things. They do not carry their own meaning with them but depend upon subsidiary facts to give them their meaning. "The" fact has meaning only among a host of relatives. (As an illustration of this dependency, one can take the great economic growth that has occurred in the desert states of New Mexico, Arizona, and Nevada since 1940. Economists attribute this growth to the same factor to which they attributed the lack of growth prior to 1940. This factor is climate. Obviously, climate has not changed since 1940. But a number of other factors have come into the picture since 1940 to alter the meaning of climate with respect to the growth of these states. The increase in retirees, the increased ability of people to take winter vacations, and a variety of changes in technology have reversed the influence of climate in this instance.) Because the individual fact must depend upon related facts for its meaning, the administrator must round up the "relatives" to tell him what the individual fact is saying. Since he cannot always identify or find all the relatives, he has to divine what the missing ones would say if they were available.

Like the fellow who raises rabbits, one wonders if our ability to generate information has not far surpassed our ability to use it. Instead of giving increasingly greater concern to the accumulation of information, the administrator needs to sharpen his skills in using it. Information is not a stock item that can be dispensed over the counter. It must be handled as a prescription and prepared for specific users. There are many kinds of decisions to be made in an organization, and these require many different proportions of information. What is information at one level is not necessarily information at another. If the concept of "echelon of decision" is valid, then a concept of "echelon of information" must be developed to accompany it. One level of an organization may need facts about a problem, but another may need instructions. The process of devising solutions is quite different from the process of utilizing them. Making a diagnosis is not the same as working out a solution. Information is the raw material for these processes, but each process has its own specifications for the information required. The provision of information is one of the most important functions of administration, and it is also one of the most difficult to do properly. Administratively speaking, passing out information is not the same as passing out handbills.

Information is the medium of administration. Administration is conducted by administering information. It is through the provision and withholding of information that administration allocates authority and maintains control of an organization. The individual member of the administrative hierarchy does his work with information and can do no more work than the available information enables him to do. His achievements and influence can be regulated by regulating the flow of information to him. His position can be completely quarantined by channeling all information around it. The level of information possessed is the insignia of an administrator and denotes his rank in the organization. Those around him defer to him according to how much information they think he is being provided. This is why the individual strives to be, or gives the impression that he is, on the "inside." People realize that what a person knows in an organization is a way of demonstrating whom he knows.

Administrative posts in an organization are created to handle information. They are required only when there is sufficient information at a particular point to require someone to handle it. The more the information, the more the administrative positions that must be set up to evaluate and act upon it. The reverse is true, and the less the information, the fewer the administrative positions required. If there were no information, there would be no need for an administrator. These simple statements seem like truisms as one reads them, but they are in direct conflict with statements being made in many corners about the coming disappearance of a high percentage of the administrators in an organization. It is being noised around that the computer is going to replace a high percentage of administrators and that the personal judgment of these administrators will be superseded by the regurgitations of an electronic data eater. No notion could be less logical. One thing the wonderful new electronic hardware can do with amazing speed is to collect and spill out almost unlimited amounts of information. If this hardware is to represent more than a remarkable bag of expensive gadgets, it will necessitate more administrators rather than fewer. If the increased flow of information is to be productively utilized, an increased number of administrative positions will have to be inserted into the administrative lineup to interpret the information and do something about it. The computer can improve administrative performance, but it will inevitably enlarge the administrative staff if administration is not to flounder in a swollen sea of data.

Along with the prediction regarding the thinning of the administrators' ranks, there is an overt implication that the machines foretell the obsolescence of the thinking man. The wizardry and significance of these machines justify all the attention they are getting, but they are only machines. Just as the substitution of the combustion engine for the horse did not make a robot of the driver, so the computer can never replace human judgment in administration. The computer can improve the administrator's efficiency, but it cannot change his role to one of a "machine sitter." There are compelling reasons why this is true. In the first place, the usefulness of the computer depends on the level of thinking of the individual using its computations. One cannot instruct the computer about what to do until one has determined what he wants it to do and where he wants to go from there. So long as the human mind has to put the computer to work, the crucial member of this combination will remain the thinking man. Somebody must feed in the questions before the computer can start spouting out the answers. Further, the computer can deal only with facts. The mind, on the other hand, has the capacity to utilize insights and understandings in lieu of facts and as a supplement to them. The computer has no set of values. This means it has no sense of what is right and what is wrong and no ability to choose between them. Also, it can handle only certain kinds of facts. Machines are, of necessity, limited to the handling of tangible, measurable data. The important administrative decisions most often draw on intangible, qualitative data that can never be coded into machine language. Some of the data are so indefinable that they have to be felt to be understood. Complicated, real-life situations require a versatility and capacity for which the human mind was specifically developed. The human mind not only programs itself but it has the faculty to do it instantly. It can immeasurably outspeed any computer because it can bypass and ignore as much or as little as it chooses. It is not restricted to "givens" and can create and conceptualize data to fill the gaps. The storage capacity of the most advanced computer is infinitesimally small when compared to the human brain. The September, 1960, issue of *Westinghouse Engineer* reports that the brain has a memory capacity for 10 billion pieces of information, while present computers have a capacity for less than 1 million. But more fundamental to the question of the role the computer will play in administration is the fact that the computer only exhibits and never reveals. Like a calendar, which can tell you the day of the month only if you already know what day of the week it is, the data the computer presents have no meaning until the mind relates them to something already known. The role of the computer ends where the role of the administrator begins. Administration is a matter of transforming the implicit into the explicit. Information only implies. It invites administration to find out. Administration must take it from there and develop the information into a definite course of action. Despite all the magic of electronics in the processing of information, a human mind is still needed to read the information and judge what to do about it.

Good judgment must formulate answers which make sense when viewed by the rationality of others. People think in part what they feel, and feelings are not very amenable to cold logic. An individual is a set of feelings in motion, and these cannot be altered at the drop of an electronic eye. A machine can't get the feel that the individual is going to put on the answer the machine grinds out. The individual projects his own feelings into what he does, and until such time as a machine is developed which conveys the likes and dislikes of the various individuals who will be implementing an answer, a human mind will have to make the final determinations. Only a human mind can perceive the essential relationships and picture the inferences that another human mind will derive.

The burgeoning scientific revolution occurring in the natural sciences has spun a halo over the scientist and things scientific. This has led to a "science rush" in almost every area of human affairs as the various professions and occupations strive to get in under the halo. Since the best way to look like a scientist is to adopt the methodology and trappings of one, number juggling and data chasing have become a national pastime. Fellows who haven't reached the level of rating a hold button on their telephone are embarrassed if they are only on their first computer. Administrators have been especially susceptible to the wired-panel-model bandwagon. Frederick Taylor gave them the trademark at the turn of the century, but they have been unable to parlay a stopwatch into very much recognition for scientific management. Actually, the net result has been that such administrators have picked up some stains where they show most on their grey flannel uniform. If past public reaction is any guide, the desire for scientific prestige can endanger the professional respectability the administrator intends to achieve by it.

Before administrators permit themselves to be forced into a scientific mold, they should examine the misconception that scientific management is an exact science, or that administration can ever be a science at all. Administration is a process of getting things done through other people and, as such, is the art of using other men's behavior. While there are undoubtedly a sufficient number of general laws of human behavior to justify the concept of a behavioral science, these laws are much too general to permit their utilization by the administrator with the same degree of preciseness with which the engineer applies the laws of the physical sciences. The administrator cannot verify his conclusions with carefully controlled experiments. It is possible for him to reasonably confirm his assumptions regarding cause and effect by observation, but it is seldom possible for him to obtain quantitative proof. The quantitative techniques of the natural scientists are applicable only to static situations in which relationships are expressible in formulas. Administrative problems are people problems and these don't lend themselves to quantitative methods. When the problems do allow a statistical answer, it usually is in a situation where the questions answered did not justify the asking. People can be counted as statistics, but they can't be counted on to act as statistics. The administrator can give them numbers, but he can never make them anything but people. Because of the problem of applying the scientific method to human action, the term "scientific management" is a misnomer. Effective administration is systematic, but it can hardly ever claim to be scientific. There is no purely scientific way open to the administrator. He need not be embarrassed because this is true. On the contrary, it is a tribute to his role to recognize that there is only a human way to handle human problems.

The top billing being given to scientific methodology in decision making is causing administrators to adopt increasingly an "embarrassed to know you" attitude toward intuition. Because intuition occurs in the absence of hard facts, or ahead of the facts, it is being written off as being in the same company as the divining rod of the well digger and the tea leaves of the soothsayer. The inability of intuition to identify the specific facts with which it associates is causing it to be increasingly considered intellectually disreputable. However, it is just this facility for producing ideas of nebulous origin that makes intuition such an extremely valuable adjunct of the administrator's judgment. It need not be loose and wayward, and when properly trained and disciplined, it can represent a highly sophisticated effort toward intellectual order. Intuitive thinking is an essential feature of productive thinking. There is nothing supernatural or mystic about intuition. It is just as much "mind stuff" as is the most direct, analytic sort of thinking an individual can do. The difference between them is in the nature of the particulars used in the thinking process. Analytical thinking can deal only with defined specifics, while intuitive thinking vastly extends the reach of the mind through the use of nonspecifics. Because it can deal with nonspecifiables, intuitive thinking permits the utilization of the thousands of bits and pieces of knowledge possessed by a person which individually are so small that the person doesn't know when he learned them or that they have been learned at all. This ability of intuitive thinking to arrange combinations of knowledge not within conscious reach really represents the individual's best source of new and innovative ideas. Because the combination occurs without the individual's knowing what he is looking for, his mind is not restricted to the same old things he has been thinking about. Also, because the combination often occurs before the individual knows what he is looking for, it permits the formation of ideas which his conscious mind would repress or disown if he attempted to build such ideas from recognized parts. It also avoids the complexities with which logical analysis would bog down his mind. Perceptions that result from marginal cues are mental "extras" and can do the administrator no harm if he treats them as tentative formulations. Once he has the idea, he has the opportunity to put it through the same analytic scrutiny through which he might put the notions that arise from his most concentrated thinking. Without an idea, he has nothing to scrutinize.

Unleashing the mind from narrow lines of logical thought is not the only mental bonus resulting from intuitive thinking. Because intuition permits the mind to leap forward without plodding through a conscious process, the individual has access to a super, high-speed perception. The fact that it works so fast is a reason that many of the clues it uses are not recognized and nailed down. It is a mental timesaver in another way. Because it is a low-pressure process of thinking, it can utilize the idling time of the mind. Those who have studied the origin of ideas insist that the best ideas most often come when the mind seems idle rather than at the time of hard concentrated thought. The process of producing ideas can perhaps be likened to the gentle rain that settles more dust than the driving rainstorm.

The defense of intuition is in no way a reflection upon conscious, analytic thought. It is rather a plea that the administrator not disown a very valuable thought process and that he capitalize on the unique contributions it can make to his judgment. Conscious, analytic thought will always be his most effective way of thinking whenever sufficient facts are available and whenever time is not of the essence. Such circumstances are not always present for the administrator, however. There are times when such a way of thinking can be clumsy or inefficient. At times, it can be like using thick gloves to pick out a needle from a sewing basket. Facts, and the events they represent, have a tendency to run together, and the administrator is often confronted with the problem of divining the significance of mixed and merged particulars. This means the administrator must, in certain instances, work with meanings rather than particulars and utilize concepts in lieu of facts. The seamless nature of events and circumstances can be an advantage to the administrator. It can force him to view some things as a whole and work with coherent entities rather than with unrelated particulars. In a way, he will have the benefit of prepackaged understanding. Understanding is largely a unification of nonspecifiables. We don't know why we know most of the things we know. We understand a person, but we cannot describe the particulars by which we understand him. We understand him by his universe rather than by his parts. Said another way, the operational principle of a combustion engine cannot be discovered by examination of its different parts. It is only when the parts are assembled into an entity that the principle is disclosed.

Too hard a search for certainty can cause the administrator to become the master of the hesitation waltz. The need to search for more evidence can become an obsession with him and produce hesitation and loss of confidence. The effective practice of administration rests on the talent for making judgments swiftly and surely. Perhaps the most important single characteristic of the effective administrator is decisiveness. This cannot be developed in an administrative storm cellar. Confidence is not the sort of thing that can be kept on a shelf. It must be used if it is to be kept strong. Admittedly, going off half-cocked is no way for the administrator to hit his target. But neither will waiting until he can shoot point blank give him many important hits—he won't get many shots. Waiting for the sure thing can cause him to tackle only problems he thinks he can solve with certainty and fail to take on the problems he should be trying to solve. Lying in wait until he is dead sure won't give him much standing with himself or with members of his organization.

How sure he can afford to be is a question that always confronts the administrator. Timeliness competes with completeness, and innovation competes with certainty. Cost is the balance by which they all must be measured. The cost of the uncertainty removed must be at least the same as the cost of the certainty added, if the removal is to be administratively justified. Loss from uncertainty is the loss associated with having to guess instead of having perfect knowledge. Not to know can cost the administrator, but this cost must be related to how much it will cost him to know. There is a range of certainty associated with each decision, and the administrator must determine in each instance at what point the payoff from further certainty ends. As Aristotle expressed it, "Every situation has its own degree of certainty, and a well-trained man accepts that degree and does not look for a greater one." Said another way, there is a difference in administration between maximal certainty and optimal certainty. The administrator is a professional risk taker, and he functions through the calculated risk. This does not mean that the administrator is ever justified in "going it" with only his hunches. It means that he needs much more than opinion but that he will have to settle for less than proof. The effective administrator recognizes that there is a wide margin of difference between being foolhardy and being foolproof.

The administrator can never be sure. He can only know an uncertain and reacting environment imperfectly, and even his most informed decisions represent educated guesses. A decision is a prediction of the future. No matter how thick the pile of facts on which he stands, the pile will always be too thin to permit the administrator to see precisely and exactly into the future. His function begins only when the clearly verifiable ends. The organization does not need direction if there is one clearcut way to go. The administrative area is the area in which choices must be made. It is an area that by definition is marked by gaps of uncertainty. They are gaps that may be narrowed by good information, but they are gaps which can never be eliminated. They can only be bridged by the administrator's judgment. In the midst of all his new-found aids, the administrator's judgment still remains crucial.

Index